T0273434

"Palmer's forthright and tender book brings to mind William Faulkner's assertion that all good writing grows from 'the problems of the human heart in conflict with itself.' During many of his formative years, the narrator straddles two worlds—the world of his large, 'loving but chaotic' and economically strapped family back home and the elite world that scholarships to Exeter, and later to Harvard and Yale, offer him . . . And though Palmer's story expands to include the larger world of racial, economic, gender, and educational challenges facing a changing nation, it's clear that, as the narrator comes to understand, 'those nine siblings—and my parents—are a part of who I am. They are my story.' And what a moving, enlightening story it is, a generous gift to us, his lucky readers."

— **Rebecca McClanahan**, author of *The Tribal Knot*
and *In the Key of New York City: A Memoir*

SCHOLARSHIP BOY

Meditations on Family and Race

Larry I. Palmer

PAUL DRY BOOKS
Philadelphia   2020

First Paul Dry Books edition, 2020

Paul Dry Books, Inc.
Philadelphia, Pennsylvania
www.pauldrybooks.com

Printed in the United States of America

ISBN 978-1-58988-145-7
Library of Congress Control Number: 2020933719

For my brothers and sisters

Contents

Author's Note

Determining the appropriate descriptor for descendants of African slaves first brought to America over four centuries ago has been a contested matter during my lifetime, each generation initially convinced that their language bestowed more dignity than the prior generation's. I certainly witnessed this growing up when "Negro" was the preferred term to "colored," at least in my family. Throughout this book, I use the term Negro for one primary reason: to remind readers how people wrote and talked about the descendants of slaves as my story unfolds. Secondarily, some terms I use comfortably today, such as black, would have been seen as derogatory by the Negroes who raised and educated me.

When a man leaves home, he leaves behind some scrap of his heart. . . . It's the same with a place a man is going to. Only then he sends a scrap of his heart ahead.

Frederick Buechner

Preface

Sitting in Boston's Logan Airport, I settle into my new academic routine to avoid wasting time. From my briefcase I pull out a stack of law student papers to grade, and push from my mind thoughts about the Exeter Alumni Association meeting I'd left an hour earlier. Consideration of the meeting's unwritten agenda—how our all boys' school was faring during its first year of coeducation—would have to wait for another day. I dive into the first paper, into what is fast becoming my passion: poring over students' written ideas.

I feel serene waiting for my flight back to Philadelphia. My job, one year after graduating from law school, excites me. And I'm finally able to afford, thanks to my assistant professor's salary, the Brooks Brothers jacket, slacks, shirt, and tie I wear, instead of the knockoff brands from my prep school days. As I slouch in my chair, red pencil poised to land, a trembling tap on my right shoulder disrupts my composure.

"If you aren't who I think you are, you have nothing to worry about." The forced calmness of his whispering voice belied the rat-tat like trembling of his index finger on my collar bone, as he continued, "I am a federal customs officer . . ."

He has a gun! President Nixon's recent announcement (September, 1970) in response to two simultaneous hijackings of American commercial airlines in the Middle East flashes in my mind: armed plainclothes federal customs officers would now be placed on certain flights and in some airports. The officer's unsteady touch feels like needle pricks in my shoulder. *He is very nervous!* I suddenly remembered that a policeman had once shot my brother Urshel in the leg. *Stay calm. Just listen.*

"I want you to get up and walk . . . slowly . . . down the corridor to your right and go into the first door on the left. I will follow behind you." In a nasal low pitch, he snarls, "Don't look back!"

Without making eye contact, I rise slowly, breathe deeply, and drop my students' papers in the chair behind me. As I stroll toward the corridor, I suppress any display of fear. I hear my older sister Lela reminding me that white people think all Negroes look alike. I'd experienced this many times: "Haven't we met before? Aren't you . . . (fill in the name of a fellow Negro student at Harvard College or Yale Law School)?" But this is not a case of mistaken identity in a social setting. This man is an armed and jumpy federal officer who thinks I'm planning to hijack a plane. *Don't let his jitters infect you. Stay calm.*

I enter the first door on the left and I now get a look at the officer as he follows me into the room and shuts the steel door behind him. Sweat beads up on his forehead as we lock eyes, my arms dangling at my sides. He shows me his badge and I glance at the closed door behind him—my exit route from the windowless room, as long as I don't upset him. He asks me my name and instructs me to show my identification. As I reach for my wallet in my back pocket, his anxious steel-blue eyes fixate on my right shoulder, a sign to pull the wallet out slowly. I show him my faculty ID and driver's license. He sighs with relief, and smiles.

"I thought you were an escaped murderer from the Walpole State Prison," he says as he shows me a profile and straight-on shot of a brown-skinned man from the maximum-security prison in Massachusetts.

"Don't you agree that you look like him from the side view, which is how I saw you as I came down the corridor?" He proffers no apology for his mistake—only justification for the detention with a tone that implied I should affirm his mistake, that he had caused no harm.

I pause before answering, afraid my fear might seep into my response. *Don't get into an argument about the degree of likeness between an escaped prisoner and me.* I stand in silence, again focusing on the closed door and the knowledge he has a gun, even though he hasn't displayed it. Anger boils up in me, but I think only of his gun. *Stay calm! Think before you speak.*

Using my best, albeit young, professorial voice, as if speaking to a student, I ask, "Is there anything else I can do for you?"

In the seconds it takes for him to step aside, open the door, and say, "You can go now," I erase his face from my mind.

As if nothing has happened, I repossess my belongings and walk toward my gate. I board the plane and immerse myself in reading student papers on the hour-long flight to Philadelphia. By the time we land, I've buried the entire incident at Logan in the deep archives of my mind.

I learned to use analysis to withhold my emotions well before this racial encounter in my early adulthood. This way of controlling my feelings began when I was a young boy dealing with my parents and siblings.

I'm one of ten. Family code name, "next to the Baby." Barry is sixteen months younger. Before going to a boarding school a thousand miles from home, I lived with my parents, Barry, and three of my older siblings, Lela, Harold, and Louise. My three eldest siblings, Lena, Al, and Willie, were married and lived, along with their spouses and children, within walking distance of our house on the west side of St. Louis.

Mother does know best as far as keeping all her sons straight. Make them into pairs: Al and Willie, the oldest two, central characters in my growing up years. Mac and Harold, a middle pairing until Mac joined the military. Me and Barry, the babies.

Two mythical brothers—Urshel and Herschel—were not around. Herschel died as a toddler, well before my parents migrated from Arkansas to St. Louis a few months before my birth in 1944. Urshel ran away from St. Louis about four years after the move. They, too, were a pair for my mother, the few times she mentioned either of her missing sons.

My three sisters were sprinkled among the boys during my mother's twenty-one years of birthing. Lena, the oldest child, married before I was born. Lela, eight years my senior, moved to Los Angeles to marry just as I left for boarding school. Louise, three years older than I, felt nonetheless like a pesky little sister growing up. Yet, she is the only sibling to ever see the boarding school from which I graduated, Phillips Exeter Academy.

As the ninth child of ten, and the sixth of seven sons, I thought I resided on the outer edge of the family's emotional dynamics. Even when I wasn't perched on the kitchen's windowsill eavesdropping on family conversations, I often *felt* invisible.

When I entered school at four and a half, many of my older siblings were my role models for how I was expected to act in the world outside home. My mother's first mantra, "clothes make the man," made me self-conscious about my appearance. She tried to straighten out a kink in my hair every time I left the house. At the same time, her admonishment to "be the best, even if you become a dishwasher," reminded me that the world might make my brown skin an impediment to her stated ambition for me to become a preacher or doctor. The way she balanced high ambitions against the reality of racial barriers helped to lay the foundation for the human being I have become.

I often withheld my feelings growing up. I internalized the tensions of America's mid-twentieth-century cultural and racial upheaval in a peculiar way because I spent my coming of age years in two different, but related, households: My Exeter parents—white male teachers and coaches—allowed me periodic visitations (vacations) with my biological parents and siblings. My combination of "parental units," as we might call them today, agreed I should aim for an Ivy League education, but the terms of their joint custody meant the work toward our agreed upon educational goal must be done at Exeter. As a scholarship boy I washed dishes, but my education was preparing me for leadership. My future beckoned me to a world unknown to me, never mind to my biological parents. My effort to succeed required that I not mix my two families, my two worlds. Instead, I kept the two worlds as separate as possible.

Life at Exeter enabled this split. As an all-boys boarding school in the 1950s, it wasn't a place where kids talked much about their most vulnerable emotions, or even superficially about their families. Rather, we filled our days with matching of wits, comradely fellowship on sports teams or in extracurricular activities, and engaging classroom and dining room discussions. At prep school, teenagers get to invent themselves, and I took advantage of that. None of my classmates even knew I had nine siblings.

And yet, those nine siblings—and my parents—are a part of who I am. They are my story.

PART I

"Get the Boy on the Train"

CHAPTER ONE

The Haircut

I<small>T WAS A</small> W<small>EDNESDAY</small> around 8:30 P.M., a week before Thanksgiving, 1958, when I walked down the third-floor corridor of Bancroft Hall toward Mr. Bedford's faculty apartment. He was on duty as dorm monitor that night—thus the open door. Jef, one of my fellow preps (what ninth graders were called at Phillips Exeter Academy), had invited his roommate, Brink, and me to spend the holiday break with his family in Salem, Massachusetts. It was the first time I had visited Bedford's faculty office and I lingered just outside of the mahogany door in the dorm hallway, an unsigned permission slip from the Dean of Students in hand.

Bedford sat at his desk, facing away from the hall, his eyes focused on some handwritten papers as I waited for him to notice me. He turned his head toward me with a glance that asked, "What's up?" his eyebrows becoming question marks as he peered over his glasses. I handed him the slip and asked him to sign it because my adviser was out of town. Bedford pushed his chair away from his desk and spun to face me, his smile so wide it seemed to touch his sideburns, "Well, I got a deal for you. Before I'll sign, you must get a haircut."

Get a haircut? There was nothing in the Exeter rulebook about the length of students' hair, only that coats and ties were required at all classes, chapel, church, and meals. I figured I had left behind this kind of concern about what Mom referred to as my nappy hair when I left St. Louis three months before. Was

Bedford, a young history teacher and the junior faculty member in the dorm, making up his own rules? I looked around distractedly for a moment, and considered whether I should bring up the rulebook. I noticed that on the right edge of Bedford's desk, the only part uncluttered by stacks of papers and books, sat a framed picture of his preschool boys—hair neatly trimmed, parted on the side.

I decided it wasn't smart to challenge him on the rules. He had my permission slip in his hand and gave no indication he was going to give it back to me. I knew from previous conversations with Bedford that he was at once the most intimidating, gregarious, and argumentative adult among the three faculty members living in Bancroft. Without much effort, he could have played the role of a lawyer in a movie. I regretted that I hadn't been able to get the signature I needed from my adviser, a bachelor who taught French and barely spoke to me (or anyone else) other than to say "good morning" and who would have signed the slip without question. Instead I was caught wondering how I could explain to Bedford why my hair was so long; how I could tell him that I was acutely aware of the fact that all the adults at Exeter—from the janitors to the principal to the academy barber to this grinning, twenty-eight-year-old, prematurely balding guy sitting in front of me—were white. How seriously I doubted any of them could possibly understand the complexities of my Negro hair.

IN MY FOURTEEN YEARS, I had never been to a barbershop. Starting when I was about four, every two weeks or so, Dad would order me to take a seat in a chair in the kitchen or find a spot in the shade of the backyard, drape one of his old shirts backwards over me like a large bib, and take out his hand-operated clippers from a canvas bag. "Hold still!" he'd bark, grabbing the top of my head with his left hand. With his right, he'd place the clippers against the side of my head and squeeze the shiny metal handles, compressing the heavy spring separating them, causing the teeth of the top blade to ratchet back and forth across the stationary teeth of the bottom. The regular rhythm of those moving blades was like the clip-clop, clip-clop of the ragman's horse on the asphalt pavement I always heard just before he turned his wagon—loaded with pots, pans, broken household appliances, and clothing—into the brick alleyway alongside our house. Any interruption of the flat staccato of the clippers made my neck stiffen, since it usually meant the blades had become entangled in some knot of tight curls that Dad called kinks. "Hold still, this is going to pinch," he'd grumble quietly, untangling my hair from the blades. He used the thicker of his two combs—the thin barber's comb was reserved for my younger brother, Barry—to pull out as many kinks as possible before restarting with the trimmer and finishing up the sides. He always paused to unscrew the wing nut holding the cover over the blades to clean them out before proceeding to the hair on top, his "hold still!" the only interruption of the wordless clip-clop of the ritual as he'd finish cutting off all but an inch of my hair.

For two weeks after every one of these cuts, I'd apply Vitalis or some type of grease to my sculpted kinks, attempting to comb and brush them into straightness. They wound up growing back problematic as ever. A week before I boarded the train for Exeter on a full scholarship, a few months after my fourteenth birthday, Dad sat me down in his backyard shop for the last time. It didn't occur to me to ask what to do about haircuts once I got to school, and Dad volunteered no parting advice.

STANDING THERE IN Bedford's foyer beneath a half-dozen uncropped inches, trying to avoid his gaze, I raised my left hand and fidgeted with the double knot of my tie before offering him a version of the truth. "I don't look bad with long hair," I began. "I brush it every morning"—Bedford burst into laughter before I could finish—"and after sports." I couldn't tell if he thought my comment was ridiculous, or if he was laughing because he had no hairstyle at all.

But then, no longer smiling, Bedford pinched his eyebrows together, the way I imagined he might when singling out one of his students in class, and looked at me. "Come on, Palmer, what's your real story? You're about to spend Thanksgiving with Jef's

parents, people you have never met, looking the way you do?
You and I both know your parents would be embarrassed if you
showed up looking like this!"

My parents had always made sure I was appropriately dressed
and groomed whenever I ventured into the world beyond our
house, even if it was only to take the bus downtown to meet Dad
after work to shop for a new pair of shoes. But why did Bedford
care about the impression I might make on the parents of one
of my dormmates? He gestured with his left hand for me to sit
in the chair at the side of his desk, so I sat down tentatively and
waited for him to resume his questions. But he didn't.

I broke the silence. "It's not really practical for me to get a
haircut before I go home for Christmas." Bedford's stare said,
"Why not?"

"Last month, I went downtown to see if I could find a Negro
barber," I said. "I asked a Negro airman I saw on Main Street if
he knew where I could find one. He told me no Negroes lived
in Exeter. The only Negro barber he knew was near his base in
Portsmouth. You know that's about fifteen miles away, so I gave
up on getting a haircut." Bedford still didn't seem convinced, so
I tried another angle.

"Just a few weeks ago, I looked through the window of the
first barbershop on Main Street at a barber giving a student a
crew cut with electric clippers. Those clippers won't work on my
hair." He looked at me quizzically. "At the second shop," I went
on, "I saw a barber giving a longhaired Exie a trim with scissors
and a comb. That comb would snap into pieces trying to untangle my hair!"

I paused in my monologue, looked down at my hands folded
in my lap, and mumbled, "And I've seen enough 'We Reserve
the Right to Refuse Service to Anyone' signs in businesses back
home that I didn't even bother to go inside."

I didn't detect any skepticism on Bedford's face as he pushed
back in his chair, gliding further away from his desk. As he
leaned back further and waited with a sideways glance for more
of my monologue, I plunged ahead, pointing out how I thought
none of the white men or boys at Exeter would notice my shaggy
locks. I pleaded that none of the other boys in the dorm, admir-

ing the side-swept elegance of their own Cary Grant styles or
criticizing each other's crew cuts, had ever said a word about
my hair.

Setting aside his usual rapid-fire method of talking, Bedford
finally said, simply, "The Academy barber cannot refuse to cut
your hair." Glancing at the picture on his desk, he continued:
"You are going to teach him, or one of the barbers downtown,
how to do it. I'm holding your permission slip until you come
back with a haircut." And he put my permission slip in his desk
drawer where it couldn't get lost in the clutter.

Dumbfounded by this unexpected assignment, I stood up
and turned around to leave the office, already figuring that Exeter's barber would be my safest way to complete it. But as I wandered back to my room, I found myself mulling over all the
things I hadn't felt comfortable communicating to Bedford during our talk.

I DIDN'T TELL Bedford how that neatly packaged airman I'd run
into downtown reminded me of my brother Mac, who was also
in the Air Force. Or how when Mac graduated from Charles
Sumner High School back in St. Louis, six years before, he'd won
a scholarship to attend a historically black college—a scholarship he turned down with the intention of borrowing money to
attend a local college of pharmacy that accepted Negroes and
whites. When Dad had refused to sign the loan papers—the age
of majority was twenty-one—Mac stormed out of the house and
joined up.

Mac, the Boy Scout with a sash full of merit badges. Mac,
the hustler with a part-time job making bicycle deliveries from
a nearby drugstore. Mac, the snazzy dresser with a mocking
tongue that he directed at me when he was not ignoring me
altogether. The few times I saw Mac after he left home he continued to snub me. Still, I eavesdropped eagerly on his conversations with others and so learned he had tested "off the charts" on
an IQ test early in his military service, that he'd been stationed
in places like Guam and Alaska, and that what he was doing
was classified. I know it was some ghostly version of Mac, well-
dressed and well-trimmed whether he was in uniform or not,

who made me realize that the Negro Airman I ran into on that October sidewalk was okay to approach about my own grooming dilemma.

I wondered what Bedford would think if he knew how Mom and Dad had argued for months about whether I should be allowed to apply to Exeter. She saw a bright educational future for me, but he worried about my tiny body—I was not yet five feet and weighed less than a hundred pounds—in a white boys' boarding school over a thousand miles from home.

When Exeter's principal visited St. Louis to meet prospective students and their parents, Dad had refused to attend the meeting, so Al, my oldest brother, went in his place. I never heard Willie, my second oldest brother and a public-school teacher himself, voice an opinion about Exeter. But, unlike Mac, he was constantly teaching me something: how to read a light meter and change a camera's settings; how trees fossilized in the Painted Desert in Arizona thousands of years ago; how to deliver a good speech (Willie had won a prize for public speaking while in high school).

When I tested high enough on an IQ test to earn a place in a gifted and talented class in 1955 as part of the desegregation of the public schools, Willie was enthusiastic and informed Mom that George Hyram, who was to be my teacher, was the smartest person ever to attend Stowe Teachers College, the segregated public teachers college named in honor of Harriet Beecher Stowe, where both Willie and Hyram had earned their credentials. When Dad questioned some of Hyram's methods, Willie leapt to his defense. It was Hyram—my teacher though sixth, seventh, and eighth grades—who introduced Exeter and its scholarship program to my mom in February 1957. I don't know what Willie told my parents once he heard about the Exeter possibility, but I assumed that he believed anything Hyram recommended was good for me.

The arguments between my parents continued even after Exeter accepted me and offered me a full scholarship in early 1958. But something happened before the summer of that year to bring about a truce. Perhaps it was Mom's determination to find a job cleaning houses to provide me with spending money.

Or it might have been the school's generous offer to provide me with a clothing allowance the first year—for those jackets and ties I would need—and to pay for my transportation. Whatever happened, Dad finally relented.

THE SUNDAY IN 1958 when I left St. Louis, I sat in my coach seat in Union Station quite a while, going over my parents' instructions in my mind. I was to change trains in Cleveland that night and take another train to Boston. Once in Boston (early the next morning) I was to take a taxi to North Station where I would board a third train north, to a small New Hampshire town that I, my parents, and my nine siblings had never seen.

I don't remember how my one suitcase—a large trunk had been shipped earlier—ended up on the overhead rack. I glanced up at it and at my new businessman's hat—a fedora—tucked in beside it. The hat had been my parents' special purchase for my entry into a world of wearing coats and ties on a daily basis. I fiddled with my tie to make sure it was straight and glanced down at my white shirt, my gray slacks, and my checkered sports jacket with handkerchief tucked in the breast pocket. I remembered Mom's general admonition about my appearance whenever I went anywhere: "clothes make the man." I finally understood why the clothes and the hat were so important to my parents as I sat there, about to set out on a life among strangers.

As the train pulled slowly out of the station into the darkness of a tunnel, I wasn't conscious of the fact that there had not been any special goodbyes to Al, Willie, or any of my other brothers or sisters. As the engine sped up and we emerged once more into the bright September morning, I could see the bridge over the Mississippi River into Illinois. I tried to imagine the new world I was about to enter, and, as the train hung there above the current, tears began to flow down my cheeks. I looked back at the smokestacks of St. Louis's factories, reached for my handkerchief, and buried my face in it against the window so that none of the people around me would notice how the confident smile I'd worn during Mom and Dad's farewells had disappeared.

The farthest east I had ever been was about fifteen miles past East St. Louis, to the Cahokia Mounds State Historic Site—the remains of an ancient Mississippian city. Dad, formerly a schoolteacher in his native Arkansas, once took my younger brother, Barry, and me to visit the large grassy mounds. Even the East Side, with its racetrack and nightclubs where Miles Davis had gotten his start, seemed like a mythical place and was off limits to the youngest members of the Palmer clan. My other forays outside of St. Louis consisted of two trips to Arkansas; a day trip on the train to Hannibal, Missouri—Mark Twain's home—that I had won by selling subscriptions on my paper route; and a family camping trip in the Missouri Ozark Mountains. I was taken aback by the vastness and flatness of the Illinois cornfields stretching to the horizon. Neither my neighborhood—turn of the century houses, early twentieth-century apartments, and commercial establishments along wide boulevards—nor Forest Park, a mile from our house, provided the wide vistas I faced through the train window. Indiana became a string of names—Terre Haute, Greencastle, Indianapolis, Anderson, Muncie—shouted out by the conductor moving through the aisle.

The *St. Louis Post-Dispatch* and a book I'd brought along to read drew me out of myself. Reading seized the space in my mind that might have longed for the gray cityscape of my neighborhood or the purple wisteria blooming along our backyard fence. As the train rocked and swayed closer to the country's eastern shore, I erased the recently familiar—Dad using his steel hand-shears to trim the grass borders around the whitewashed trunks of our two maple trees; Willie instructing me on how to capture the beauty of a flower in the Missouri Botanical Garden with his 35-mm camera—to make space for new surroundings, panoramas, and people. My fickle teenage heart had already committed itself to a place where the books I used in my courses would be purchased by the scholarship office, where I would have my own room for the first time in my life, where I would be able to play a sport nearly every day, where all my teachers would be men like Hyram, and where Mom and Dad would not argue about my future in my presence as if I were not in the room.

The transfer in Cleveland, at about 9:00 P.M., went well; again, someone helped me with my suitcase. I took my assigned

seat and fell into a rocking sleep. When I awoke the next morning, a different conductor explained that I should get off at Back
Bay Station in Boston rather than South Station, which is the last
Boston stop. He told me it was an easier taxi ride to North Station, my ultimate destination, from Back Bay. I thanked him as
he helped me retrieve my things from the overhead rack.

My confidence restored after a good night's sleep, I started
down the aisle, dragging my suitcase behind me as the train
slowed to a stop at Back Bay. It was at this moment I noticed
him—my image of the prep school boy coming down the aisle of
the adjacent car toward me. He was a tall white teenager in a blue
blazer, blue button-down shirt, striped tie, and tan raincoat, and
he had his own suitcase in his hand. As we approached each other
at the exit door, I said, "Hello," remembering Dad's admonition
never to say hi, "Could you tell me how to get to North Station?"

"Sure, I'm going there," the prep school boy replied. "Would
you like to share a cab?"

He introduced himself by name and as a senior at Phillips
Academy at Andover, another New England boarding school
and Exeter's archrival. He spoke easily and assuredly. His questions were all friendly, let's-get-to-know-each-other type questions: Where are you from? What school are you going to? What
year are you? So, I asked him the same type of questions as we
boarded the same Boston and Maine train. I noticed this older
teenager of the prep school world did not wear a hat. I made an
entry in my mental notebook: leave new hat in closet at school.

I said goodbye to him when he disembarked at the station for
Andover and was left to complete the last thirty minutes of my
journey alone once more, gazing out the window. The smokestacks of the red brick factory buildings in Lawrence and Haver-
hill reminded me of the shoe factories near downtown St. Louis,
but as we crossed into New Hampshire, horses and cows and
barns with their silos dotted the landscape. At the Exeter stop,
I dragged my suitcase off the train without noticing if any other
boys climbed down with me. I got into a taxi (after the driver
put my suitcase in the trunk) and said, "Take me to Bancroft
Hall, please," amazed at how one twenty-four-hour-plus train
trip could change so many things.

"YOU MUST BE PALMER," a smiling, sparkling-eyed man said, in a familiar Midwestern accent, as I entered the dormitory. "I'm Ted Seabrooke," he continued, as he extended his hand. "I saw you get out of your taxi from my office window. Welcome to Bancroft Hall!" I shook his hand hoping my own face reflected his infectious smile. He told me that he knew St. Louis well. Before coming to Exeter, he'd coached wrestling at a high school in Granite City, Illinois, just across the Mississippi River. The ever-present voices of my parents or older siblings that usually whispered to me what I should do or say when I encountered a stranger disappeared from my consciousness. My fourteen-year-old gut told me: listen to Seabrooke.

I managed to transport my suitcase and myself to my room on the fourth floor by taking an elevator that the janitor unlocked for me. I unpacked and mingled with the other new students. Most of us were preps. There were a few tenth graders, known only as "lowers," and a few eleventh-grade "uppers" and twelfth-grade "seniors." As we introduced ourselves to each other, the first question after "Where are you from?" was "Are you a scholarship boy?" The dorm reverberated with conversation all morning, right up to lunchtime: What sport are you going to play? Who do you have for math? Who's your advisor?

We were doing more than making conversation. We were sizing up each other's verbal skills in anticipation of our future competitions in the classroom. The verbal jousting continued as I sat down with six other preps for my first meal. I had already met three of them while reconnoitering the dorm. Jon, like me, was a scholarship boy from Salem, Massachusetts. Jef (for Joseph E. Fellows III), whose father had gone to Exeter, was also from Salem. His roommate, Brink (for Van Wyck Brinkerhoff IV), whose father also had gone to Exeter, was from San Antonio, Texas. Brink, Jef, and I were the smallest of our group; we must have looked like little boys playing dress-up in our jackets and ties. Jon, with his strawberry blond crew cut, was the tallest and from afar no doubt looked like a senior eating with the preps. Dick, Bill, and Ben, other preps at the table, all introduced themselves and volunteered where they were from.

Suddenly, in the midst of all the animated conversations

around the table, Brink said to someone on his right, "You, Nigger!"

Just as suddenly, a deep New England silence absorbed every decibel of prep chatter. All eyes focused on me, the only Negro in the dining room. I looked past Brink's brown crew cut and noticed Seabrooke smiling at his two teenage daughters at the faculty table in the corner before centering my gaze on Brink's face. Speaking without thinking, I said, "Don't use that word." Then I continued in an even softer voice, saying, "It hurts my feelings." Brink mumbled a fumbling apology, and the preps' chatter resumed within minutes, albeit at a more subdued level.

Brink's response—the fact that he expressed genuine embarrassment and vulnerability, rather than attempting some elegant verbal twist to remove the social sting of what had just occurred—actually drew me to him. At that moment, responding to Brink, I had to bury my father's fears about this world I had chosen to inhabit. I made an unspoken vow never to tell anyone in my family about this incident. I also vowed never to tell Seabrooke or anyone else at Exeter about Brink's use of the word "nigger" to denigrate a white boy in my presence, hoping to preserve the possibility of a future friendship uncomplicated by racial suspicion.

Exeter seemed a world away from the rest of the country's racial tensions and conflicts: Emmett Till's murder in 1955; armed troops escorting nine Negro teenagers into Central High School in Little Rock in 1957; the bill enacted by the Arkansas legislature in 1958 opposing desegregation of Little Rock schools. The fact that my parents and all my older siblings had been born in Arkansas made such events regular topics of Palmer family conversations. Toward the end of these discussions, a parent or older sibling would inevitably extract some moral from a particular news story that young Barry and I should take to heart, lapsing into a sing-song central Arkansas drawl to explain how to deal with whites in general or how to distinguish "okay" white people from those who might try to harm or insult us.

I HADN'T HEARD a single reference to race at Exeter since that first day in September. But here it was, November, and I found myself on the ragged edge of a conversation with this white teacher about my Negro hair, trying to convince him of the importance of my visit to Jef's home with Brink without having to break those promises I'd made under my breath or to explain how much it meant to me that Brink and I had become friends in the first place. I guess if it was a haircut that he wanted, a haircut he would get.

When I got up my nerve the next day to go to the barbershop in the basement of one of the main academic buildings, my confidence was briefly shaken by the age of the barber. The white-haired bespectacled man looked like a retired barber at best. Maybe I should have gone downtown to find a younger man with steadier hands. I pondered this as he smiled kindly, and then he startled me with a question: "How do you want your hair cut?"

Dad had never asked me what I wanted my hair to look like. Staring into this barber's mirror, I imagined myself transformed into a movie star like Harry Belafonte. But my immediate problem brought me back down to earth in a hurry. "Have you ever cut a Negro's hair?" I asked the old man tentatively. "No," he replied gently, focusing his pale eyes on my reflection in the mirror. "What do you think would be the best way for me to begin? Clippers or comb and scissors?" "Clippers," I replied, a bit more confident, "but let me comb it out first." I took out the sturdy Hercules comb I had brought with me, worked out all the kinks I could, and told the barber to leave about three inches on the top and make the sides a bit shorter.

I could see his reflection as he examined various comb-like attachments on the shelf behind him, picked up one of them, and attached it to his electric clippers. (Dad didn't have any attachments for his hand-helds.) In a moment of truth, the barber flipped them on. I could barely see the teeth of the rapidly moving blades or how they worked, but I imagined the motor replacing Dad's heavy hand. Its noise and the singing of those fast-moving blades reminded me of June bugs—the flying beetles Barry and I used to catch and put into jars back in St. Louis. The buzz of these electric blades was nothing like the slow clip-clop of Dad's clippers.

I scrutinized the barber's every move in his large mirror,

more astonished than frightened. He used various plastic attachments to cut my sides, stopping occasionally to ask if he had taken off enough. I could never actually see what Dad was doing when sitting bibbed for a trim back home. My neck was relaxed because, somehow, I knew there was little chance those electric shears would clog in my hair. The barber found the top more of a challenge. Even though he used several different guards, he had some trouble cutting the hair evenly. There were no gaping holes, only little valleys dipping here and there that I could probably obscure through vigorous combing, brushing, and hefty amounts of Vitalis.

LATER THAT NIGHT, after dinner, I knocked on Bedford's office door, trying to anticipate what he would say about my haircut. "Come in!" he shouted through the closed, but unlocked door. "Palmer," he began in his usual impassioned manner as I walked toward his desk, "did you see this morning's *Boston Globe*?" Bedford was a walking and talking encyclopedia on what was changing in the world, gleaned from his absorption of both the *Boston Globe* and the *New York Times* every day. Before I could answer, he went on to tell me about another French colony gaining its independence from France. I assured him I would read the *Globe* but began to wonder if he understood why I was there. He pushed his chair back from the desk, extracted my permission slip, and without so much as a word about my hair, signed it and laid it in my upturned palm.

CHAPTER TWO

Where Are You From?

WILLIE'S ROLE in my ascent to Exeter remains obscured in the shadows of our lives. When he summoned me to his side for some lesson about the importance of paying close attention to the world, I felt the sudden thrill of being an object of his attention myself. Look, he would say, his voice a throaty whisper. And, already a scholarship boy in the making, look I did, attentive as a little professor.

Willie's first venture into raising my consciousness occurred when I was just six years old. One day he grabbed me by the hand and told me he was going to take me to see something truly amazing in the darkroom at the photography studio where he had a part-time job. (He was a full-time student at the local teachers' college.) Speechless, I tightened my grip on his hand as a signal that I was up for this adventure, even though I had no idea what he had in mind.

We walked to the studio on Kingshighway Boulevard about a block away from our house on Maple Avenue. I remember standing on the sidewalk outside, facing the squat building, listening to the traffic at my back and admiring the large pictures of smiling people in the shop's window. I was feeling brave enough to let go of Willie's hand as, with his signature "Boooooooooy, c'mon" and a sideways jerk of his head, he herded me inside.

A man behind the counter, who I guessed was Willie's boss, greeted Willie and told him the darkroom was all ours. What was a "dark room," I wondered? How could you see enough to work there? I looked around the brightly lit room excitedly. Off to one side there was a stool that sat just in front of a long, gray curtain hanging on the wall. Willie explained how people sat there to have their pictures taken by the camera mounted on a black and silver tripod that stood nearby. *Willie has one of those three-legged things at home for his camera!* On each side of the stool stood a tall shiny pole. Silver shades mounted on the poles, surrounding clear unlit bulbs full of strange-looking wires, gazed down at me like glittering sunflowers. *WHERE is the dark room?* I grew more curious. Willie must have noticed my wandering eyes because he chuckled and told me the darkroom he had promised me was in the back.

I followed Willie around the counter and down a narrow passageway. He stopped in front of another curtain, a black one, and told me to stay close to him as he pulled it to one side. He tugged my hand as he did so, urging me to follow him into the shadowy space the curtain created around a closed door. Total darkness descended when he let the dark fabric fall behind us. *Was this the dark room?* I heard Willie rattling the door's knob and suddenly his hand appeared, bathed in an eerie red light that now streamed into our curtained cavern. *What are these strange smells?* Willie urged me on again with a tug on my fingers, this time into the darkroom itself, as he quickly shut the door behind us.

"Stand still. It's going to take a few minutes for your eyes to adjust to this light," he said. I had to open and close my eyes a few times before I could begin to make out shapes and depth. There were clothespins holding pieces of paper on lines strung around the room. Willie dropped my hand. I sensed he was moving away. I followed the sound of his footsteps and could make out the back of his head in the red dimness. I focused on where he stood and could see his hand reach up. I heard a faint clicking noise. A dim white light came on and beamed down onto a narrow counter similar to the one out front.

A cloudy whiteness seemed to seep into the red atmosphere hovering over everything in the room. I looked around and noticed that the pieces of paper on the clotheslines had pictures of people on them. I could make out Willie's face, too, now, wrapped in its red halo. He stood next to the machine that was spilling white light down onto the counter. Willie explained in quiet tones that it was used to enlarge photographs.

I could feel the concrete floor beneath my feet. It felt like the floor in our basement at home, but was hidden in the deep shadows beneath the counter.

As he excitedly adjusted various levers and buttons I could not see from where I stood, Willie announced he was about to astonish me. His voice grew more and more enthusiastic as he explained he was going to show me how a picture taken with a camera became a photograph on a piece of paper.

He continued to lecture the air above my head, tossing out terms like developer, fixer, stop bath, and silver bromide. Since I would not grasp most of this chatter until much later, I just stood there, barely nodding in response, skeptically unimpressed. But when Willie's chatter disappeared into the deep red silence, just at the moment he placed a sheet of the slick photographic paper into the solution in a tray on the counter, I leaned in for a closer look. Murky gray shapes began to form over some parts of the paper, as if someone had spilled ink there. The hue of a hazy sky took on the curves of an oval. Parts of the sheet continued to darken while others grew paler, brighter, white nearly—even in the dim red light. I gulped, flabbergasted, as I realized that a face, a smiling face, was now looking up at me from the bottom of the shallow pool.

The soft clatter of Willie rummaging for a clothespin to hang the dripping photo with the others on the line was the only noise that broke the silence. I stood there, speechless, until Willie started toward the door. Suddenly I looked around and realized my eyes had fully adjusted. I could see everything in the room, right down to the floor. But there was no time left for exploring that day. Willie, I'm sure, had lots of other things to do, so I dutifully followed his back, out through the door and the black curtained vestibule.

Although we never went back to the darkroom, this solitary experience became my touchstone for everything Willie tried to teach me about photography over the years. When we talked about why I needed to learn how to hold the camera steady and how the picture would come out fuzzy if I moved the camera when I pulled the shutter, he reminded me that the pictures we had seen in the darkroom were clear because the camera had been mounted on the tripod I had seen at the shop. I remember how he urged me to hold a camera in my hand long enough to feel my arms become as steady as his tripod.

At first I didn't fully understand what he was talking about when he showed me his light meter and explained how it helped him determine how long the shutter on the camera should remain open (or, how fast it needed to open and close). This, in turn, controlled the image the film captured. Or why he insisted that I should always take a light meter reading very near to a person's face as well as in the background. But I got a better inkling of the importance of the light meter when he explained that too much light would blow out the white areas of the picture when it was developed in the darkroom. He further explained that too little light would lead to too much black in the image. And so, he unpacked for me the difference between underexposed and overexposed in this context.

The most important thing to remember, Willie told me, was that the final image that emerged in the developing solution in the darkroom depended on what the photographer had seen long before he looked through the viewfinder of his camera. He loved to illustrate this, often during long walks around the botanical gardens, where we would wander the rows of flowers looking at each of them carefully before choosing a particular subject and using his camera to focus in on our selection. Having an eye for photography meant, for Willie, seeing the actual flower in terms of the capacity of the film in the camera, and the precision of its shutter mechanism, and the controlled chemical processes that would produce the final image.

When we were shooting pictures indoors, that long-ago visit to the photography studio framed Willie's lessons on how I should use a flash. He reminded me that the two shaded lamps in the studio that had looked to me like sunflowers were actually giant light bulbs used in taking close-up pictures of people's faces. The photography studio used the sunflower lamps and a background curtain to get those clear and bright pictures I had seen in the shop's windows.

I was always thrilled when Willie allowed me to use the light meter before we adjusted the camera settings. Learning to test the light on a person's face had been my favorite lesson among the many that my de facto mentor had taught me during my elementary school years. Each time I approached some random cousin at a barbecue or descended on the out-of-town company gathered on the front porch to gossip, as I brought the meter close to their faces, I could hear Willie's quiet instructions, and see that face emerging in the solution tray.

A HALF-DOZEN YEARS or so after that memorable day in the darkroom, I was enjoying the summer break following my first year of enrollment in a school with a program for gifted students. It had been my first year attending a different school from Barry, and I'd quickly realized life away from him, without a perpetual sidekick, could be very liberating. It took some effort to adjust. I had to develop ways of doing things on my own. I no longer had to check in on him during recess, or lollygag with him at lunchtime, or walk home with him at the end of the day. But, truth be told, I was very pleased with this newfound autonomy.

That summer, Willie and his family took a trip to the Painted Desert in Arizona. When they returned, Willie called to tell me he wanted me, only me (not Barry and me), to come to his house to see the slides he had taken out West. I told Willie I would call him back, white-lying when I added "as soon as I finish my chores." I had already finished them, but I needed some time to figure out how to escape the house without Barry. I went to find him and saw from the top of the porch stairs that he was over in the backyard next door, playing catch with the boys who lived there. Back inside, I called upstairs to Mom that I was walking over to Willie's for a quick visit. I left out the part about the slides. I didn't want her to remember that she hadn't let me go on the Arizona trip with Willie and his family because I was Barry's designated playmate for the summer. I knew any reminder of Barry would elicit her knee-jerk instruction to take him with me to Willie's. I hastily called Willie back and told him I was on my way.

The long walk to Willie's house gave me time to reflect on

what I might have missed that summer besides an unknown landscape—deserts and mountains. I wondered wistfully what it might have been like to spend that much time with Willie, his wife, Irma, and my niece, Pam. They had been gone for over a month.

Willie had definitely fallen off the adult pedestal where I'd always placed him when he failed to use his verbal skills to push back against Mom and persuade her to let me go on the trip. Part of me knew he had tried to argue that the trip would be good for me, that it would expand my knowledge of geography and earth science. But another part of me was angry that he didn't challenge Mom's notion that I had to be Barry's round-the-clock summertime companion. Didn't he know I was tired of being Barry's babysitter! I tossed the thought that the shared time and taking all those pictures with Willie would have been amazing right out of my mind by telling myself he'd only wanted me along to babysit Pam. Still, the idea of viewing his slides and visiting for a while all on my own took away my self-deflating resentment about being treated as nothing more than a handy babysitter, and instead filled me with genuine anticipation.

When I arrived at his house, Willie told me that the slide projector and screen were set up in the basement because it was darker there. The only light in the windowless rec room at the bottom of the stairs was the projector's beam on the white screen that Willie had placed in front of the television set. Two folding chairs flanked the small card table on which the projector sat. With a wave of his hand, like an usher in a movie theater, Willie invited me to take the seat to the right of the projector as he plopped down in the other chair.

On the phone, Willie had said he couldn't wait to show me the slides from his trip to Petrified Forest National Park, and his voice was as animated as it had been when he first told me he was planning the trip and invited me along. But, as he put up the first slide, he seemed calmer. His voice was uncharacteristically even and clear as he described each projected image, lingering over why he had chosen a particular angle at the entrance of the park or a certain grouping of stones. His voice descended almost to a whisper, as if he were in church, when the shape of a petrified giant redwood appeared. He told me about the tree, wondering aloud what it must have been like centuries before. My eyes were glued to the image as he described the film speed, the time of day he took the photograph, and the various light meter readings he'd recorded before shooting. Then there was silence.

I don't remember any goofy interjections of "Bo-o-o-o-o-oy, I wish you could have been there!" from Willie during our private viewing. Nor do I remember any sense of being bored with his detailed explanations of each slide. I recalled how excited I got whenever Willie had handed me his camera and allowed me to shoot some film. The experience gave me a glimpse of an unfamiliar, serious side of my brother, and helped convince me that he might have wanted my company on the trip because I, perhaps I alone, was genuinely interested in his photography. Interested in him.

I DREW UPON all the insights and advice Willie had shared with me over the years when, early in my first semester, I interviewed to be a photographer for the *Exonian*, the student newspaper at Exeter. The photography editor, Tom, asked me about my previous experience, and I reeled off stories about what Willie had taught me, emphasizing the fact that I had not actually developed film or made prints before. I told Tom what I knew about light meters and cameras, and about the cameras I had used, which included Willie's 35mm Pentax camera as well as my own Kodak Brownie, an inexpensive and small box-like camera that, in those days, children just beginning to practice photography received as gifts.

Tom seemed impressed and offered to be my mentor, promising to introduce me to lots of new cameras—his own and the newspaper's—and to teach me how to take sports pictures, if I was interested. Interested?! It was the most exciting thing an upperclassman had said to me since I had arrived at Exeter two weeks before. Tom wanted someone to cover the sports beat, particularly in the spring when he was hoping to be on the varsity track team and would often be tied up with meets on Wednesday and Saturday afternoons.

Tom taught me to use the Academy's doubled-lensed, German-made Rolleicord. He explained that, with the Rollei, once I saw the image I wanted framed in the viewfinder I should push the shutter that operated the lower lens to capture the image on film. Tom noted this twin reflex system was excellent for action photos, since the photographer never loses sight of the subject (even a moving one) to the sort of temporary blackout that accompanied the opening and closing of the shutter in a single lens camera. I was excited as my horizon of photographic knowledge expanded.

Our first assignment together was to take pictures of a soccer match against another New England prep school. I arrived at the soccer field a bit early and waited eagerly for Tom, who showed up with the Rollei strapped around his neck along with a set of large binoculars. He would later explain how we could attach the binoculars to the Rolleicord's twin lenses to get quality close-ups of the game action. As he strolled, silver tripod hoisted over one shoulder, toward the Exeter bench where I stood waiting, I noticed the light meter that also dangled around Tom's neck and thought of Willie.

Tom mounted the camera on its tripod and attached the binoculars over the two lenses with black rubber connectors. Then he flipped open the Rollei's bracketed top, turning it into a kind of reverse periscope for viewing whatever was in the camera's field of vision. When Tom invited me to take a look at what he had focused on I was stunned by how much clearer and sharper the images were than any I'd viewed with my Brownie or even with Willie's Pentax, and I told Tom so. With a knowing smile on his face and understated accent he replied: "German engineering."

After satisfying himself that I understood the basic operation of the camera—how to press the shutter and quickly advance the film after each shot—Tom took his light meter and pointed it toward a spot on the field where the Exeter players were warming up, and took a reading. He told me what the f-stop should be for the 400 ASA film he'd decided to use and asked me to set the camera up. At this point, Tom took over the equipment, advising me that it would take some time for me to develop the skills in eye/hand coordination needed to overcome the primary challenge of all sports photography: reading the future.

While the teams warmed up, Tom modeled for me how to follow the action with my eyes before beginning to look down into the camera. He told me to watch a boy dribbling a ball who was about to pass to another boy, urging me to visualize the shot I wanted to take before the action actually got to that point in the play because, just at the moment I pressed the shutter, I had to stop swiveling the camera on the tripod or the picture would come out blurry. He encouraged me to practice reading the body language of the boy dribbling while simultaneously locating the eventual recipient of the pass—all this before I took my shot.

Once the game began, Tom shot several rolls of film from various spots around the field. I observed the play closely, not as a partisan for Exeter, but through Tom's eyes. I wanted to learn to see what he was looking for in action shots. Most of his pictures were, understandably, focused on Exeter players. But, as Exeter fell behind by two goals in the match, he shifted his attention and began taking pictures of encounters between Exeter players and the opposing team, where the opposing player was, visually, the obvious winner of the encounter—an opposing halfback, say, taking the ball away from an Exeter forward. Tom stopped to explain that the picture in the paper had to fit the actual sports story. If Exeter ended up losing, the photo he eventually selected for the paper might need to communicate something about the team's loss.

During the last quarter, Tom let me shoot an entire roll of film. I knew this was not in anticipation that I would get a picture good enough for the paper. Tom seemed both patient and confident I would learn. As I moved the camera around to capture views of the action, Tom would suggest adjustments I should make in positioning and aiming the camera. He might sometimes shout out commands like: "Focus on the goalie!" in anticipation of a shot on goal. It was reassuring that his instincts were only right about half the time. It helped me stay confident that I was equal to the challenge of learning this new way of seeing.

After the game, we went back to *The Exonian* darkroom and developed our film. Tom printed out contact sheets that contained small prints of all his pictures, the old-school analog of digital thumbnails. We studied the sheets together. Tom told me he had to make a pretty quick decision on which picture to use because the next day's paper was due at the printer downtown before ten o'clock that same evening. (*The Exonian* was published every day except Sunday, so shooting pictures for the school newspaper took up my entire free Wednesday afternoon.)

Tom's selection process started with eliminating all th e bad pictures. He explained why several pictures flunked out. One was way too blurry. In another he missed the actual kick he was after, although the player was crisply in focus. He'd shot too early in a third picture—the ball was not anywhere near the goalie's hands. We used a magnifying glass to look more intensely at five or six good shots. He chose a picture that showed an Exeter player taking the ball away from an opponent. We put the negative in an enlarger and made a print.

I asked him how he knew what size to make the print and Tom explained that the paper's layout editor had told him before the game what size print he needed for the back page of the four-page edition. While the print dried, Tom took my roll of film and made a contact sheet of my shots. He gave me a critique of what had gone wrong with some of them. My most consistent mistake was not stopping the camera the split second before I took the shot, resulting in lots of blurry pictures. But he was generally pleased with my first attempts to capture the action.

All fall, Tom and I worked on improving my skills at sports photography both on the field and in the darkroom. We shot football, soccer, and cross-country pictures. By the end of the semester, I was taking the pictures by myself and doing all the developing and printing. Tom, as photographic editor, selected the shot for the paper.

Over the course of spring semester, Tom made a wide selection of cameras available for my use and took time to teach me some of the nuances and idiosyncrasies of each. First among these was the Academy-owned Graflex Speed Graphic, which felt like a tank compared to the Rolleicord I had grown accustomed to wearing around my neck. I had seen the Speed Graphic in movies, witnessed its attached, handheld flash, raised above

*Larry and his friend Brink, working on a sports photography
assignment for the school newspaper. This photograph appeared
in the 1960 yearbook.*

the head of some fictional newspaper photographer, exploding
in the faces of generic gangsters leaving downtown courtrooms.
The Graflex's design—higher resolution film than the Rolleicord,
wide angle capabilities, and easy viewing mechanism—meant it
was used in a variety of settings for portraits, some sports events,
and what Tom called "time-lapsed" still photography.

Mounted on its tripod, the Speed Graphic's wide angle capabilities were perfect for capturing a shell full of four long-armed prep school boys powering their sleek boat over the Squamscott River, which makes its way through the marshes to the Atlantic Ocean a dozen miles away. In the world of ubiquitous digital photography and disposable cameras that we inhabit nowadays, my excitement at the prospect of using this famed American-designed, large-format machine with its oversized negatives might seem a bit wonky. But that was the late 1950s. And I was over the moon.

I NEVER BOTHERED to tell Willie (face to face, or in writing) that I was using some of the finest cameras made in the world. I never sent him a copy of the print of my first photograph that appeared in the school newspaper. I didn't even tell him when I became the assistant photographic editor or when one of my photos for *The Exonian*—a shot of four boys in a crew shell—was selected for the yearbook my upper year.

At the time, I blamed my failure as a correspondent on the intensity of my schedule. Chapel attendance was required Monday through Saturday and began at 8:00 A.M. Classes were scheduled between 8:30 A.M. until noon, six days a week. After lunch, a two-hour period was reserved for required sports activities, except Wednesday and Saturday afternoons. Two afternoon class periods started at 4:30 P.M., except Wednesday and Saturdays, although most students only had one afternoon class period, usually the 5:25 slot. (If you were taking fifth year Greek or Latin, you might have a 4:30 class.) Most clubs and extracurricular activities took place after dinner between 7:00 and 8:00 for preps, who had to check in with the teacher on duty in their dormitory by 8:00 every night (unless they had permission from the dormitory faculty or were attending the Saturday night movies in the gym). Church attendance was required on Sunday, except for Jewish students who could attend their Friday night services.

Unscheduled time was a fiction, even though there were no required study periods at Exeter. I had at least one free period every morning, Monday through Saturday. I could go downtown, pick up my mail, or stop in the Academy Grille for a cherry coke.

I might stop in the Grille one day a week, but if I did not spend most of my free time during the morning studying I would not be prepared for my afternoon class or the next day's classes. The method of instruction in which twelve or so boys and a teacher sat around an oval Harkness table to probe the assigned materials encouraged preparation, if for no other reason than to save oneself the embarrassment of being unable to participate if the teacher directed a question at you, or asked you to respond to another student's comments. The hectic schedule, however, did not stop me from sending an occasional short note to Mom or Cynthia (a girl I knew from grade school back in St. Louis).

I would like to think I failed to share stories about my new adventures in photography with Willie because I didn't want to make him feel bad being stuck back at home with his old Pentax. At the time, I assumed it was the expensive technology alone that made great photographs. I may even have presumed, like any proud, competitive sibling, that my action shots were somehow better than, and not simply different from, my brother's still photography. I truly believed that Willie would have been dissatisfied with his 35mm Pentax if he knew I had my hands on Tom's 35mm Leica or his Rolleiflex, the professional model of the Academy's Rolleicord. Willie's lessons in life and photography faded into the shadows along with many other things I left back home. But there was something besides the distance, something in Willie's attitude and actions toward me that had left me troubled and noncommunicative and made the passions he'd tried to share feel more and more like hand-me-down clothes that didn't quite fit. Even before I left for Exeter.

AROUND THE SAME TIME that Willie first swept me into his passion for photography, I became aware of his other deep passion: Omega Psi Phi fraternity, his notion of a brotherhood beyond our biological brotherly companionship.

One evening after supper, I watch Willie and about eight other college-age boys carrying gold bricks march past me in the hallway. At the door to the basement, like soldiers responding to a command, they make a sharp right turn and start down the stairs. Two other boys, carrying narrow gold and purple boards with handles, follow the line into the bowels of the basement. I begin to follow them. "Don't go near the basement!" barks my older sister, Lela, who is finishing up the dishes. I ask her what is going on, and she tells me it's none of my business. *There must be something bad happening if Lela and Willie want to keep it a secret!* I keep quiet, knowing I will be able to eavesdrop on conversations among my parents and older siblings.

The next morning, Willie leaves for his classes at teachers' college, still carrying a gold brick. He looks down at me, grins, and says, "The brothers really used those paddles last night. I'm gonna need a pillow to sit down today!" *Is he serious or joking?* As he walks out the front door, my mind latches onto the words, "paddles" and "brothers." *If those boys are Willie's brothers, are they also my brothers?* As soon as I ask myself the question, I know the answer: no. *Are those gold and purple boards I saw last night called paddles? Did those two boys beat Willie with those paddles?*

I'm afraid to ask anyone because I don't know who is in on the mysterious bad things happening. Nearly every week over the winter, the line of boys snakes its way into the basement after supper. Each boy carries a brick in one hand, and in the other a heavy, old-fashioned train lantern. I was so taken by the gold bricks the first time I saw the line, I must have missed the parade of lanterns.

I overhear bits and pieces of conversations between Willie and our parents as he reports on the basement activities and college. As a fraternity "pledge"—Willie's word, which I don't understand—he has to carry his brick around at school and walk in a line with other pledges between classes. One morning, a week or so after Willie's remark about needing a pillow to sit, Dad asks Willie if his butt is black and blue. Willie shakes his head from side to side and denies having any bruises, adding that none of the other boys do either. *Willie and the other boys are being beaten right in our house!*

One Saturday morning as I sit spooning cornflakes into my mouth, Willie speaks directly to me. He rolls up his tee shirt sleeve and proudly displays a horseshoe-shaped red blister on his arm; my mouth opens wide in shock. Before I can ask who did

such a thing to him, Willie beams: "I'm no longer a pledge. Now
'a brother.' An Omega!" He explains that the Ω on his arm repre-
sents the last letter in the Greek alphabet.

I imagine Willie roped and held down by other boys, the hot
brand sizzling into his arm. *I don't want anybody branding me
like a steer in a cowboy movie! Why would he want anyone to
do this? Does Willie believe our brotherhood would be stronger
if he could paddle me in the basement? Would he let his Omega
brothers brand me?*

These doubts and confusions left me guarded and insecure
around Willie. A very impressionable child, I fretted so much
about the paddles and branding irons, I never considered what
the gold bricks and lanterns might have meant for Willie and
those other boys in the basement. Did Willie allow his frat brothers to brand him to symbolize that his body no longer belonged
to our parents, but to a brotherhood of educated boys? If Willie
ventured beyond St. Louis, did his seared Ω assure him that he
could find other educated men who had taken the same pledge
he'd made in our basement? Maybe Willie touched his seared
arm to remind himself of those who would shelter with him in
the uncertain, uncomfortable, and perhaps even hostile new environment beyond the segregated college he attended. Was he
being courageous? Or was it fear?

My own unspoken fear of fraternity-inflicted violence may
have predisposed me to be hyperaware of a need for rules and
limits. It may have been this that drew me to a sport like wrestling, a sport where elegance and brutal physicality merge within
a controlled set of fundamental movements or forms, all of which
entail risk. Accidents will happen, but the rules and the pre-
scribed forms combine to limit risk.

I barely acknowledged Willie's repeated, "You should become
an Omega when you go to college." I became indifferent as
Harold, and eventually Barry and my nephew, Cornell, joined
Omega Phi Psi, the first Negro fraternity, founded in 1911 at a
historically Negro university, Howard University.

Attending Exeter inoculated me, to a great extent, against
Willie's recruitment efforts, as I wasn't exposed as frequently to
his exhortations of Omega this or Omega that. I was simply not

around. More important, I recognized I was in an all-male environment where hazing was one of the few offenses in the rulebook for which a student could be expelled. I was confident that the faculty members who lived in my dorm would not have tolerated any of the older boys even picking on the younger boys. Escaping the Omega pledge line that Willie pioneered in my family, to my way of thinking, was just one more advantage of being a scholarship boy far from home.

MY RELUCTANCE TO communicate with Willie about my new photographic experiences probably also had a great deal to do with my own self-consciousness about money, and my growing sense of the great privilege my access to the best photographic technology in the world at the time represented. Tom's personal camera collection and the Academy's great equipment were luxury items I knew no one in my family, not even Willie, would dream of owning or using for recreation—what photography for the school newspaper was for me.

Such were the ghosts I carried around with me at Exeter. I was haunted by the fact that I purchased my Brownie Kodak with money I saved from my paper route while Tom's parents paid for his Leica and his Rolleiflex. Not thinking about the very different economic circumstances of my photography mentor made life at Exeter easier, smoother for me. As if I were somehow born destined to be there.

Furthermore, from my first day conversations in Bancroft Hall, I wore my status as a scholarship boy as an internal badge of honor. Like me, about every fourth boy answered the "Are you on scholarship?" question with a confident, "Yes." I knew the parents of the non-scholarship students had more money than Mom and Dad. I assured myself that being a scholarship boy meant I, especially as a very small prep, was recruited by the Academy because of my academic potential. The Director of Scholarship Boys' job, as distinct from that of the Director of Admissions, was to find and encourage boys like me to apply, whether we lived in Minnesota or South Boston. At a more practical level, I would soon learn who the other scholarship boys were because we were all assigned unpaid "scholarships jobs"—

waiting on faculty in the dining room, working in the kitchen, working in the library. (My prep scholarship job was working in the Bancroft kitchen, but I later moved on to the library.) The fact that my father worked in the post office, another prep's father was a banker in New York City, and another's was a public high school principal in a small Indiana town was irrelevant. More apparent than our economic backgrounds, our answers to the "Where are you from?" question revealed that none of our parents were around. Seabrooke, the other two faculty members in our dorm, and by extension, the men of the faculty, were the adults who ran this show.

CHAPTER THREE

Wrestling

Early my first fall, Seabrooke, the varsity football coach, made it clear that he liked that I was small, even if being big was an advantage in football. In addition to coaching football, Seabrooke was assistant varsity lacrosse coach in the spring, and wrestling coach in the winter. When he talked about wrestling, he enchanted boys who had never thought of wrestling as anything other than the entertainment version they might have encountered on TV. Not a real sport. I was no exception.

"Don't get yourself injured this fall; you have a great future as a 115-pound wrestler," he told me a day before my very first class. He recommended I play soccer as my required fall sports activity four afternoons a week. I signed up for soccer.

Brink, my dormmate, told me that Seabrooke had also spoken to him about coming out for wrestling in the winter. Brink was small too, although perhaps an inch or two taller than my own four feet, eleven inches. I don't know if Coach Seabrooke also advised Brink to play soccer. If he did, Brink didn't follow his advice. He chose football. He was, after all, from Texas, where college teams won national football championships. In Seabrooke's eyes, the two smallest preps—Brink and I—were spending our first fall sports season simply getting in shape for wrestling, which would begin sometime in mid-November. In my first year at Exeter, Brink would become my main wrestling partner.

Seabrooke, one of three faculty members who lived in Bancroft Hall, reinforced his message about my potential as a wrestler throughout my first weeks of prep school life. I encountered him almost daily: in the dining room; in the common room (a sort of living room next to the dining room, where the only television available for the forty boys in Bancroft was located); at 8:00 P.M. check-in when he was the faculty member on duty; or along the paths between Bancroft and the athletic facilities. The Bancroft faculty ate nearly all their meals at the faculty tables in the Bancroft Hall dining room. Seabrooke might pause at our prep table to let me know he was following my progress as an athlete ("I heard you scored your first goal!") before joining his colleagues and members of his own family at a faculty table.

COACH SEABROOKE BELIEVED that wrestling was all about conditioning your body and training your mind to react instantaneously to physical and visual stimuli. If you felt the slightest pull on your body from your opponent on top, you must quickly "switch" by throwing your arm across his arm into his crotch, in order to end up on top. On the other hand, if the nerves in your body felt the slightest push, you must quickly grasp your opponent's arm, press it into your solar plexus, and "roll" the opponent onto his back. Working on one's feet involved understanding how to move so that your opponent responded in a way that allowed you to "take him down."

Each day before we entered the wrestling room, we ran a mile in the indoor cage on the wooden track above the dirt track. "That's ten laps, gentleman, half of the lap you sprint, the other half you jog," he proclaimed. "For you preps," looking straight at me and Brink, "the reason for the sprinting is to build strength and power so you can execute a move in a flash. The reason for the jogging is to build endurance so you will be mentally and physically able to go nine minutes in a match with only two one-minute rest periods, or wrestle three times in a day in the New England Interscholastic Wrestling Championships."

Seabrooke seemed focused on preparing Brink and me for a sports career beyond the wrestling practice room, which meant wrestling before spectators. He arranged several exhibition matches for us whenever the opposing team had a kid around 100 pounds (the smallest weight class at the time was 115 pounds). Seabrooke must have been in touch with other coaches to make sure they brought the 100-pound kid along in the bus. He would also arrange for us to wrestle exhibition matches against each other before the starts of our official home varsity matches if the visiting team didn't bring a 100-pounder. One of us seemed destined to become the 115-pound varsity wrestler the next year. Although we were only preps, Brink and I were essentially wrestling six days a week whenever there were home meets.

IN MY QUEST for all things new, I yearned to be outside in the New England winter, and a few weeks into my second wrestling season I decided to try hockey. The hockey rink at the time was neither covered nor enclosed. A year earlier, some of our New England dormmates had introduced Brink and me to skating on the frozen Exeter River on Sunday afternoons. We purchased hockey sticks and used skates. We would skate for miles up and down the river, passing the puck back and forth as we experienced the quiet of the New Hampshire woods. By December of my sophomore year, a few weeks into wrestling practice, I thought to myself: if I could skate for hours on the Exeter River, I would be a natural at hockey. I rehearsed my conversation with Coach Seabrooke.

There might have been some deeper motivation for my decision to quit wrestling: the fear of actually facing a teammate, probably Brink, in a challenge match to be on the varsity or even the junior varsity team. It was early in the season, and there hadn't yet been any challenge matches to establish who the number one wrestler in each weight class was. Both Brink and I were heavy enough to be 115-pounders. I'm not sure if I was more afraid of Brink beating me, or my beating him. The latter might damage our friendship, the former my ego.

I told Coach Seabrooke about my desire to try hockey without any fear of emotional reprisal from him. When I broke the news to him one day before practice, he was in his usual good-humored manner, at least initially. He appeared serious, however, when he looked me in the eye and told me I could come

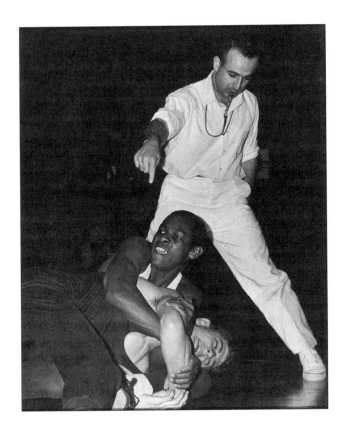

back anytime I wanted. I took him at his word. After only a few weeks, I switched back to wrestling, realizing I was only an average skater. When I reported back to the hot sweaty wrestling room after the first set of challenge matches, Seabrooke told me that I could always continue to skate on Sundays when the river was sufficiently frozen. Brink was the varsity 115-pound wrestler that year, and I was third-string. I still don't know why I took a two-week sabbatical from wrestling. I was changing in ways I did not fully understand.

I MOVED UP to the varsity wrestling team my upper year as the 121-pounder. Brink and I still practiced against each other, even though he wrestled as a 133- or 138-pounder. At the heavier weight, he made the junior varsity team (meaning he didn't win enough challenges to wrestle at the varsity level). He was very good at pinning his opponents to win a match. I, on the other hand, won my matches without ever pinning any opponents.

I can still hear Seabrooke calling to me, "Stick him! Stick him!" when I had an opponent in a position to put his shoulder blades on the mat for two seconds. Inevitably, I would only gain points for a "near fall"—almost pinning the opponent and ending the match—before letting my opponent roll over to his stomach.

But my strengths (and my delights) as a wrestler were my ability to "escape" from the bottom position and my ability to take down my opponent from the standing position. Early in my career, Seabrooke converted me from an "Energizer Bunny" wrestler, constantly on my feet running around the mat the entire time in bursts of energy, into a multiple-geared cobra, able to strike in a flash from what might appear a dreamy slow step. Essentially, Seabrooke coached me to move in a way that would hide my speed and quickness from my opponent.

An opponent who wanted "to lock up"—putting our heads together with our arms around each other's necks—might feel me join in his little slow, lumbering dance. I could feel if he took three steps every time we moved to his right, but only two to his left. So, I would slowly work him toward his left and just after he landed his second foot, I would lower my left arm and drop to my left knee while pulling his head across his chest with my right hand. My goal was to snatch his right leg with my left hand and bring him to the mat. If my opponent countered, or I missed, I would move away and then come in close for another tie-up. If my opponent reached up with his right arm to lock-up, I would quickly knock his arm up in the air, slide across his body on my right knee, end up behind him, and throw him to the mat.

I spent numerous hours working with heavier opponents in the wrestling room on various tactics and moves from the standing position. Seabrooke made sure I never used the same takedown moves from week to week, and I knew how to defend against any attempts to bring me to the mat from the standing position. I was convinced no one could take me down.

My upper-year invincibility on my feet remained intact until I met Carlos Ramos from East Providence High School in Rhode Island. I knew he was supposedly one of the best wrestlers in New England, but I had beaten another supposedly outstanding wrestler from Rhode Island a few weeks before. Seabrooke had warned me he was very good at riding with his legs (scissoring his legs around an opponent's body before moving his victim into a pinning position), so I would need to escape as quickly as possible when on the bottom. As I looked over at his slender, long body, I noticed his dark wavy hair, his milk-chocolate-colored skin, and his handsome face. I realized he was not "Negro" or "colored," but of Portuguese extraction, regardless of what the crowd of whites gathered in the small gym in the cage might think. Ramos earned his first points by taking me down; he accumulated points for a reversal when he was on the bottom; gained riding points for being on top longer; and he also received points for several near falls. I remember spending most of the match doing neck bridges to avoid being pinned. I lost the match on points by a wide margin. Afterward, Seabrooke, ever encouraging, said, "You might get a chance to wrestle him again at the Interschols," meaning the New England Interscholastic Wrestling Championships, in March.

WHEN THE SEEDING came out for the championships, Ramos was ranked number one in our weight class. I don't remember where I was seeded, only that in order to have a rematch with Ramos somewhere in my bracket, I would first need to beat a prep school kid I'd already beaten earlier in the season. As three or four other Exeter wrestlers who'd been selected to compete in the tournament and I began preparing, Seabrooke used my defeat by Ramos to encourage me to become a "pinner." When I made the excuse that I wasn't strong enough to pin most opponents, he argued that I was much stronger than Ramos. How else could I have spent several minutes bridging and avoiding being pinned in two of the three periods? Seabrooke wasn't ignoring my first opponent, but used the week before the tournament to work on getting me to pin from my take-down moves, especially with my first opponent, and possibly with Ramos. He told me I had great endurance for a single match, but to win the championship required me to win three matches in a single day. Pinning my first opponent was an energy saver for my rematch with Ramos.

The much-awaited rematch with Ramos never took place. The Friday after practice, I weighed 126.5 pounds on the scale in the Exeter gym. Seabrooke told me not to eat or drink anything until after the weigh-in the next morning in East Providence, the site of the tournament. On our way through Massachusetts, our bus stopped at a Howard Johnson's for breakfast. We had checked my weight again early that morning before leaving Exeter. I was still at 126.5 pounds. The other wrestlers all ate a regular breakfast. Seabrooke told me I could have only a piece of toast, which I did. When we arrived in East Providence for the weigh-in, I stepped comfortably on the scale. To my dismay, I was just over 127 pounds. In those days, there were no second chances in New England wrestling to run a few laps and weigh in again. I was disqualified for failure to make weight. My body simply would not cooperate in my attempts to stay below the required weight of 127 pounds, having weighed 121 at the beginning of the season in December.

My other teammates were in a state of shock. I was supposed to end up at least in fourth place, points toward a possible team championship. Seabrooke, however, did not look disappointed. He patted me on the back and said, "Our scales must be off. You are a great wrestler; you are going to win a championship next year. Go get yourself some breakfast."

Within a week, I was easily over 140 pounds. My teammates elected me captain of the team for the next year. They must have noticed the transformation in my body more than I did, as my increasingly muscular physique all season announced to the world that I had reached puberty at last. "Body fat" had not yet become a common phrase, but I had very little of it. Seabrooke, the experienced football, wrestling, and lacrosse coach undoubtedly noticed my growth spurt. He was pleased that physical awkwardness was not part of my particular growth leap my last two years at Exeter. He wasn't at all concerned about my weight.

I WAS WRESTLING at the 147-pound class my senior year and usually weighed about 152, two pounds under the 154 limit, the day before weigh-in times. I had won all my matches without pinning anyone going into the final match against our rival, Phillips Academy at Andover. The Andover captain, who also was Negro, was my opponent. I lost the match on points. I was particularly surprised that I lost a point for stalling—not trying to wrestle—when he was riding me on top. I had never been called for stalling in my four years of wrestling. The loss meant I would not be seeded number one in the New England Prep School Championships the following week as had been expected. (The Interscholastic Championship of the previous years, which included high schools and prep schools, had been dissolved into several different tournaments.)

When the tournament selections came out on Monday, I was seeded number two and the Andover captain was seeded number one. Coach Seabrooke alarmed me at the beginning of practice when he called me over to sit down on the mat next to him. "Let me see your right knee." I took off my sweat pants and watched as he felt the puffy tissue. "You still have water on the knee. You are not to practice today and probably not until Thursday or Friday." I hadn't paid much attention to having slammed my knee into the floor instead of the mat during practice the week before the Andover meet because my knee didn't hurt (or I didn't register the pain) when I walked or ran. My heart must have missed a beat as I realized I might not be able to wrestle in the tournament on Saturday. Seabrooke could read my mind.

"You are a much better wrestler than that Andover kid. Your problem was the water on your knee prevented you from bouncing off your knees in the takedown position and when he was riding you. That's why you got called for stalling. You couldn't push off your knees. Once your knee heals, you will be able to take him down anytime you want. Just remember everything we worked on last week. You don't need anything new for him. What you need is rest and to have the trainer look at the knee every day."

By Thursday, I was back running the three miles a day I'd done all year for conditioning without even being out of breath. I worked out with our 167-pound wrestler and found I could execute my takedown moves and my escape moves with precision. I was at my peak that first weekend in March, exactly where Seabrooke had told me he wanted me to be in the fall when he refused to move me from the heavyweight intramural football team that served as our school's junior varsity up to the varsity football team. I had suffered my first athletic injury during practice before the Andover match without knowing how one slight malfunction in one limb could affect my performance. I had no trouble making weight that Saturday morning of the tournament.

With two of our wrestlers seeded number one, including my friend and dormmate, Brink, at 138 pounds, we could easily win the team championship if I upset the Andover captain and Brink and my other teammate, at 115 pounds, won their championship matches. Things went well until Brink lost in the finals just prior to my match with the Andover captain. My teammates were excited about my rematch in the finals, despite the lack of the possibility of a team championship.

I, on the other hand, was calmed by the lesson my first athletic injury had taught me about my body. I might have been able to imagine my right knee sliding along the mat before I sprang off it the previous week, but my brain couldn't register the pain as it smashed into the mat. Neither did my brain comprehend my inability to push off one of my knees when I tried to quickly bounce from a crouching position to stand. In my first two matches that day, I sensed the difference in my body compared to the previous week. I relied totally on Coach Seabrooke to understand what my body could do in relationship to the body of the Andover captain.

Coach Seabrooke had changed my warm-up routine for the tournament by eliminating anything that might display my energy or quickness—the opposite of his strategy in previous matches. In the past he had, for instance, told me to skip rope as a warm-up exercise to signal the quickness of my feet to my opponent's coach, perhaps provoking him to say, "Be careful when you're on your feet with this guy. He's really quick!" My teenage-opponent would probably hear something like, "That kid is better than you are, so be careful." This defensive attitude formed a mental cloud over any attempt to take me down, visible in the way he would cautiously move in those initial seconds of our encounter in the center of the mat.

At the New England championships, my warm-up routine was more yoga-like for my first two matches. Perhaps Coach Seabrooke had surmised that my unexpected loss to the Andover captain had generated a buzz among the opposing coaches: "Palmer got called for stalling last week. He must be hurt or tired out." Or, my slow stretches might have led those coaches to tell their wrestler, "This kid Palmer has lost a step or two, try to take him down," causing an aggressive approach by my opponent that only set him up for me to take him down. I won my first two matches easily, without any ostentatious display of my athletic prowess.

I remember one wrinkle Coach Seabrooke added to my warm-up for the championship match: He told me to keep my baggy sweat pants and shirt on while stretching out and to stop as soon as I broke a slight sweat. The Andover captain was a display of muscles in his long black tights and sleeveless wrestling shirt with "Andover" embossed across his chest (wrestlers didn't wear singlets back then) as he jumped up and down. Coach Seabrooke gave me last minute instructions as I took off my sweat pants: "This guy is confident he can take you down. But he has very heavy feet. Take him down in the first fifteen seconds and let him up as soon as the referee awards you points."

I walked slowly to the center of the mat, shutting out all sounds in the gym before turning on a set of mental headphones tuned only to Coach Seabrooke and the referee. I heard the referee's whistle, then silence. However the Andover captain moved his body, I had an entire repertoire of moves Coach Seabrooke had trained into my nerves and muscles from which my body, not my mind, could choose.

I did not have any preconceived notion of how I was going to take him down. His body's motions communicated to my body how to dislodge him from his center of gravity. With no mental effort on my part, the short dance we did in the center of the mat ended with the Andover captain down on his stomach and me on top of him. "Let him up," I heard Coach Seabrooke shout to me. I pushed myself away from my opponent and returned to the center of the mat and waited for him.

What happened next is buried somewhere in my memory. At some point during the nine-minute match, I remember Coach Seabrooke calling to me to "stick him," meaning to pin his shoulders to the mat. But the ability to totally dominate another boy's body and ignore the pain in his face was something I'd never been able to incorporate into my own body, despite Coach Seabrooke's best efforts. I won the match on points, like all my other victories. I took off the mental headphones as the referee held up my hand, the sign of my victory, around nine o'clock that Saturday in March 1962. I could hear the cheers as I walked across the mat and hugged Coach Seabrooke. I said to myself, "This is it. I'm never getting on a wrestling mat again."

I QUIT watching my diet and found myself putting on weight very rapidly without adding much fat. I was more in tune with my body and could sense its health and fitness. Coach Seabrooke let me know that if I stayed in shape, I would have a good chance of making the varsity lacrosse team that year.

Prep year, I initially signed up for baseball in the spring, thinking it wasn't much different from the softball I'd played one summer. I quickly discovered a difference between slow pitch softball and baseball: I lacked the hand-eye coordination that would enable me to hit the fast spinning baseball. As I struck out every time I attempted to hit that first week, I noticed the intramural lacrosse players running and passing the balls among themselves. I had never played or even seen lacrosse before, but I decided I would learn something new—a sport no one in my family knew anything about. I went to the gym office and switched my spring sport to lacrosse.

My intramural coach told me that as a small player I should learn to play attack, one of three players who stay near the opposing team's goal. When I tried out for varsity my senior year, Seabrooke and the head coach, a member of the religion department faculty who had coached me in football, suggested that I try out for midfield—the players who roam the entire length of the field—because of my size, speed, and endurance. I took their advice and was selected for the varsity team.

In one of my first varsity games, we played against the Boston Lacrosse Club (BLC), a team consisting of former college players who competed against other clubs in the northeast, some colleges, and a few large prep schools. We had no expectation of beating these men, some of whom were good enough to later join the first professional lacrosse teams in the mid-1970s. Our coaches assured us the experience would sharpen our skills against our prep school or college freshman opponents. A good college player could use those curved wooden sticks with leather and string webbings for heads to throw a lacrosse ball between 80 and 100 miles per hour. Their passes and shots on goals, our coaches explained, were not only faster than we might have ever seen, but also more accurate. Their last words before breaking our huddle on the field were something like, "Don't get discouraged."

Less than two minutes into the game, BLC scored two quick goals off both face-offs. Our coaches called a time out. We circled around our head coach again, waiting for his wisdom, his "adjustment." He looked at me and said, "Palmer, once their face-off man puts his head down, shift down to the end nearest the midfield line before the referee calls, 'Set!' As soon as the referee blows his whistle, take out their face-off man as he rakes to his left. We've got to slow down the goals off their face-off wins! Okay, let's go!" I was taken aback.

As I scampered back to my original spot on the side face-off line, I replayed the moves BLC's face-off man had used to score on the previous two face-offs. Both times he had expertly gained quick possession of the ball. He had run down the field toward our goal like he was a point guard leading a fast break in basketball, with the Exeter face-off man trailing behind. Less than three passes later, BLC scored.

As the face-off men hunkered down into their positions for the third match-up, I slipped down the line just before the referee shouted, "Set," exactly as our coach had instructed. I leaned on my wooden stick and crouched down so I could get a quick start. At the sound of the whistle I shot up from my stooped position, imagining not only the point on the field where I would encounter the BLC face-off man, but also his solar plexus, which I calculated as the center of gravity of his compact body. As he started to sweep the ball with the backside of his stick toward his left while still slightly bent down, I drove my shoulder through his midsection just as I reached my top speed. His body rose from the ground as if someone had grabbed his waistline from the sky. I saw his loose-fitting padded leather gloves fall to the ground as his body relaxed into a sitting position, momentarily seeming to float in the air. As he descended, he landed on his butt and fell to his back like he was about to form a snow angel. His helmet unbuckled as his head hit the grass and dirt surrounding the face-off spot. The referee blew his whistle. The BLC players moved toward their fallen star. I stood frozen and watched as the face-off man resisted assistance in getting up. He picked up his gloves and helmet and walked over to me and smiled. "That's the best hit I have ever seen!" he said before trotting off the field.

Prior to that moment, I had always attributed my athletic success at Exeter to my "finesse" and coachability. The previous fall, for instance, during my only year playing football, when I gained seven or ten yards on a play designed for five yards from my halfback position, I chalked it up to my quickness, not to my ability to run through the arms of would-be-tacklers. When my coach recommended to Seabrooke that I be moved up to the varsity team midseason, Seabrooke's refusal reinforced my concept of my body as not particularly strong. "I don't want Palmer to get hurt," I remember him saying. Most likely, he also added something like, "Let him have fun running over the JV guys this fall and getting in shape for wrestling." After all, it was fun scoring lots of touchdowns. I had what I would later describe as the ability to instinctively feel, without any anger or antagonism toward anyone, that the space another human body was trying to occupy actually belonged to me.

Before the hit against the BLC face-off man, I had assumed he was taller and broader in the shoulders than me. In fact, I was about three inches taller and thicker in the upper body. Had this been wrestling rather than lacrosse, we were not in the same weight class; he was at best a 138-pounder and I was closer to a 167-pounder. Nonetheless, I was surprised by the amount of raw physical power I could unleash. I realized I was no longer the little brother or the small prep. I was a boy in a man's body, capable of physical harm.

I was uneasy with the smiles and backslaps from teammates, and the "good job" from our coach when I got back to our bench. Their admiration of my ability to take out a player rumored to have been an All American in college frightened me. I had a new responsibility: controlling my suddenly discovered physical power. At the time, my hit was legal—a face-off we won because the rules about stoppage of play for loss of equipment gave us possession of the ball. However, recent rules changes would make a hit similar to the one I most remember illegal. A player with his head down is now defined as "defenseless" and can't be body-checked at all. If this took place in a game played today, I could be charged with a form of targeting a defenseless player and penalized with several minutes in the penalty box or ejection from the game. I take little pride in my surprise body-check that sent the BLC player flying through the air. Had my take-out occurred in a game with average high school or prep players, I might have seriously injured someone.

I was selected for the All-Prep team in lacrosse and went on at Harvard to win three varsity letters in lacrosse; I was also selected for the All-Ivy League team twice. But my career as an athlete started with Coach Seabrooke. He liked that I was small as a prep; he liked that I was big and strong as a senior even when my mind could not fully imagine what my body was capable of doing. He accepted me.

I never shared with Coach Seabrooke my intention to end my wrestling career. I knew I had disappointed him when I politely refused to consider his offer to get me a partial athletic scholarship at a big-time wrestling school, like Wisconsin. (Seabrooke had been an All-American wrestler at the University of Illinois and knew lots of college wrestling coaches.) I did not want to disappoint him further when he mentioned how he was looking forward to the ways I would develop as a wrestler at Harvard. I allowed his fantasies of me to live on.

He wrote in my yearbook:

Larry:

When you were a Prep & wrestled vs Andover, I told the Andover coach that you would be a N. E. Champion. It couldn't have worked out better. You were a good capt. on a good Exeter team. You & Brink were my 1–2 punch & are both on the All Exeter Wrestling Team. I expect to see you whenever you are in town.

Ted R. Seabrooke

CHAPTER FOUR

Troublemaker

WHAT'S LOUISE DOING HERE? I thought as I watched her switching along the path from Elliott Street toward me with nine-month-old Charles, Jr. (Chuck) on her right hip. She was dressed as I imagined she would be for church in a two-piece sleeveless suit with gold trim that blended into the tan skin of her arms, her fitted skirt cut just below her knees accentuating the curves of her slender figure. Her hot-comb-straightened and curled hair enveloped her oval face, and I noticed how her fuchsia lipstick picked up the red highlights in her cheeks as she approached. The word "pretty" floated into my head as Louise closed the distance between us.

I stood with my dormmates near the entrance of Bancroft Hall, the four story, Georgian-style building of red brick with green doors and white trimmed windows where I'd resided my four years at Exeter. Fresh from our graduation ceremony, my fellow classmates and I had removed our graduation robes, but were still all dressed in dark slacks, white shirts, and those thin ties of the 1960s.

"We just came to say goodbye," Louise apologized, as she turned and glanced back over her shoulder to her car parked on Elliott Street. I followed her eyes and saw her husband, Charles, Sr., seated in the driver's seat. I waved at Charles, a Navy seaman stationed near Newport, Rhode Island, but turned quickly back to my sister as she explained, "Charles has to get back to the base because he's on duty tonight."

I bombarded her with a stream of nervous chatter: "I didn't know you were coming to the graduation ceremony. I didn't see you sitting with Mom and Dad. When did you get here?" But my declarations were only half true. After she and Dad arrived the day before, Mom had mentioned to me that Louise would be coming to the ceremony. When I did not see her seated with Mom and Dad, I had assumed that some disaster had prevented Louise from attending after all. Mishaps seemed to have followed her around ever since she was a child. Maybe that's why her sudden appearance outside of Bancroft filled me with something akin to dread.

ONE OF HER CALAMITIES killed our first dog, a German Shepherd named Roscoe. She didn't literally kill him, but I always believed her bad luck led to his early demise. Louise was about ten years old—and I was about seven—at the time of Roscoe's passing.

Roscoe was fun to play with even though he was not friendly to strangers. I devised a game of chase with him and Barry in our well-fenced backyard. The playing field included the grassy patch near the back porch, the porch itself, and Roscoe's doghouse, which stood beside the porch, its roof just inches below the three-foot high porch deck. The object of the game was to get the ever-barking Roscoe to chase one of us up the porch steps just as the other vaulted over the railing onto the roof of his doghouse. As soon as Roscoe sensed the first intruder on his rooftop, he ceased his chase up the stairs, barked even louder, whirled around, and bounded toward his house. The rooftop intruder would then jump to the ground and run toward the porch steps with Roscoe in hot pursuit. The second intruder, tracking Roscoe's chase carefully, always jumped onto the roof just as Roscoe was about to catch his other prey. The sound of our feet hitting Roscoe's roof always made him turn on a dime and head back down the stairs.

Police dog that he was, Roscoe's instinct was to chase down the new offender on the roof, not necessarily the one who had just jumped and run. Barry and I could waste whole afternoons running in that fixed circle, up the stairs, onto the deck, over the railing, onto the doghouse, across that familiar ground, up the back stairs. Roscoe's mad dash up the stairs, his comic skidding and sudden turns kept us laughing, unafraid of his vicious barking.

One November day, Barry, the dog, and I paused, mid-chase in our invented backyard game, as if on command, and Roscoe's barking ceased. Louise had emerged through the back door, pleading to join our game. I hesitated and took a careful look at her. She wore a long winter coat with a fake fur collar. I couldn't imagine her jumping over the porch railing even if she'd had on a short jacket. But she flashed her pearly white teeth and added a bit more information to her plea. She said that Mom had told her it seemed we were having so much fun—they could both hear our laughter and the barking through the closed door—that Louise should come outside and join us. Once I heard it was Mom's suggestion, I decided it would be useless (if not unwise) to say no.

Perhaps I gave Louise only a partial explanation of the game, the part about running up the stairs, hopping over the rail, landing on the pointed roof of his doghouse, and jumping onto the ground to entice Roscoe to chase her up the stairs before the next person leaped onto his dog house. I might have forgotten the part about the complexity of timing her jump so Roscoe would turn away. Or perhaps with three offenders on the loose, Roscoe (or we?) got confused.

The fateful moment came on Louise's first attempt at leaping over the railing. I was laughing too hard to notice exactly how it happened, but somehow Roscoe put his big paw down on the crown of her head. Blood flowed through Louise's dark brown hair, not yet hot-comb-straightened and curled the way she would wear it as a teenager. Her tears washed over her cheeks until they glistened. Louise's wailing summoned Mom, who used gauze to stop the blood flow and then applied an ice bag to her noggin. There was nothing to stop Louise's tears as she gave her version of the mishap, blaming the entire accident on the dog.

Mom listened to Louise's story and asked her a few questions about what Roscoe had done. Louise told Mom that she had been afraid Roscoe was going to bite her. I wanted to correct Louise and assure Mom that Roscoe had never attempted to bite either Barry or me as he chased us around the porch and in the yard. But he had bitten someone who had approached our front porch several days prior to the incident with Louise. I stood silently as Mom acted as both judge and jury, pronouncing Roscoe's sentence. I failed to come to his defense despite all the fun I'd had before Louise asked to join the game. Mom told us that when Dad got home later that afternoon, she would tell him to get rid of the dog. Roscoe was gone before supper. Dad told us after he got back, with just a tinge of sadness, that he had taken Roscoe to the pound.

Even though Dad didn't say it, we knew Roscoe was as good as dead. I always assumed that he would have been euthanized at the shelter simply because of his size. He was over ninety pounds. On top of this, I believed Dad would have told the truth (as Mom had relayed it to him) if the shelter operators asked any questions about why he wanted to give Roscoe away. The dog had one human bite on his record and, according to the ten-year-old Louise, he had attempted another. This was in the days before German Shepherd rescue groups or no-kill dog shelters. So, I blamed Louise for Roscoe's death (or at least for his disappearance from our lives).

The summer after Roscoe's demise, Barry and I took turns nearly every day pitching old tennis balls to each other. Since we had no catcher as backstop, our turns hitting were limited to ten swings. The objective of our game was to see which one of us would hit more balls over the garage, which we agreed constituted a home run. The easier the pitch to hit, the fewer times whoever was batting had to stop to retrieve his own missed balls or not swing at a bad pitch. We didn't mind the interruptions to retrieve the tennis balls from the back alleys, since actually getting the ball high enough to clear the one-and-a-half story garage was sufficiently difficult that only about a third of the balls ended in the back alley. With three old tennis balls, the pitcher had an incentive to throw balls easy to hit while competing to be home run champion for the day.

One day, I was up to bat, digging into the dirt, as Louise walked down the back-porch steps and asked to join our game without even knowing what we were playing. I had never seen her hit a tennis ball, Wiffle ball, softball, or real baseball. Louise couldn't hit. She couldn't climb either of the two maple trees. Nor could she throw a football. The only thing she could do was roller skate on the sidewalk. Unlike Mom, she was no tomboy.

Mom would occasionally stop whatever she was doing in the kitchen and come out to take a turn at bat in our game. She would lean her stout body into the imaginary plate on the backyard sidewalk; choke up on the bat; peer over her glasses at the pitcher; and usually connect the fat end of the bat with the ball. Barry and I served as catcher and pitcher when Mom batted. Of course, if I was the pitcher, I always threw the ball very slowly since she made it clear she wanted to hit the ball. She even managed to hit a few home runs.

Louise, on the other hand, was a skinny girl with little apparent athletic ability who was trying to join our game for the first time with no clue about how it worked. So, I made my decision without even looking to Barry for approval of my assertion of power as the bigger and older brother. "You can play catcher," I told her.

I once more went through the motions of digging into the batter's box, a patch of dirt near the backyard sidewalk that served as home plate. Barry put the tennis ball in his mitt and imitated a baseball announcer like the ones we'd heard on KMOX radio calling the St. Louis Cardinals games. "Here's the wind up . . . and the pitch is on the waaay . . ."

The next thing I heard was the crack of my bat hitting Louise's left temple, followed by the backdoor hinge screeching and Mom yelling as she ran down the stairs. Once again, blood was streaming from Louise's head, this time running straight down her face. Mom stared at me, still holding the bat, and offered her own analysis of what had happened: "Larry, you've got to be more careful!"

I wanted to ask, "How was I supposed to know she didn't know how to squat like a catcher?" but I refrained. Once again,

I stood in silence. I was afraid that if I contradicted Mom's interpretation of how the accident occurred, I would suffer the unpleasant consequences. But I didn't like being blamed for Louise's mishaps one bit.

WHEN I WAS FIVE OR SIX, I was under the back porch, sitting on the bottommost concrete step leading down to the basement entrance. I had chosen the concrete floor and walls of the well of the basement entrance as the spot for my match experiment.

I struck a kitchen match against the steps and observed the flame carefully. I let it burn down until it nearly reached my thumb and index finger, then threw it into the drain hole at the bottom of the stairs. I lit another, and then another, and another, trying to understand how the matches Mom used to light the gas burner on the stove worked. I must have reached match ten when Louise appeared at the top of the stairs.

"BOY, I'M GONNA TELL MOMMA ON YOU!" she shouted. "YOU KNOW YOU'RE NOT SUPPOSED TO BE PLAYING WITH MATCHES. GIVE ME THAT BOX!"

I handed over the matches without mumbling a word. The way she shouted told me there was little chance I could explain my scientific experiment or avoid her enforcing Mom's rules. I followed her up the basement stairs and on into the kitchen. I contemplated asking Mom for mercy, but Louise cut off any chance for negotiation as she announced, "Mama, Larry was trying to burn down the house by throwing lighted matches down the drain under the porch!"

Mom studied me through her glasses and ordered me to remain in the kitchen. She left me standing in front of the screen door and went outside. I watched her pull a thin branch from the maple tree nearest the porch. As she walked back, I tried to prepare my defense. When Mom shot me another stern glare as she entered and grabbed my arm, I realized Louise's version of the story had already determined my punishment.

Mom's maple branch, her switch, would do its own talking. She whacked me once on the back of my calves and then once on my bottom. I gave out the loudest screams I could muster, thinking she might stop. But Mom remained calm and continued rotating her lashes between my calves and my bottom. I wasn't counting them, but she might have been, because she suddenly stopped. I screamed through my tears, "I didn't know playing with matches was wrong!"

"I know you didn't," she replied in her matter of fact manner, "I just want you to remember from now on." I wasn't sure what she wanted me to remember. That playing with matches was wrong? That experiments like mine could be dangerous? But one thing I did remember was that Louise was a tattletale.

I TRIED TO HIDE my irritation at Louise's sudden and unexpected arrival on the steps of Bancroft Hall. I hadn't mentioned to my dormmates that she might be coming to the ceremony. As she stood next to me, little Chuck getting fidgety in the hot June sun, I tried to pretend my older sister didn't embarrass me. My voice sounded false to me when I asked her about her arrival time at Exeter, though I attempted to convey both delight and surprise. Looking back, I realize I was performing for the audience of my classmates standing there on Bancroft's lawn.

"We drove up this morning. We were sitting in the far back . . . uh, we only got here just as the ceremony was beginning." She smiled. The tale of her late arrival did not ring true to me either, and her "beginning" seemed an exaggeration. I hadn't seen her come into the assembly, which had been held on the lawn in front of the main academic building, a Georgian structure with an iconic bell tower. I suspected she had missed the entire ceremony.

Louise broke the momentary silence by turning toward my classmates and announcing, "Hi, I'm Larry's sister." And then, before any of them could reply, she turned toward me and continued, "Gotta run!" and with a quick glance back at my classmates, added, "Nice to meet you all."

She shifted Chuck to her left hip, hugged me, and sashayed back down the path to the car. I wanted to yell at her retreating figure, "I haven't introduced you," but shouted instead, "It was nice of you to make the trip from Rhode Island." She waved to me once more before she installed herself and the baby in the front seat next to Charles and their small white car disappeared down Elliott Street.

I tried to pretend the quick encounter with Louise hadn't happened, thinking that Louise seemed like a pesky little sister, always showing up to disrupt my plans. I imagined what a disaster it would have been if she had arrived in time to engage in casual conversation with my friends. She probably hadn't even heard of Dartmouth (where Jef was headed) or Tulane (the school Brink had selected). It could have been worse.

In March 1961, during spring break of my upper year (eleventh grade) at Exeter, I happened to be home for Charles and Louise's unannounced wedding. Their ceremony took place in our living room on Maple Avenue. Five of my older siblings were already married, but I hadn't attended any of those ceremonies. Either I had not yet been born, or had been too young, or the weddings had taken place far out of town. The day after the wedding, Dad helped Charles pack up the small car, and my sister and her new husband left for Rhode Island.

I knew very little about Charles except that he and Louise had been dating during Christmas vacation of my upper year. I didn't pay attention to Charles's comings and goings because at that time I paid very little attention to Louise or anything she was doing. Barry told me Charles had been a star running back on Soldan High's team, and that he was enlisted in the Navy and was home on leave for the holidays.

I only began to take emotional stock of Louise and her situation around 10:00 A.M. on New Year's Day when, still attired in holiday party clothes from the night before, my nearly-twenty-year-old sister walked through our front door. She moved silently past where I sat on the steps toward the kitchen. I don't know what made me get up and follow her down the hall. By the time I entered the kitchen, Louise was standing at the end of the table nearest the back door. Mom stood in front of the stove. I stopped at the other end of the table, near the hallway entrance.

I saw Mom's eyes flare and her lips tighten as she nearly shouted at Louise, "Where have you been all night?"

"We went to a club in East St. Louis and decided to have

breakfast at a hotel," Louise offered in a surprisingly confident voice. Mom's stout body erupted violently, taking several quick steps toward Louise. Louise's face contorted in fear as Mom drew back her arm. My sister stood as if frozen. Her passivity prompted a deeply visceral response in me, and I launched my body at an angle, trying to intercept my mother before she crashed into Louise's petite frame. Mom's open left hand collided with Louise's right cheek, sending her stumbling. Mom's right hand was balled into a fist, ready to lash out again. But before she could land another blow, I managed to hook my right bicep over her extended right arm, swing around behind her, and hook my left arm over hers, restraining her firmly.

Louise ran from the kitchen. Mom struggled to free herself from my grip while screaming something at Louise's back about not getting pregnant. For a few seconds Mom continued to struggle to free herself from my clinched arms. In those moments of silence, I was tempted to trip Mom and pin her to the floor as if she were a wrestling opponent. I wanted to hurt her for slapping Louise almost literally off her feet. Fortunately, my mind took control of my rage, and I just squeezed her tighter.

Mom must have realized what I also sensed: she weighed more than me—probably a hundred and sixty pounds—but I was stronger than she was. I was not going to allow her to beat up Louise. Finally, Mom quit struggling, a signal of her submission to my physical restraint; and I, overwrought, released my awkward grip around her full bosom.

I went back into the foyer, overwhelmed that I had openly defied my mother's authority to physically punish Louise. More amazing was my instinct to follow Louise into the kitchen in the first place. I had feared verbal fireworks, at the least. That fear helped me, in that moment, overcome my bad habit of ignoring my sister long enough to rescue her from a beating. I really had protected her.

ONCE UPON A TIME, a long time ago, on a sunny summer day in Forest Park in St. Louis, I sat in Mom's lap, snuggled up against her ample breasts. Something stirred me as I nestled in her lap; not a wake-up shaking, for I wasn't asleep. The message from

Mom's chubby arms became clear: she was pushing me off her, sliding me down her thighs. Was it someone else's turn to climb onto her lap? My younger brother's? My younger niece's? The new baby's or my nephew's? Or could she just be tired of holding me?

As soon as I slid to the bottom of her legs and my feet hit the ground, I wanted to keep gliding, to run to the next plaything in my imagination—a see-saw, a swing, a shimmering tower to climb. But there was no playground at the picnic site, only the long sloping hill in front of me. My feet felt the urge to run away—or just to run to some place down the hill. I took off. I was four.

"Not so fast!" I could hear Mom shouting as my skinny legs and knobby knees began churning, powered by some mysterious engine inside me. The park's grass was short enough to allow my white high-tops to float above the green cushion as I picked up speed. I flashed by family members gathered in the shade of maple trees, swerved around picnic tables loaded with fried chicken, deviled eggs, and pitchers of Kool-Aid-laced lemonade, dashed beyond the white stone barbecue pit where Dad and maybe Uncle Ike were doing up some ribs, neatly dodged my older brothers Mac and Harold playing catch on the edge of the gathering.

I could see the finish line at the bottom of the hill as I found a higher gear, pumping my arms in crosses in front of my short-sleeved shirt. I arrived at the iron railing setting off the picnic site from the sidewalk and the street.

Willie, his camera dangling around his neck, emerged from his 1938 Ford as I stopped at the rail, not breathless, but relieved to have escaped I-don't-know-what. Louise appeared stage left. She must have already been at the bottom of the hill, and I hadn't seen her as I started to run. Or maybe I had her in my mind's eye when I felt the urge to run down the hill to someplace or someone.

Willie must have spotted her too just as I arrived at the railing. He told us to pose for a picture in our summer finery. Saying "no pictures, please" was no use with him. Louise was in a sleeveless dress, standing along the rail, looking directly into

Louise, 7, and Larry,
about 4

the camera with the whole of her seven-year-old self. I—my left index finger in my mouth—looked slightly away from the camera, down the sidewalk. I leaned into her left side, my right arm hidden behind her back. I was happier than I had ever been.

CHAPTER FIVE

My Brother's Secret

BARRY GRABBED MY ARM as I walked through the front door, whispering that he had something he had to tell me about Al. I had just arrived for spring break my second year at Exeter. Barry gave me a look I recognized from when we were kids engaged in mutual daydreams about fielding grounders according to Al's instructions. But Barry wasn't wearing the dimpled smile that had accompanied our daydreaming sessions. In its place, I saw a knot between his eyebrows that worried me. I stood there trying to imagine what Barry knew about Al that I didn't, until Barry sighed, "Come out to the front porch."

I dropped my suitcase in the hall foyer, followed him out into the mild March St. Louis air, and sat down with him on the top step. I was riveted by my brother's ominous tone and, for one anxious moment, wondered if anything had happened to Al. I quickly dismissed that possibility, since no one in my family would ever have selected my younger brother to deliver bad news about my hero, Al. Pushing aside my anxiety I realized how deeply curious I was, but I tried to appear relaxed as I casually asked, "What's up?"

Rather than answering me, he asked if I remembered a "fast girl" we knew at Washington Elementary, Sondria. The word "fast" made me hesitate. I'd never heard anyone at Exeter use it to describe a cute girl who might be freer with her kisses or affection than most teenagers, but I quickly remembered those Maple Avenue connotations. I nodded my head. She certainly was cute. At that moment, Barry blurted out the news that Sondria was our niece. My tone grew more anxious as I asked him to explain. Barry paused for what felt like an eternity as the faces of my oldest siblings raced through my imagination: Lena . . . Al . . . Willie. Barry finally spoke. Sondria was Al's daughter.

I knee-jerked a sophomoric "No way!" If Al had sex before he was married, did it mean I could have sex before I married, in violation of the morality code that hung in the air but was never explicitly expressed at Maple Avenue? The school physician at Exeter had explained in health class how babies were made, but informal sex education in the dorm, built around images of Playboy bunnies, included casual references to rubbers as one means of preventing pregnancy. It was clear to me that few of my dormmates planned on remaining virgins until they married, if they could help it. As a small fifteen-year-old without a girlfriend, I was not brought into conflict with the moral code I had mentally internalized. At least for now. I wanted, instead, to focus on my brain, not the feelings that might be growing in other parts of my body. I gave up exploring my nascent sexual feelings, at least openly.

Barry assumed a more authoritative posture, straightening his upper body and turning to face me, and dropped what was, for me, the real emotional bombshell. Al had told him a few days before I arrived home. Barry knowing Al's secret before I did hurt more than anything. I admired Al so much, I thought, or perhaps dreamed, that our relationship was special, despite the complex social and emotional dynamics of our family. Whatever his reasons for concealing his fatherhood, I thought he would have wanted to share this important news about his life with me himself. Thinking of those family dynamics, I wondered out loud "Why did he tell you?" *Why couldn't Al at least have waited a few days and told us together?* I sat there in stunned silence as Barry told his version of Al's story.

Al and Bernice, Sondria's mother, had known each other as teenagers in Arkansas, and she, like our family, had moved to St. Louis toward the end of World War II. Sondria had been conceived when Al was on leave from the Navy and Bernice was between marriages. Bernice was not simply a family friend Al had known back in Arkansas—though she had always been described to me and Barry that way. Sondria had been born when I was two years old and Barry was one. Bernice's husband at the time, whose name I never remembered, agreed that Sondria should use his last name and be raised as his child. With Sondria about to enter high school, Al and Bernice decided that it was time to tell Sondria the truth about her parentage.

Bernice had always wanted Sondria to know Al and our family. Even after Al married (when I was about five or six) he visited his "old friend" Bernice's house regularly, and so had frequent contact with Sondria. Before I left for Exeter, he sometimes took Barry and me on these visits, which were usually quick, unannounced stops—"pop calling" in Al's Southern parlance. The brief and friendly small talk I observed, punctuated by lots of smiles among Bernice, Al, and Sondria, never suggested that Sondria was anything more than the daughter of a family friend from Arkansas. And Bernice's husband didn't seem to mind our visits.

Years before, Bernice had deliberately enrolled Sondria in Washington Elementary (despite the fact she lived outside of its district boundaries) with the hope that Sondria would get to know Barry and me. In fact, she often ended up assigned to Barry's classroom. Barry was a year older than Sondria, but both ended up on track to enter Soldan High School the same year. Al and Bernice were afraid that, once in high school, Barry and Sondria might develop a romantic interest in each other. Did Barry also think Sondria was cute? Together, they both broke the news to Sondria that Al was her biological father, and then Al told Barry. Al asked Barry to tell me as soon as I got home from prep school. Evidently, Mom and Dad had known about Al's blood relationship to Sondria since the day she was born.

I sat frozen to the wooden step, mesmerized by Barry's monologue. I didn't ask any questions, even though many bubbled up from the swirling pool of tenderness and jealousy and insecurity I found myself dog-paddling through, trying to figure out how all this new information might impact my relationship with Al. Besides, I was afraid Barry would leave something important out of his story if I interrupted him for any reason.

In those days, we knew about the incest taboo without knowing the exact language to describe the prohibition of a sexual relationship with certain biological relatives. I experienced a growing sense of befuddlement that Barry, the little brother I had shepherded through childhood, was warning me, his role model (or so I imagined myself) not to develop any romantic interest in Sondria. Eventually my impulse to interject was too strong to resist, and I blurted out: "Did Al say why he wanted you to tell me, rather than Mom or Dad?"

Barry's response indicated he was as confused as I, though perhaps for different reasons. Barry guessed that Al might have thought Barry would understand my reactions to the news better than anyone else because we had been raised like twins until the day I left for Exeter. Surely if I hadn't been away, Al would have told me himself! If I had been around, would Al have given me time to ask him questions? Had Al asked Barry to tell me as a way of bypassing Mom? I found myself obsessing about how Mom might have broken the news of my brother's out-of-wedlock child. She would have certainly added her own moral lesson for me: don't follow in Al's footsteps by getting a girl pregnant before you marry her.

The emotional energy I expended as I tried to analyze my jumbled feelings about Al and Barry, Mom and Dad, and Sondria made me restless to change the topic. I asked Barry how Sondria took the news, wondering whether they had suddenly become bosom buddies or confidants over the previous few days. He appeared a bit irritated—perhaps by the awkwardness of the role he had been asked to play—and the knot between his eyebrows reappeared before he spoke again. He told me to ask Sondria herself if I really wanted to know, because Mom had invited her to Sunday dinner after church! We exchanged bewildered glances as Barry got up from the porch step and went back into the house, leaving me to speculate on how Sondria's inclusion at the Palmer dinner table my first Sunday home from Exeter was supposed to help me accept her as a member of our family.

I HEARD my new niece's name exactly once more between this conversation with Barry and her arrival the next Sunday at around 2:00 P.M., when, an hour or so before we would be sitting down to our meal, Mom told me to set the dining room table with an extra place for Sondria next to Louise's regular spot. Unspoken messages hid behind Mom's simple directive. There were no "regular spots" for anyone at the dining room table, because we used the dining room mostly for extended family dinners on holidays. On those occasions, Louise, Barry, and I usually ate at a card table in the living room; we weren't old enough to sit at the big table where Grandma Lela (when she was living with us) and my three married siblings who still lived in St. Louis (along with their spouses) dined with Mom and Dad. I translated Mom's order as: set the dining room table the way you would the kitchen table where we usually eat Sunday dinner, but add a space for Sondria.

Mom's second coded message was a warning: eating in the dining room meant Sondria's first meal at Maple Avenue was a special occasion where our best behavior, including conversation topics appropriate for honored guests, was expected. A further subtext: control your mouth and let the adults lead the conversation. It went without saying that we were not to discuss how Sondria might feel about suddenly discovering she was part of the Palmer clan, the question that had been pressing on my mind since my talk with Barry. That we were not to talk about it was confirmed by the fact that no one on Maple Avenue even mentioned Sondria's name.

I rushed to the door when the bell rang. I offered Sondria a hug that I hoped would instantaneously transform her from "fast girl" to niece, then unwrapped myself nervously from her returned embrace. I tried to ease my own awkwardness with a tentative "Welcome to the family." She smiled—she has Al's smile—and told me she had known I was Barry's brother since we were all together at Washington. She teased me, pointing out how I'd never seemed to notice her. I responded jokingly that I was two years older and paid no attention to runts like her. We laughed as I took her coat, hung it on the coat rack in the hall, and escorted her directly into the dining room rather than the kitchen where Mom was putting our standard Sunday fare of fried chicken on a platter.

These allusions to our newly discovered kinship, made when I first greeted Sondria at the door, were the only mentions made of her new status in our family. The dinner turned out to be very formal, with carefully selected topics of conversation—school experiences, the sermon at our church, polite inquiries about the service at the church Sondria and Bernice attended—all announced by Dad from the head of the table. The questions I wanted to ask Sondria about her feelings, and about Al, remained tucked inside. Was she disillusioned like I was that Al had concealed his fatherhood? If she was angry about his deception, could she forgive him? Could I?

As soon as we finished dessert, Mom called Bernice to pick up Sondria. It was apparent that Mom and Bernice (and perhaps even Al) had arranged for Sondria's first visit to Maple Avenue to be brief. I realized that if I thought a meaningful conversation with Sondria might help me resolve my own mixed feelings about Al, I would have to find a way to talk with her outside the company of the family. Talk as one teenager to another.

I didn't know how to address my hurt feelings directly with Al. Not only was it emotionally too hard to confront my oldest brother, it was logistically impractical: I didn't live at home; I spent only a few weeks of vacation in St. Louis during the school year; and Al was either working or occupied with his own family. By the time I got home for the summer, other issues had erupted in my fickle teenage heart.

I DIDN'T HAVE an opportunity to talk to Sondria either during the remainder of my spring vacation, or at any point while I was still a teenager. Sondria and I had our first chat about Al when I was twenty years old—Al's age when Sondria was born—and a junior at Harvard. By then, Sondria had had a major fight with Bernice and was living on the third floor of the Palmer house on Maple Avenue. I sat with her in the bedroom that Barry and I had shared before I went away to Exeter and finally asked about her relationship with Al. Listening to her version of the story, I noted some discrepancies from what Barry had told me five years earlier.

It turned out she'd never been told (had never even thought) that Bernice's second husband was her biological father. In her mind, he was her stepfather. Bernice had told Sondria that her biological father was Bernice's first husband, who, for no other reason than being a bad person, had never wanted to see his daughter. Sondria told me how she broke down, cried, and eventually became angry when Al and Bernice told her the truth. Sondria asked them both why they had lied to her all those years. Bernice had shot back in anger; she hadn't wanted anybody to call Sondria a "child out of wedlock," especially once she started school. Sondria speculated that her mother had mistakenly believed she would, or should, actually be grateful for the deception, and described how Bernice wept as Al stood there, mute, by her side.

Sondria went on to say that Al had remained calm; that he had tried to soothe her. He explained that after Bernice remarried he agreed to keep Sondria in the dark out of respect for her mother's wishes. They tried to reassure Sondria of their good intentions by pointing out that Al had always paid Bernice "child support," even though Sondria grew up thinking she was the dismissed daughter of some unknown man. No one had ever led her to believe she might be Al's. Not the child of her mother's "friend from Arkansas."

Had Barry been confused about this point? Or had he just failed to understand all the nuances of the story Al had shared with him so many years ago? Maybe I had been distracted and missed what now felt to me like an important detail. The words "child support" sent my mind racing to another place.

I had often wondered why Al had never attended college after leaving the Navy. I viewed Al as the more "intellectual" of my two oldest brothers. Willie, the college-educated schoolteacher, was always trying to teach me something. Al, by contrast, seemed more interested in playing with ideas with me. I was struck by how Al had used a course on Mark Twain he'd taken in an adult education program as a springboard for conversations with me about *The Adventures of Huckleberry Finn* when I was a freshman at Harvard. I sometimes imagined Al sitting in a college dorm room, talking to a classmate about the issues of their times, engaging in conversations like the ones I was enjoying about civil rights, the French war in Algeria, or the meaning of films from France, Italy, and Sweden. I leaped to the idea that Al was forced to find a job upon discharge, rather than use the GI bill to go to college, because he had a daughter to support.

From Harvard, my mind carried me to my earliest memory of Al and the yellow pants he had made for me, the week I'd been hospitalized with a concussion. That was just before my fourth birthday. . . . Did he use his GI Bill to take tailoring lessons rather than go to college?

Listening rather distractedly, I didn't fully process the significance of Sondria's descriptions of her deep sadness at the sudden news that Al was her father. As she relived her discovery of Al as her biological father, she began to sob. Her tears jolted me to tune back in and hear her talk, almost urgently, about her desire to get away from St. Louis, to go live in Texas with Bernice's mother, and to finish high school there.

Sondria did move to Texas, and I lost contact with her until after I graduated from law school and she returned to St. Louis. I was pleased to find that with time she had come to share my strong affinity for Al. Her father. My brother.

THE SUMMER BEFORE I entered kindergarten, I watched as Al, with Dad and three of my older brothers, built a cement block fence to replace the rusted wire fence clinging to the old, rotting wooden post along the alleyway. I had set up my observation station on the steps of the back porch to see if I could figure out what they were doing. I noticed that in the confusion of trying to understand Dad's barked orders, while Urshel, Mac, and even Willie sulked in silence, awaiting clearer instructions, Al, whistling a song, seemed to understand what to do with very little direction from Dad, like the junior boss of the work gang. As the work pace hastened and the sun got hotter, Al asked me to help.

Al took a blue handkerchief from his hip pocket and wiped his forehead as he walked back toward the house to start his second row of cement blocks. He looked down at me on my perch at the bottom of the stairs and said, "Larry, be a good gopher and go tell Mom to fix us some ice water." I jumped up and ran to the kitchen to pass his message on to Mom. She emptied ice from trays in the icebox into a pitcher and filled it with water. I tried to pick it up with one hand, but it was too heavy. I tried to grip it with two. Mom saw me struggle, came over, and took the pitcher. She picked up a glass and walked out onto the porch and called to Al. I tagged along behind her, a little embarrassed I had not been able to lift the pitcher of water. Al hurried over and met Mom at the bottom of the stoop, taking the pitcher, already sweating from the heat, and the empty glass from her. As he turned and walked toward my father he looked back at me, laughed, and said, "When you're a little bigger, you'll make a good water boy!"

A few months later, on a fall afternoon, Dad, Willie, and Al were planning to cut down the silver maple tree near the garage. It stood taller than our two-and-a-half-story house; the other two maple trees along the new fence were barely two stories high, and didn't represent the sort of danger my father recognized in the towering shape of the older tree. Dad feared that, in a thunderstorm, the tall maple might fall onto the house or the garage.

As preparations began, I ran down the sidewalk to ask Al if I could be the water boy. He looked down at me with a concerned frown, a look of alarm in his usually smiling eyes, and chided me gently, "Oh, no little brother." He explained that cutting down a tree was too dangerous a job for a "little fella" like me to be around, and he told me to go back and stand on the porch.

Before I could answer Al, Dad intervened with an agitated "No!" ordering me to go inside because there would be tree limbs flying all over the place even before they went at the tree's trunk. I tried to hide my disappointment and offered Dad my obligatory "Yes, sir." As I started back down the sidewalk toward the porch, I heard Al call out to my back that I could watch from the kitchen window. I turned around and mumbled a dejected, "Okay."

From my perch in the kitchen windowsill, I watched Al sling a rope over his shoulder and climb up the tree. He disappeared into its silver green leaves, just starting to fade toward autumn yellows and burnt oranges. Suddenly the rope slithered back down through the multicolored foliage. Willie grabbed one end

of it and tied it around a single-handled saw. A few moments
after Al pulled the saw skyward, the leaves near the top of the
tree started to shake. Dad moved up the sidewalk toward the
porch, turning around just as he reached the bottom step. He
tilted his head back and trained a studious gaze upon the treetop
where Al worked, hidden.

Dad shouted something into the sky just as a large branch
came crashing down into the yard. Al's head appeared in the
opening. He released the saw, letting it dangle in the branches
below as he disappeared again into his leafy cave. After a while,
Al's hand emerged and grabbed the saw's handle. A few minutes
later, Dad shouted again and another thick branch, with multi-
ple tentacles reaching out in all directions, fell into the yard. Al's
head and upper torso were clearly visible. I could see that he had
used the other end of the rope to tie himself to the trunk of the
tree. He untied himself, secured the rope to a large branch, and
lowered the saw into Willie's waiting hands before he vanished
again, downward, into the branches. Once Al had lopped off a
third of the tree, he lowered the saw for the last time, and finally
lowered himself to the ground to consult with Dad and Willie.

After a few minutes of quiet debate, Willie slung the roll of
rope over his shoulder and climbed up the tree. He tied one end
of the rope around what remained of the tree's top, dropped
the other end down to Dad, and climbed down out of the tree.
He and Al took the long two-handled crosscut saw and walked
around the maple. Dad picked up the one-handed saw and
marked a spot on the tree with a few strokes. Even with the yard
full of felled branches, the giant maple still blocked my view
of the top of the garage and towered over the two other maple
trees that stood near the new fence. Al and Willie took the two-
handed crosscut saw and began sawing through the cut that Dad
had started. Back and forth they went, faster and faster, as if to a
tune that kept speeding up.

My brothers stopped to rest for a while, stripping off their
flannel shirts before getting back to their sawing at the trunk
in their white tee shirts. Dad watched closely as they sawed
through the thick tree trunk, and soon signaled for them to stop.
Al picked up several steel wedges and Dad instructed him where

to place them. Willie handed Al a sledgehammer, then he and Dad grabbed the rope secured to the tree's top and started walking toward the house. With the narrow ends of the wedges firmly inserted into the partial cut in the tree trunk, Al started taking huge, mean swings at their wide bases, driving them deeper into the tree trunk slowly, like giant nails. Willie and Dad, standing in front of the porch steps, pulled on the rope together, the task requiring the combined strength of their bodies. My eyes shimmied along the rope, starting at the point where it emerged from their knotted fists, following its upward slope into the tree that began to waver as if blown by a strong wind. But there was no wind. The leaves in the other two maples hadn't stirred.

Al stopped, stood up straight, and shot Willie a glance, then waved to signal he was almost finished splitting the trunk. Willie pushed Dad toward the next-door neighbor's slatted fence, gave the rope a downward yank, and then ran down the stairs to the basement entrance underneath the porch. Al gave a few more whacks at the wedges. I looked up just before the maple tree—its many branches streaming a rainbow of silvery green, yellow, and burnt orange—fell to the sidewalk with a booming crash. The tree's crest landed just a few feet from the bottom of the back-porch steps. Willie emerged from the basement stairwell, grinning. As he and Dad closed the distance between them, my father's rounded shoulders seemed to relax for the first time. Al stood tall and erect near the stump of the maple and smiled with his arms stretched out like wings, hugging the big new sky he'd helped to uncover.

The backyard remained off limits for several days as Al and Willie chopped up the tree and burned the branches and logs in the ash pit at the end of the garden. I couldn't see the roaring fire from the kitchen window, but I could see the smoke billowing above the garage. They chopped up the stump and dug it out enough for Dad to plant a dwarf apple tree in the silver maple's place within a month of its felling. I didn't understand then that the felled silver giant must have been severely diseased. It was over fifty years later, when a neighbor's large oak tree fell into my own backyard on a sunny and windless day, damaging my garage, that I saw, first hand, how termites could weaken an apparently healthy tree. Dad (and perhaps even Al and Willie) had enough experience from their Arkansas farm life to recognize such things.

As I GREW OLDER, I discovered the incidental benefits of removing that old maple tree: most notably that it left more playing space in our backyard (which stretched a good fifty feet from the bottom of the back-porch steps to the garage door and maybe thirty feet across from our cement block fence to the neighbor's wooden one). Realizing its silvery branches no longer crowded over the concrete pad in front of the garage (a perfect surface for bouncing balls), Al installed a basketball hoop there; its shiny orange rim sparkled against the whitewash of the garage. I was about ten when our home court hosted its first game.

The day Al put up the hoop I was so preoccupied with watching him install it I didn't notice the brand new, dimpled, black-lettered basketball until he picked it up and announced he was going to teach Barry and me how to shoot. He bounced the ball to me and told me to bounce it back to him, which I did gingerly. I marveled at how smooth and light it felt in my hands.

We started with the two-hand set shot, popular among college and professional basketball players in the 1950s. To demonstrate, Al dribbled the ball on the concrete a few times, then, still dribbling, quick stepped onto the sidewalk connected to our makeshift court. He stopped about ten feet away, turned around to face the basket, and told us to pay close attention. Using both hands, he pushed the ball away from his chest, lifted his arms above his head, and sent the ball sailing in an arc that connected with the rim of the steel hoop. As the ball fell through the white net and bounced back toward him, Al stepped up and caught it, then bounced it to me, instructing me to give it a shot.

I grasped the ball, held it against my chest, and started to walk, without dribbling, toward the spot where Al had stood. He laughed as he told me to come closer to the hoop, explaining that where he had stood was too far away for me. I walked about half the distance to the hoop for my first-ever basketball shot. I tried to imitate the motions Al had made with his hands and body as I launched the ball upwards. It arced feebly and landed at the bottom of the garage door. Barry, standing off to my right, laughed. But Al didn't.

He motioned with his right hand for me to come a little closer as he picked up the ball with his left hand and instructed me to do the two-hand shot a little differently. He proceeded to show me how to bend my knees and crouch down, holding the ball between my legs. Rising out of my squat as I swung my arms upwards my underhanded release gave the ball more momentum as I let it go. On my first attempt from a crouching position the ball landed on the closed garage door just below the basket. Al smiled. He came over to me before my next try and adjusted the depth of my squat and told me where to focus my eyes as I went through the motions of throwing the ball toward the rim. He then said something I wouldn't appreciate for some time: "You will start to feel the power in your legs and back go up through your arms." I believed him.

He let Barry, who had been observing my lesson, have a few tries at shooting the ball underhanded. Al moved Barry about a foot closer to the basket than he'd placed me. Barry's shot hit closer to the rim, but neither of us succeeded in getting a single basket that first day, though we kept at it until Al announced he had to go home to his wife and kids. He said that he'd be back on Saturday to check on our progress.

Through the falls and winters of our preteen years, Al advanced our basketball skills: dribbling, driving the basket (we had to open the garage door for those drills), jump shots, rebounding, and guarding without committing fouls. By the time we moved up to the ten-foot-high hoop on the school playground, I knew the rudiments of the pick-up shooting game, HORSE, which was sometimes used to decide who would be captains of the teams in a pick-up half-court game, who were then awarded the prize of selecting their respective teammates in a schoolyard draft.

Springs and summers, Al switched to working on our baseball skills, particularly fielding. He started by throwing us groundballs. Once we got the knack for putting our bodies in front of the moving ball, Al gradually increased his throwing speed, each lesson more and more challenging. Al would hit grounders toward me so I could practice getting out of my defensive crouch, running toward the ball, fielding it with my glove and throwing it to Barry on our pretend-first base to make the out. If I failed to pick up the ball cleanly, or it went through my legs, Al would tell me how to correct my mistakes. Barry and I would switch positions to ensure we got equal training. Al always left us with homework (like fielding backhanded when balls came zinging into our right sides) until our next lesson. And he warned us to be careful throwing the real baseball to avoid breaking any of the garage windows.

The lack of space in our small backyard didn't stop Al from turning it into a version of a sports training facility for Barry and me.

IN THE SUMMER of 1957, Al started a snow cone business to supplement the income from his job at the cable wire factory. When he asked me—not Barry and me—to work after supper with him, I readily accepted, even though I already had an early morning paper route. There were no parental objections or even discussions about whether I could accept Al's offer. He had either pre-cleared the plan with Mom, or he had enough authority within the family to decide on his own what was good for me. Al and I discussed what he wanted me to do and how he would pay me a percentage of the profits, after he figured out and deducted his expenses, for any evening that I worked.

Several nights a week, after a very early supper, I would walk nearly two miles to Al's house. He lived in a neighborhood known as The Ville, a residential and commercial district that had been the educational and cultural center for Negroes in St. Louis since Reconstruction. Al was convinced that there were plenty of people in The Ville—relatively prosperous Negroes like himself with steady employment in steel mills, auto plants, and meat packing houses—with the means to purchase after-dinner treats, in the form of snow cones, for themselves and for their children during the hot summer months. So, he purchased a small white truck equipped with an ice crusher, icebox, and storage space for the syrups, paper cones, and other equipment necessary to drive around the residential streets until dark, hawking bits of frozen bliss. That summer I learned how to operate the gasoline powered ice crusher, pour the appropriate amount of syrup, and quickly make change on sales.

Al drove the truck slowly through the neighborhood, often whistling a tune, while I rang a bell and yelled out, "Snow cones! Snow cones!" Al often put me in charge of counting the number of cups and measuring the amount of syrup at the beginning and end of each evening. I also kept track of the ice expenses in a little notebook he kept in the glove compartment. The job provided extra practice for my arithmetic skills that summer. Al was always friendly and personable. He might greet a customer whom we hadn't seen in a while with, "I haven't seen you in a few days. I hope everything is okay. Do you want a grape like the last time?" I tried to follow what appeared to be Al's first principle of customer service: get to know your customer and remember their individual preferences.

Al would drive me home after we had cleaned up the truck and stored the supplies in his garage. I usually walked through the door at Maple Avenue by nine-thirty or so, my share of the night's profits jingling in my pockets. If Al had wanted to paint a sign on his small white truck, I guessed it would read, "Palmer Brothers Snow Cones." I imagined he would want the wording to live up to his Arkansas nickname, Brother, or, as Barry and I called him, "Bro." Al (the name my brother used when referring to himself), was my father's namesake—Arglister L. Palmer, Jr.—and he was always willing to shoulder the responsibility that name implied, extending a helping hand to any of us in need. But he was special to me. If I'd had my way, that fantasy sign on the white truck the summer of 1957 would have read: "Palmer and Son Snow Cones." Such was my selfish, childish desire. In those days, in the fictional ideal childhood I fabricated for myself, Al was always the stand-in for my aging, high-strung father.

Not long after our summer snow cone business, as my application to Exeter entered its final stages, Al was called upon to stand in for Dad at a meeting with Exeter's principal, William Gurdon Saltonstall, when he visited St. Louis.

Earlier that fall my teacher, Dr. Hyram, had arranged a meeting between Mom and me with Hamilton ("Hammy") Bissell, Exeter's Director of Scholarship Boys, at the offices of the St. Louis branch of the Urban League. Two representatives from the League, who served as Hammy's contacts for locating promising Negro applicants in St. Louis, also attended. That day Hammy was in recruiter mode as he explained why he thought I might be a good candidate for Exeter. He seemed particularly impressed that I was a paperboy as well as an excellent student. He explained the timetable for the required tests and the application process. At the end of the meeting, Hammy indicated that he wanted my parents and me to meet the principal of Exeter who would be coming to St. Louis for an alumni event a few weeks later. The Urban League representatives said they could make their offices available for the meeting with Saltonstall, and the arrangements were made.

Later that evening at the dinner table, Mom told my father about the meeting scheduled with Principal Saltonstall. Dad's irritated and gruff, "I'm not taking a day off work to meet whatever his name is!" suddenly made me aware that he had been totally silent about Exeter until that moment. "But, Bud,"—it was one of the few times I heard Mom call Dad by his Arkansas nickname—"it's important that both of us be there to meet Mr. Saltonstall. I am sure the other fathers will attend the meeting. You don't want them to pick one of the other boys over Larry, do you?" Dad ignored her pleas and asked Barry about his day at school. I don't recall anything Barry said, but I remember rehearsing in my mind what I would say when Dad asked me about mine. I carefully avoided any additional mention of my meeting with Hammy Bissell that afternoon, sensing that any reference to Exeter might bring on another of Dad's angry outbursts. I asked myself if Dad was, for some unfathomable reason, questioning whether I should even apply to Exeter.

As the date for the meeting with Mr. Saltonstall approached, Mom told me that Al, my oldest brother, would attend in Dad's place. I had no idea whether Mom had solicited Al's help, or how Dad had reacted to Al's willingness to take time off from his own job to attend the meeting. I suspected there was an ongoing argument among the Palmer adults about my application. Dad had said nothing to me about Exeter since his initial, abrupt dis-

missal of the opportunity to meet Saltonstall. Nor had he spoken
to Mom about it, at least not in my presence.

Al's attendance at the meeting with Saltonstall signaled to
me that he was in favor of my applying to Exeter. When all five
feet, eight inches of Al rose from his seat to shake hands with
the six-foot-three, white-haired, bushy-browed Saltonstall, I felt
certain he would know how to present Dad's questions and concerns without fussing or sounding anxious. Al used his most gentle voice to make excuses for Dad's absence. Saltonstall seemed
to accept the idea that Dad had been unable to get the day
off, and expressed the hope, with a twinkle in his eye and a sly
smile, that he would meet my father on another occasion soon.
Al chuckled as if he and Saltonstall shared an understanding of
what the meeting was all about. I didn't understand then that
Saltonstall meant to express his hope that I would apply. At the
time, I was simply relieved to see the confident light in Al's eyes
as he relaxed into his usual calm demeanor.

"Salty," as I would later know the principal, proceeded to
extoll the virtues of Exeter: the small classes, the sports, the
music, living with other boys. After his sales pitch, he asked
Mom and Al if they had any questions. Al took the lead, at first
asking rather straightforward questions about the length of the
vacations in the winter and spring. He then moved on to what
I guessed were Dad's concerns: what was the racial climate
for a small Negro boy like me? Salty conceded that the Academy had only a few Negro students, but assured Al that recruitment efforts were underway to make sure I would not be the
only Negro student in my class. He pointed out that Hammy Bissell was traveling the country trying to find not just other Negro
kids, but scholarship applicants from all sorts of backgrounds.
I was quickly sold on Exeter, but felt I had to be careful not to
show my enthusiasm at home. I left the meeting determined to
let Al battle with my father over the merits of the school and
whether I should attend.

FOUR YEARS LATER, as I was about to leave for my freshman year
at Harvard, Mom asked Al to talk to me about the dangers of
premarital sex. She wasn't worried about the college girls I might

meet in the fall, but about a high school sophomore named Cheryl who, Mom was certain, had bewitched me that summer. I have always assumed she expected Al to play the "Sondria Card" when he took me aside one August evening to talk to me in the lawn chairs out back.

I wasn't sure how much Mom had told him about the continuous verbal fisticuffs we had been engaged in about Cheryl since June. These arguments usually started with Mom's accusation that I was having sex with Cheryl, then progressed through Mom's fears that Cheryl would end up pregnant and I would not be able to attend Harvard. I didn't bother to deny Mom's assertion that I was having sex with Cheryl. Rather, I countered by angrily questioning how she could know I was having sex with Cheryl. Mom claimed she could tell I wanted to have sex with Cheryl—which was certainly true. Such was our impasse.

I could have admitted I was still a virgin and lowered the level of hostility in these conversations, but I took sinister pleasure in keeping Mom in the dark. Her criticisms of Cheryl and lack of trust felt like an all-out assault on my own judgment. Perhaps Mom thought her constant harping about how my future would be ruined if I had sex with Cheryl might actually serve to restrain me. She didn't pause to consider that I honored her moral code and also believed that sex before marriage was wrong. As far as I could determine, so did Cheryl. Cheryl was the first girl that got my passions raging, but I was actually still afraid of ending up in hell. Mom had watched my five older brothers go through puberty and had ample experience observing male hormones gone wild. She could see the telltale signs, including my defiant refusals to answer her questions. I'd invited Cheryl to a family picnic in Forest Park without telling Mom (or anyone else in my family), and I suspected that this had motivated my mother to call in reinforcements in her war against my budding sexual desires. So there Al sat.

I stared at him skeptically as darkness crept over the backyard. I viewed him as Mom's ground attack, so I steeled myself to resist my true desire to talk to him about Cheryl. I remembered how Sondria had described mistrusting Al for deceiving her, and wondered if I could trust him now. I didn't need him to give me a Miranda-type warning, "Anything you say to me may be reported back to Mom." I was ready with my mental tools of deflection, but without the sharp edge of anger I had used all summer with Mom. This was, after all, Al.

Unlike me, Al seemed very comfortable in his own skin as he began to talk. He nearly succeeded in disarming me with the gentleness of his voice, but I fought back with an inner mantra. Be strong! I was so busy preparing myself for a hypothetical tirade about Sondria and his mistakes and the circumstances that had led to her birth that I almost missed the two brief sentences he spoke: Mom, he explained, was worried about my relationship with Cheryl. And he had no intentions of telling me what I should or should not do about it.

We sat there in deep silence for a few minutes as I tried to figure out what to say. I failed to consider whether Al was waiting to see if I wanted to talk about my relationship. I was feeling too defiant to ask myself whether it would be a good idea to talk to him about it. I also failed to consider that Al might have thought Mom's approach to my blossoming sexuality was inappropriate or, at the very least, not good for me. It never occurred to me that Al might have interpreted Mom's request to talk to me literally, that he had no intention of delivering any "Let's not have any more Sondrias in this family" messages. Al rose, and, without further comment, walked up the back-porch steps, and went into the kitchen. I sat staring across the lawn at our neighbor's fence, disappearing in the early evening darkness, thinking about how Al had fulfilled the letter of Mom's law by taking me aside to talk. But the spirit of those two sentences had been his own.

CHAPTER SIX

Alone

I GRAB HAROLD'S HAND through my mitten as we reach the bottom of the front stoop of our house at 4956 Maple Avenue. I look to our left, toward Kingshighway Boulevard and see children in colorful stocking caps high stepping with anticipation along the sidewalk. To our right, more children march along the sidewalk, past the other three turn-of-the-century houses on our side of Maple, toward Hoffman's Market on the corner of Aubert. We join this growing throng floating past our house like minnows headed toward a shoal, and wait our turn to cross at Aubert and continue along the other half of the 4900 block. As we step off the curb, I realize Harold is taking me across the border of my known world.

I squeeze his gloveless hand once more through my navy-blue mitten as he speaks to other children he knows. We make our way to the end of Maple at Euclid Avenue. I notice some boys chasing another boy. They run a zigzag among the walkers on Euclid as Harold continues talking. I don't hear anything that is said because I am nervously searching for the boy being chased. I notice the walkers ahead bunching up. They seem to be gathering in a swirling pool that empties into a narrow passage. Their chatter becomes subdued as more and more of them climb a set of stairs and pass through a gate in a black iron fence into an asphalt lot. Harold leads me a few steps further and stops in front of the main entrance of a three-story brick building. We walk up a long flight of stone stairs. Harold pulls the top of his pea coat together, releases his grip, and opens a heavy green door with "Washington Elementary" carved in stone above it. My first day of school, January 1949.

Harold takes my hand and walks me down to the end of a shiny first-floor hallway. At the kindergarten room he reminds me again who my teachers are, says goodbye, and assures me he'll be back at lunchtime to pick me up. I march across the threshold by myself.

Miss Curry and Miss O'Fallon, my kindergarten teachers, greeted me with smiles. "You're Louise's little brother, aren't you?" Miss Curry asked.

Miss O'Fallon laughed and asked, "You're Harold's little brother, aren't you?"

"Yes, ma'am," I answered confidently, although I didn't see what was funny. Miss Curry was just as Harold had described her: a tall and wide, fair-skinned woman with freckles. No lipstick. And short black curly hair. She showed me where to hang up my brown wool jacket and cap. My mittens were attached to the sleeves of my jacket by a short piece of elastic with clips like the ones on the ends of suspenders. Miss O'Fallon also fit Harold's description: brown-skinned and heavily powdered with almost purple lipstick. She was both shorter and less stout than Miss Curry. Miss O'Fallon took me over to the blocks and told me to build a house until the other children arrived. I soon moved on to puzzles, writing my name, and peering through books with lots of pictures.

Recess came too soon. The teachers on the playground indicated they knew who I was by their delighted, "Aren't you one of Mac's brothers?" or "Isn't Lela your sister?" often followed by "All you Palmers favor one another!" I always replied politely. I didn't see Harold or anyone his size outside with us. Then I remembered that the kids on the second and third floors had recess at a different time. I studied the other kindergarteners around me and some other kids who appeared to be, at best, first or second graders. I decided to join a game of hopscotch.

Back in my first-floor kindergarten room I had a fleeting image of the boy being chased on our way to school. I couldn't tell if those boys, who were more Harold's size than mine, had been playing a game or if they'd been trying to catch the zigzagging boy to hurt him. Harold had warned me to stay away from kids who fought, but he didn't tell me if I should worry about the big kids or just kids my own age. Still, I was comforted knowing that Harold was only two floors away and went back to my kindergarten activities less anxious.

Five and a half years later, a now sixteen-year-old Harold whispered, "Wish me luck" as he turned left and walked across the alleyway toward the apartment building. I watched from the stoop as my brother's plaid, short-sleeve shirt, his creased tan khakis, his high yellow ears, and his close-cropped hair (parted neatly to the left) gradually faded into the heavy flow of Negro school children swirling past him in the other direction. No one had told me directly, but I knew that Harold's stroll toward Soldan High School that morning in September 1954 marked the beginning of a new era in the educational lives of the Palmer children.

I had known since June that Harold would be transferring from Charles Sumner High, the all-Negro school he'd been attending, to Soldan. All summer our house had buzzed with conversations about what the United States Supreme Court's decision in *Brown v. Board of Education* in May 1954 would mean for Harold, Louise, Barry, and me. After Lela's graduation that same year, I had heard Mom remark to Dad, "Well, Bud, I guess that's the last graduation we will attend at Sumner." So, I knew that I wouldn't be following in Mac and Lela's footsteps there. But Harold was already enrolled at Sumner and doing very well. My parents wondered out loud if he would have a choice to stay at Sumner once the desegregation plan went into effect in September. But it soon became apparent that they had decided Harold would transfer to Soldan, within walking distance of our house.

Mom seemed to possess a great deal of knowledge about the voluntary desegregation plan the St. Louis School Board had devised. She was active in the Parent Teacher Association at Washington Elementary and its equivalent at Sumner High. As a former elementary teacher in Arkansas, Mom seemed to exist in a hybrid category, somewhere between parent and teacher. She remained friends with Miss O'Fallon long after I left her kindergarten room. I'm sure Miss O'Fallon gave Mom valuable insider information about what the Negro teachers were thinking and discussing as the voluntary desegregation plan was being developed. Additionally, when I was in second grade Miss O'Fallon had married Charles Oldham, a white lawyer active in the local civil rights movement. Besides her connection to the Oldhams, Mom was also president of our local block association, active in local Democratic Party politics, and an election worker in our precinct. She fed tidbits from her various sources to my father as the calendar ticked down to the implementation of *Brown* in St. Louis.

As Harold disappeared from view that day, I waited for Louise and Barry to join me on the bottom step. When they arrived, we followed our usual route to Washington Elementary. My fifth-grade teacher, Miss Razz, explained the significance of the day before she started our lessons. "As of today, the process of eliminating 'white schools' and 'colored schools' has begun." I was mesmerized by the way she fluttered her long eyelashes, stretched her slender body to look—at me?—over her black cat-eye glasses. "All schools are made," she continued, "out of the same bricks."

The high schools were desegregated on that very day, in accordance with the city Board of Education's plan, which she explained to us. "Next fall, some of you," she took care to enunciate clearly and slowly, "will be transferred to other schools, most likely Clark Elementary, so you will not have to cross Kingshighway. And some of you will remain here at Washington."

I assumed from all my eavesdropping at home that I would remain at Washington. No surprises there. But then Miss Razz told us something about the plan I'd never considered: some of the teachers at Washington would be transferred to other schools.

My heart skipped a beat. Part of me was afraid of being in a class without a teacher who already knew Harold, Mac, Lela, or Louise, or who wasn't aware of the Palmer clan's reputation for producing good students. But what still stands out in my memory is my apprehension about losing the beautiful Miss Razz, with her no frills or nonsense style. Even now I can see how she made it clear that day, with just a flutter of her eyelashes, that there would be no questions allowed about the desegregation plan. Our arithmetic exercises were more important.

Six months later, Mom told me Miss Razz had recommended that I be tested to determine if I would qualify for a special class for "gifted" sixth graders being constituted the next fall. I just assumed the gifted class was part of the elementary school desegregation plan. The day I was pulled from the classroom to meet a psychologist for the test, Miss Razz was a bit mysterious in her explanation about where I was going.

"Larry has to go take a special test in the principal's office," she assured the class. "Nothing is wrong."

Of course, nothing was wrong! I never misbehaved. I'd never been sent to the principal's office. And Miss Razz had surely never stood me in a corner or used her long stick to whack me for some misdeed. I imagined that Miss Razz avoided mentioning the gifted class to the other students because they were not being considered. It didn't occur to me until much later that her lack of full disclosure, her uncharacteristic aura of unease and embarrassment, might have been due to some inkling that this was a new way for the Board of Education to segregate elementary students—post racial desegregation. Instead of looking at the color of our skin, the powers that be would divide us into categories on the basis of an IQ test.

When all was said and done, I was offered a place in a gifted class. The letter from the Board of Education indicated there were several gifted classes for sixth graders in various schools throughout the city, but they had assigned me to a class at Bates Elementary—a forty-five-minute ride via public transit from our house. The letter also indicated that, if my parents accepted the offer on my behalf, they would be responsible for getting me to and from school.

Mom and Dad did not discuss the cost of transportation. It seemed a forgone conclusion I would go to a different school the next fall, just as it had been foreordained the previous autumn that Harold would transfer to Soldan. I only overheard my parents discuss one question: could I make the bus trip by myself? Not surprisingly, Mom proposed a test to answer this, and sent me on a trip downtown by myself to meet Dad at the post office to buy a new pair of shoes. Not surprisingly, I passed that test, too.

THE NEXT FALL I walked by myself toward Kingshighway to catch the bus long before Harold, Louise, and Barry left for school, no sea of children's faces floating down Maple Avenue toward me as there had been for Harold the previous fall. I was less concerned about the possibility of entering an integrated school (Harold had already done that the previous fall with no visible adverse effects) than I was with breaking the family pattern of attending Washington Elementary.

I boarded a city bus on Kingshighway heading north, still trying to anticipate what it would be like to be assigned to a teacher Mac, Lela, Harold, or Louise hadn't met first. The only thing my new teacher would know about me was my IQ. She wouldn't say anything like my kindergarten teachers or the teachers on the playground had on meeting me my very first day in school back in 1949: Aren't you Harold's—or fill in the blank's—little brother? I transferred to a bus on the Natural Bridge Boulevard line headed east, toward downtown, with more eagerness than apprehension about meeting my new teacher and new classmates. In some ways, I was looking forward to not being Barry's big brother at school, free from the responsibility that went along with that title.

I got off the bus and walked the remaining few blocks to Bates without recognizing any of the Negro children walking along with me. The letter from the Board of Education had not mentioned who my teacher would be, but did give my parents the room number of the gifted class on the school's second floor. Lunchbox in one hand and a notebook in the other, I scampered up the stairs. Only about half the desks in the classroom were occupied. I was early for the first day. I took a seat in the front row—where I always sat—to the left of the teacher's desk, and waited in silence for the rest of the kids and the teacher to show up. Gradually, other students filled in the rows behind me. One white girl, who I would soon discover was Cynthia, took a front row seat as well. I glanced behind me and realized Cynthia was the only white kid there.

Just then a Negro man walked through the door behind me to the front of the room, his back erect like a solider, and stood at attention in front of the desk; a soldier guarding a fort. My teacher is a man! I must have been expecting that a "smart kids'" teacher would be some combination of Miss Razz and Mom. I knew male teachers existed—like my brother, Willie, and Mr. Banks, who lived next door to Lena. And I'd had a substitute male teacher once when Miss Razz was away for a few days. But something struck me about this short—shorter than any of my brothers—brown-skinned man. Was it his thin mustache and large blue-gray glasses? Or how his light blue, short-sleeved shirt was open at the top? There was certainly nothing special about his navy pants, brown belt, brown penny loafers, or his black hair with strands of gray that picked up the blue in his shirt.

I knew Mom would quiz me about my teacher's appearance, so I struggled to find a way to describe his hair. It stood straight up, like he did. It wasn't brushed back flat on his head with the help of grease or tonic, the way Dad wore his. It wasn't cut close to his head with a part on his left, like Harold's. And it wasn't shiny and smooth enough to have been processed with chemicals, the way Negro entertainers like Nat King Cole wore theirs. As he began to speak, introducing himself as George Hyram, I came up with a description to satisfy my mother: He has good hair. About three inches on the top, brushed up, and with neatly trimmed sides. I could add his skin color and clothes for Mom later, after I got this most important detail out of the way.

My amazement at George Hyram's maleness only grew as he began to tell us about his background. Other teachers had never told me where they'd most recently studied (the University of Paris in Hyram's case). Nor had they ever mentioned their graduate work (Hyram was finishing up his doctorate in education at St. Louis University). He had served in Army Intelligence during World War II. I was totally impressed (I believe the teenage word at the time would have been "snowed") by Hyram's résumé. The program he laid out for the year (far beyond the normal sixth grade curriculum) excited me: French lessons; systematic logic exercises designed for elementary age children (Hyram's area of study); periodic class discussions with experts from St. Louis University. Beyond that, he would be our teacher until we all graduated and went on to high school!

Hyram also spoke about the racial composition of our class of twenty-one black students and one white student. Cynthia had originally been assigned to a gifted class in another school, but her parents had fought with school officials to have her assigned to our class, nearer to her home. Cynthia was not the first white kid my age I had encountered. Rocky, a summertime playmate who lived in the apartment building across the alley from our house, was "white" and I was "colored," in the school district's lexicon. When school started, Rocky had walked west to Clark Elementary School (reserved for whites), while I walked east to Washington Elementary School. I also knew that even before public school desegregation in St. Louis, some Negro kids were in classes with white kids. The Negro kids in the house next door walked along Kingshighway Boulevard toward Saint Marks' Catholic School. A cardinal had ordered the parochial schools desegregated around the time of my birth. My cousin who was blind went to the Missouri School for the Blind, which, as I discovered when I attended a Christmas play there in the early 1950s, had both white and Negro children in the same classroom.

EARLY IN OUR first year together, George Hyram asked our class "what is sound" in such a way that his words ended with an exclamation point rather than a question mark. I intuited from what he'd said on the very first day of class that he wasn't looking for a dictionary definition. Yet one eager-to-please girl got up from her desk and walked over to the dictionary stand. "Something audible," she said, reading from whatever version of Webster's we had in our classroom. "But what if you were deaf or trying to communicate with someone who was deaf?" Hyram shot back, not to the volunteer dictionary reader, but to all of us.

I thought for a minute that he could see the explosion of ideas going through my mind. The fervency underlying his question had launched an inner dialogue before any student spoke: Was the song I hear sometimes in my head sound? Was the galloping of a horse I hear when reading silently about a person riding a horse sound? I was too awestruck to speak and watched others express their cleverness, trying to grapple with various perspectives on sound. An eager-beaver boy exclaimed, "It's the waves, the sound waves that your ears hear!" Hyram expressed his skepticism by removing his glasses and glancing out the window. Some kindhearted girl explained gently to the eager-beaver that he couldn't use "sound waves" to define "sound." The animated discussion went on for the next twenty minutes before Hyram suspended—not ended—the conversation. We had just experienced his way of introducing a classroom conversation that would reappear throughout the school year, supported by various guest participants.

What I still find so striking about those many inquiries into the nature of sound is the realization that this was Hyram's notion of fun. I was hooked. Hyram encouraged us to engage in verbal and mental gyrations with each other, and with him and other adults, because he enjoyed—perhaps at some deep level, loved—thinking. I sensed he wanted us to fall in love with thinking as well. He was never going to test us on "what is sound?" Rather, the discussions about sound were Hyram's unique method of providing a foundation for what he hoped we would learn in this new class for "gifted children": how to live with a many-faceted question. Occasional discussions of sound continued to erupt, without any visitors present, during sixth, seventh, and eighth grade—to Hyram's delight.

THE FOLLOWING FALL, our gifted class at Bates was transferred to a new Washington Elementary School, built across the street from the early-twentieth-century building of the same name that I had entered as a kindergartener. All the Palmers now walked to school: Barry and me to the new Washington; Louise and Harold to Soldan and Harris Teachers College, respectively. As part of the desegregation plan, Harris, run by the Board of Education, absorbed Harriet Beecher Stowe College, which had been run by the Board for Negroes. Thanks to the construction of the new Washington, I no longer faced the long bus ride to Bates each day. While I found myself back in my neighborhood for school, my friends were all students in Hyram's class.

Dr. Hyram—he had received his doctorate in June 1956 and insisted on being called by his newly earned title—painted a very different future educational path for me than the one Harold was pursuing, or the trail Willie had blazed. It appeared I would indeed graduate from Washington Elementary (like Mac, Lela, Harold, and Louise before me). But Dr. Hyram told the entire class, not just me, that he was recommending I apply for a scholarship to attend Phillips Exeter Academy for high school. Like many topics raised in Hyram's class, this was unfamiliar territory.

I reported at dinner one evening in February 1957 that Hyram was going to recommend I apply to a boarding school in New Hampshire. I can't remember any immediate reaction—positive, negative, or indifferent—from anyone at the table. I do know that Hyram wrote Mom a note—she saved it for me—asking her to call him about Exeter.

As a seventh grader at the new Washington, I no longer spent two hours a day commuting by bus, and used those hours to follow Harold's path in another way: I took on a part-time job. Harold worked as a grocery store cashier. I worked a morning paper route that took me about an hour. This first job marked the end of my twenty-five-cent weekly allowance. Provided I could get all my customers to pay up, my profits each week exceeded two dollars, some of which my parents insisted I put in my savings account.

Getting up at six every morning gave me a chance to see more of my dad. He reeked of Ben-Gay and Mennen's After Shave as he took his regular seat at the head of the kitchen table for a pre-dawn breakfast that only he and Mom had shared prior to my paper route. I usually arrived at the kitchen table before him, and sat silently after he said grace, trying my best not to inhibit his conversation with Mom. Over the course of that school year, my attending Exeter would drift in and out of these conversations. Mom embraced the idea of my applying to Exeter as soon as she heard about the success of Exeter graduates in gaining admission to Harvard. Initially, Dad was silent as Mom pointed out Exeter's advantages. But I noticed a worried look on his face, his mouth often full of eggs, grits, sausage, and toast or biscuits. No hint of a smile emerged beneath his Clark Gable mustache as Mom waxed on about Exeter's virtues. Rather, something like fear hid beneath his clean-shaven face. On the rare occasions when Dad did speak about Exeter, he remained noncommittal, at least when I was within earshot.

I suspected Dad's reticence was because my application to Exeter was really Dr. Hyram's idea. Dad was often skeptical about my enthusiasm for all things Hyram—Dr. Hyram told us today about Ghana's independence; Dr. Hyram did a logic exercise with us today; Dr. Hyram gave us some dictation in French—at the dinner table. I was already convinced that I should go to boarding school. I believed that anything Hyram thought was good for me (educationally), was in fact good for me. My parents and all my older siblings wanted me to be a good student. Therefore, I should go to Exeter. And so I dismissed Dad's uneasiness and latched onto the support of my mom and my older brothers.

DAD'S STANCE on the matter was not so easy to overcome, but he did eventually assent to my leaving home. I turned my paper route over to Barry a month before his twelfth birthday, and I went off to Exeter in September 1958.

On my first trip home in four months, for Christmas break, my afternoon train was several hours late getting into St. Louis. I was taken aback that no one was at the station to meet me. On the last leg of my journey back across southern Illinois, I had imagined Mom calling every hour to see when I would arrive. I fantasized that she'd be anxious to see how much I had changed in the four months I'd been away. But I quickly pushed away my sense of disappointment at her absence and sprang into action. If I could get myself to Exeter, New Hampshire, surely I could get myself from Union Station in St. Louis to our house on Maple Avenue. I dragged my suitcase to a payphone and called home.

My excited, "I'm here!" was met by Mom's calm reply to take a cab home.

I would have had to anyway, since Dad and Harold, the only drivers in the family, would still have been at work or in class at that time of day. When I entered the otherwise empty house, Mom was preparing supper. She gave me a light kiss on my cheek and went back to stirring something on the stove. I disappeared to unpack and await the arrival of Harold, Dad, Barry, and Louise.

That evening, at supper, I sat at our oval kitchen table in my regular spot on Harold's left. Dad beamed at all of us before bowing his head to say grace. "Heavenly Father, we thank you for this food . . . ," he began, as my mind wandered back to images of the round dining room tables in Bancroft Hall at Exeter. No grace before meals there; only chapel before classes convened around oval Harkness Tables. Dad's soft ". . . in Jesus' name we pray" woke me from my reverie just moments before his resounding "Amen." As he lifted his head, his eyes glistened as if he were holding back tears of joy. He smiled, and, once again looked toward Harold opposite him at the end of the table, and to me at Harold's side. An eerie, momentary silence engulfed us all. I could not remember ever witnessing such muteness around our kitchen table.

I glanced at Mom, who diverted her eyes to Barry, seated on my other side. It was Harold who finally broke the unusual silence, attempting to start a typical family conversation by retelling an incident that had occurred in one of his classes at teachers college that afternoon. Dad, in a surprisingly gentle voice, interrupted him. "Harold, let Larry talk first, he's home after being away." Harold gulped. I watched the right side of my brother's smooth face flinch and his cheek puff out slightly as his teeth clenched. His eyes, squeezed almost shut, flickered with anger even as his upper lip trembled with sadness. Then the tears began rolling down his cheeks as he turned his reddened eyes toward me and bolted from the table.

Dad's moment of dinnertime joy and Harold's wounded reaction to it hung like a cloud over the next three weeks of my

Christmas vacation. After this upsetting dinner scene, I became increasingly cautious about the way I talked about my Exeter experiences with everyone in my family. I responded carefully to questions, trying hard to strip any sense of wonder and marvel from my voice. Over that Christmas 1958, I convinced myself that boarding school was going to be an experience I could not readily share at home. All my feelings about the stimulating people I was meeting at Exeter, about the exhilarating (and often difficult) days of classes and soccer, about my disappointments when I didn't earn all A's, about my haircut dramas, even about the architecture of quaint New England houses, would have to be just that: mine. Alone.

CHAPTER SEVEN

The Attendance Card

EARLY IN SPRING SEMESTER of my senior year at Exeter, the last of the students and faculty having left Phillips Church, I approached the school minister, "Freddie" (as I only called him outside his presence) Buechner. Frederick Buechner, a published novelist as well as an ordained Presbyterian minister, arrived at Exeter at the beginning of my prep year, 1958, to be the school minister and to teach English and religion.

I was the head student deacon and carried the attendance cards I had collected from the other student deacons. I don't remember what role we played in the service (passing out bulletins, taking up the collection?): my stroll down the aisle to meet the deep-set, blue-gray eyes of Frederick Buechner concerned our secular duties as attendance monitors. I asked Buechner if I could meet with him to discuss a problem during that morning's service.

I had expected an appointment in his office/classroom, where we had met before to discuss my paper in his course. Buechner was generally reserved and somewhat shy, and I did not associate him with spontaneous acts of generosity and openness to students the way I might other faculty members, like Bedford or Seabrooke. The weariness underneath my otherwise calm voice may have signaled both the urgency of my request and my need for a more private space to discuss the matter. He surprised me with an invitation to join him and his wife for dinner that Sunday evening. "Come over after vespers," he added in a voice more cheerful than the literary solemnity of his preaching voice that morning. He had seen me many times, along with perhaps two dozen other boys, at the short voluntary vespers services before Sunday dinner. I had nearly five hours to reflect on the morning service attendance problem.

The Academy required every boy to attend a religious service each weekend. Students could choose to attend local churches, or the Friday night Jewish services, rather than the Academy's reformed protestant church, Phillips Church. A student could simply inform the Dean of Students' office which service he would be attending during any given semester. Each boy attending Phillips Church sat in a particular pew, in an assigned seat. Each boy had the responsibility to sign in by writing his name in the appropriate space on the attendance card for each Sunday. The deacons collected the attendance cards in certain sections of the sanctuary and noted the absences for their assigned rows. The boys attending local churches or Jewish services had their own sign-in systems. Skipping religious services was the equivalent of missing a class in the school's disciplinary system. As head deacon, my usual routine included reporting any absences to Bob Kessler, Dean of Students, sometime Sunday evening after 8:00 P.M., but before my 10:00 P.M. senior check-in time.

On that April Sunday morning, the choir practiced a hymn as a few early arrivals took their assigned seats. The church was almost full when I noticed a prep I knew leaving the church through a side door just before the last-minute crush entered. I knew that he usually attended the Friday night Jewish services. Immediately after the service, Jim, one of the other deacons, showed me an attendance card from his section and said he believed that the prep I had seen leaving before the service had signed in for the captain of the football team (I'll call him "John")—and then scooted back out. John's signature was on the attendance card, and neither of us could recall seeing him in church. I hadn't been looking for him, since he wasn't in my assigned section. Jim was a member of the varsity football team, as well as my varsity wrestling and lacrosse teammate. John was also on the varsity lacrosse squad. Jim asked me what I was going to do, knowing only the two of us were aware of a potentially forged signature. We didn't need to tell each other we couldn't say a word about the incident. I didn't know yet what I was going to do. I told Jim to wait.

BUECHNER LIVED at the end of Tan Lane off Main Street, across from the main administration building. I walked past Phillips Church and replayed my conversation with Jim. I tried to unscramble what I knew had happened from what I suspected. As I walked past Dean Kessler's house, just beyond Phillips Church, my entire Exeter career flashed before me.

I was on my way, along with about sixty of my two hundred plus classmates, to Harvard in the fall. I had won a New England Prep School Wrestling Championship in early March. I was a dorm proctor in Bancroft Hall, and a member of the Herodotus Society, the history and current events club. I had grown over six inches in the past year to nearly six feet, and weighed close to 170 pounds. I had just made the varsity lacrosse team. As my American history teacher, Henry Bragdon, had told me, I was well liked and respected. Not necessarily popular. By most measures, I was part of the Exeter establishment. My attendance report to Dean Kessler, which I hadn't yet given, could change my standing in the student community.

Expulsions late in the spring semester had occurred in previous years. After a certain number of absences involving classes, sports, and religious services, Dean Kessler would recommend to the faculty some disciplinary action ranging from "restrictions"—early check-in or no weekends away—to probation for a period of time, or expulsion—or, as it was called, "being fired." Reporting a student as absent from church, in and of itself, had no immediate consequence unless the student had other absences, behavior problems in the dorm, or subpar academic performance. If that were the only absence, at worst the faculty advisor might simply tell the student to set his alarm on Saturday night. But a fraudulent sign-in, particularly an upper classman using a prep as the actual perpetrator of the fraud, would be a big deal, an offense that could lead to expulsion.

Being selected as a deacon, like being a chapel monitor or a
proctor (who checked in lower classes in the dormitories), was a
badge of honor on the college résumé and an indication the faculty trusted you to be part of the (fairly) benevolent progressive
disciplinary system. I hadn't paid much attention to what might
happen to students I reported as absent to Dean Kessler. Not
until that Sunday.

John was headed to Yale, along with about thirty-five of our
classmates. He was a chapel monitor, too; in fact, he took attendance for my row in the Assembly Room. He was white, from
Virginia, and wealthy. His parents flew up for every football
game his senior year. He was clearly very popular among the students, but I knew very little about him. He wasn't, for instance,
one of the students I would encounter around the newsroom of
the *Exonian* during my time as an active photographer for the
newspaper. He was not someone whose interpretation of current
events I might have disagreed with at a meeting of the Herodotus Society. He definitely was not among "the wonks"—the boys
who wore slide rules on their belts and earned nearly straight
A's—whom I secretly admired. I stereotyped him as one of "the
jocks," a label I would never have applied to myself, despite my
athletic abilities. In a flash, it occurred to me. I didn't like John.
My awareness of this made me cautious as I entered Buechner's
home, concerned my judgment of the facts might be clouded.

IT WAS THE ONLY TIME during my four years at Exeter that I ate
a meal with a faculty member, or stepped into a private living
space. I had been in faculty offices in Bancroft Hall, but these
offices were next to the dormitory entrances. I had no idea what
other parts of the apartments looked like. I admired the mono-
grammed sterling silverware as Buechner asked me about my
classes and my college plans. After a relaxed dinner, he invited
me into his study for our discussion.

He reached for his pipe, focused his gaze in my direction,
and asked me to tell him what was bothering me about the service. Something about the way he looked at me freed me to talk
about the ambiguity of what Jim had told me about John and
what I had seen. He listened carefully to my story and asked

me what I was going to do. He allowed me to think out loud as I tried to be fair in my assessment of what I knew and of how Jim would need to be involved in any formal accusation. I didn't want to accuse John of using the prep to sign in since I hadn't witnessed it myself. On the other hand, I wanted John to know I would be watching his behavior, a signal that I had reason to suspect his cheating on the attendance card. Since John was my chapel monitor I would see him the next morning and ask him, "How did you enjoy the service at church yesterday?" In the end, Buechner left what I said, or did not say, to Dean Kessler up to me.

On my way back to Bancroft from the Buechners', I delivered my written attendance report to Dean Kessler without mentioning anything about John. I then went to see Jim to inform him of my plan to warn John. He seemed both relieved and concerned. Jim knew John better than I did and wasn't sure he would understand the subtle irony in my question. At the same time, Jim was grateful that he wouldn't be called before Dean Kessler to tell him what he knew about John. That we wouldn't be forced to be accusers, at least not for the moment.

THE NEXT SUNDAY, the same prep, a bit sleepy-eyed with uncombed blond hair and his raincoat collar pulled up over his tieless neck, arrived early. Jim and I watched him walk over to the empty pew, pick up an attendance card, sign it, and walk out of the church. As soon as he left, we walked over to the pew and looked at the card and saw only John's name. When it came time to collect the attendance cards, we had both noted that John wasn't seated in his assigned spot. My attempt to warn John to cease and desist using his prep stool pigeon to sign in for him had failed. Perhaps he heard my question as license to miss church each Sunday without any consequences. After church, I first reported this repeat-incident to Buechner and then walked down to Dean Kessler's house to do the same.

I apologized to Kessler for disturbing him before lunch, but told him I had a serious attendance problem to report. His stern eyes seemed to soften as he invited me to sit down. He let me tell my story without interruption. As I relayed the events of that morning, I felt neither righteous indignation nor any fear of the consequences for my "squealing" on John. I was numb to any emotions. I felt I had no choice, once Jim and I had witnessed the fraudulent sign in. As I stood up to leave, I handed Kessler the attendance card with the fake signature. Kessler assured me that he had all the information he needed, and he would handle the matter from that point without involving Jim or me. He also, his eyes perhaps dropping into sadness, thanked me for bringing the matter to his attention so promptly.

BY MONDAY AFTERNOON'S lacrosse practice, word had spread that John and the prep who signed him in were being brought before the faculty. I felt some pretty hard stares from some of my teammates, especially those who lived in John's dormitory. I overheard rumbling about the possibility of John being expelled. None of the boys in the locker room said anything to me, and I tried not to respond in any way to their prolonged glares. I had a momentary fear about what might happen on the field—Mondays were usually hard contact days. I reminded myself that the head varsity coach was my advisor in Bancroft Hall, and Seabrooke was the assistant head lacrosse coach. One or both would likely notice any attempts at physical retaliation. Panic about John, or his jock friends, quickly faded.

I lived in self-imposed semi-isolation for a day or two while the faculty debated the matter and announced a verdict: Eight weeks of restrictions (twice the normal amount) and eight weeks of probation for John—effectively the remainder of the semester. He would be allowed to graduate, provided no further violations, and Yale would be informed of the disciplinary action. The prep who forged John's signature also received probation and restrictions, but for a shorter period of time. Even after the expulsion cloud over the community lifted, I didn't discuss my role in what had happened with any other student or member of the faculty. We—Jim, John, and I—went back to the other activities of our final semester at boarding school.

PART II

Straddling
Two Worlds

CHAPTER EIGHT

Separation

M OM TOLD LOUISE, BARRY, and me to go sit on the front porch until the fried chicken she always cooked on Sundays, after church, was ready. It was a week before my fourth birthday, a sunny June day in St. Louis. I followed Louise and Barry through the screen door. They climbed into the two steel chairs on the shaded side of the porch. I crawled into one of the matching chairs on the opposite side of the porch, facing them, my chair hot from the sun. Louise and Barry sat comfortably in their chairs, so I left my spot to see if I could squeeze into Louise's shaded chair with her, but she pushed me away.

Barry's knotted brow and dimple-less cheeks told me not to try the same move with him, so I started to walk back toward the chairs in the sun. I remember looking down the steps that led to the street. They were partially shaded by the porch roof. I was thinking about sitting there until I noticed Louise shift in her chair.

She'd gotten out of her seat and was perched on the banister, about six feet above the front lawn, her legs dangling over the back of her empty chair. I bet she could see past the apartment building next door, all the way to the gas station at the corner, maybe even the cars whishing by on the four lanes of Kingshighway Boulevard. I went back to my chair and grabbed both armrests. I pulled myself into the seat and looked over the back of the chair; I could see the apartment building on the other side of the alley. I stood up in the seat of the chair. I lifted my right knee onto the banister—it overlooked the brick alleyway fifteen feet below—and started to twist my body toward Barry and Louise.

When I opened my eyes—I have no idea how many minutes, or hours later—I was on my back. I rolled over and saw, through narrow white slats, a room I'd never been in before. Everything in the room was white and brighter than a cloudless June day. I tried to sit up, to get on my feet. My head hit a net. I stumbled back to my knees and screamed, "Barry, Barry!" as my tears began to flow. I could hear Barry's voice crying "Larry, Larry!" from a long corridor, but couldn't see him.

A week after my twenty-hour coma, I overheard my parents talking about the white couple who lived on the second floor of the apartment building across our alley. They'd seen me trying to get onto the banister and had run downstairs just as my head hit the pavement. Although they had never entered our house before that day, they ran inside to get Dad, and drove us to Children's Hospital rather than the city-owned Negro hospital—assuring Dad the hospital wouldn't turn us away.

When Barry and I weren't quite ten, we shared a fantasy that when we were older we would find two sisters to marry and live together at the house on Maple Avenue. In our mutual daydreaming, we imagined ourselves sharing the Palmer house, albeit with a few architectural add-ons. The backyard would be converted into a paddock for our horses and serve as a landing pad for our helicopter, which we would reserve for longer trips, including transporting us to and from our jobs downtown, where we imagined there would also be a helicopter landing pad. We never envisioned any details about our wives, probably assuming they would stay home, take care of the house, cook the meals, and care for our horses and children. Our brides' most important characteristic would be that by saying "I do" at our double wedding they were also agreeing to the living arrangements Barry and I had pledged to each other. In our younger years, we imagined ourselves always together—without any other member of the Palmer clan. Our happily-ever-after fantasy of perpetual togetherness no doubt grew from the fact that, before I went away to Exeter, the sixteen months' difference in our ages didn't

*Barry and Larry on
the front porch, 1948*

mean much to us. We were nearly the same size and had similar physical abilities. My clothes were perhaps one size larger
than Barry's, but I (and everyone else in the family) viewed us
as twins.

So, when Al coached me on how to field a groundball, Barry
received the same instruction. In the summer of 1956, Barry and
I joined a summer softball team at Washington Elementary. He
played shortstop, and I was the catcher. In one game, Barry hit
a grand slam home run after I led off the inning with a single.
At the dinner table that evening, I served as Barry's press agent,
describing exactly how the ball sailed over the head of the left
fielder. It felt to me, in my retelling, like I had hit the home run
alongside him. I was his first run batted in. Barry allowed me to
engage in my fictional participation in his grand slam, offering
an effusive description of how I'd tagged out a runner at home
plate and, in his view, saved our team's victory. My memories of
Barry are filled with such moments: sharing small joys and supporting each other. But a cardinal family rule cast a shadow over
them: Because of those sixteen months, it was my responsibility
to remember that we were not emotional equals. Most important: I was expected to take care of him.

One morning a few weeks later, my parents went shopping and told Barry and me to cut the grass in the backyard while they were away. I started on my half—the larger half—as soon as the dew had dried. Barry, meanwhile, was playing with the neighbor boys in their backyard. They had concocted a new version of the game of tag, the object of which was to get back to a base before the person who was "IT" could tag you with a tossed baseball glove. With two boys running around the yard from makeshift base to makeshift base—any random patch of bare dirt or convenient tree branch would serve—desperately avoiding the third boy with the glove, the game combined some aspects of dodge ball with running the bases in baseball.

I glanced wistfully through the picket fence at their newly invented game just as Barry dodged a toss of the glove, ran toward a base, and slid into it. After I finished my portion of the mowing, I called to Barry and told him to come home and finish his half. He ignored me and continued to play. I knew Mom and Dad would be returning soon and would be upset if we hadn't completed our morning chore. I didn't want to hear Dad fussing at me because we hadn't finished cutting the grass. I couldn't figure out how to get Barry to help, but I didn't want to finish the entire yard myself.

Clutching the handles of the push mower, I watched Barry slide into another base, his head flung defiantly back. This time the glove hit his face. Barry got up, screaming that he couldn't see. I let go of the mower and ran through a hole in the fence, grabbing my brother. Walking him back through the gap in the fence, I took him into the house to wash his face. After a cold scrubbing, Barry could see out of one eye, but his other eye was bloodshot and swollen shut.

I was so caught up tending to Barry that I didn't hear my parents pull up outside and enter the house. When Mom and Dad learned what had happened, they took Barry to the hospital and soon returned with a diagnosis and a prognosis. The leather baseball glove had burst a blood vessel in one of his eyes on impact, so Barry would have to wear a patch and remain quiet for a few long, boring days. He also had to stop playing softball on the summer team we had joined. And, even though the doc-

Larry and Barry on the front porch with their parents and sister-in-law, Alma, 1955

tors assured Mom and Dad that Barry would make a full recovery, there would be consequences for me as well. Since Barry couldn't play softball for the remainder of the summer, my parents pronounced, neither could I. Dad then proceeded to give me a whipping with his shaving strap for allowing Barry to play the game next door when, as he explained, he should have been helping me cut the grass.

I cried bitterly and yelled, more at what I saw as the injustice of the punishment than in reaction to the physical pain. That night, after Barry and I said our prayers, beginning with the familiar "Now I lay me down to sleep," and I managed not to choke when I got to the "God Bless Mom and Dad" we had been taught to add at Sunday School, I took up my complaining once more. Barry listened to my moaning with something more than an eight-year-old's sense of compassion before agreeing, "It's not fair."

Barry's acknowledgment of my hurt allowed me to temporarily bury the rage I felt toward him for disobeying my order to stop playing and cut his half of the yard. Not until I was in

college did I realize "his half" was my own made up rule for
the task Mom and Dad had assigned to us that day. Their rule
read: Larry is the head of the Larry/Barry conglomerate, and
Larry is solely responsible for its successes and its failures. That
day's beating turned out to be my last; but I never played softball again either.

NOW PRETEENS, Barry and I sat down to play Chinese checkers at
the kitchen table one Saturday morning. I had already delivered
my morning papers and needed to kill some time before heading
out to collect subscription fees from my customers. Barry and I
had just started another game when we heard a rumbling above
our heads. We jumped up and moved to the hallway door to see
who was running down the stairs. Mom, dressed only in her tur-
quoise bathrobe, rushed past us out of the house through the
front door. I was astounded by the speed at which Mom moved
her stout fifty-four-year-old body, though I knew she had been a
tomboy as a child. I also knew she could still choke-up on a bat
and hit a baseball, though I'd never seen her run the bases. As
the door slammed shut behind her, we turned to see Dad hob-
bling down the stairs as fast as he could—his .38-caliber pistol
jostling around in his raised right hand—his face partially covered in shaving lather and a bit of blood oozing from a nick just
below his chin. Dressed in a sleeveless undershirt, his suspenders hung down the sides of his trousers.

Fifty-eight and generously pot-bellied, Dad gasped for air as
he reached the front door. He stopped on the porch, his shoulder
blades moving up and down slightly with his labored breathing,
and gazed for a few moments in both directions up Maple Avenue, unsure of Mom's getaway path, then roared, "Woman, you
could have killed me. Slapping me while I was shaving!" As he
reentered the house, he looked down the hallway toward Barry
and me, huddled together in the kitchen doorway. Dad's face
was ashen, his forehead squeezed into a frown that framed the
saddest expression I'd ever seen. He walked slowly back upstairs,
the pistol dangling at the end of his right arm. He didn't say a
word to us.

Barry and I looked at each other for answers about what had just taken place, to say nothing of Mom's whereabouts. I assumed the argument my parents were having in their bedroom—none of which I overheard—was about my going to Exeter, so I wasn't about to go upstairs and ask Dad. It felt dangerous, especially for me, to inquire about a fight I believed concerned my future. And I wasn't about to let Barry go upstairs either.

The image of Dad's .38-caliber pistol, a gun usually hung in a holster in the bedroom closet, remained fresh in my mind. Barry and I had sneaked a peek at it once (and at Dad's shotgun) when Mom and Dad were busy working on some project in the backyard. I'd all but forgotten about the pistol because I'd never seen Dad handle it, but I'd seen him with his shotgun on numerous occasions. He used it on hunting trips and for shooting a few shells into the air from the front porch in celebration of the New Year. My agitated thoughts floated toward Mom, shaping themselves into silent questions—Where could she have gone in her bathrobe? Was she ever coming back?—until Barry interrupted.

"What are we gonna do?"

"Wait."

"For what?"

This last query stumped me, so I formulated an answer I didn't really believe was true: "Until Mom comes back and tells us what happened."

I was fairly certain Mom would come back and get dressed once she thought it was safe to return, even if she might mysteriously disappear again. She was fastidious about her appearance in public, so she would need to be smartly dressed, her face adorned with foundation cream and powder, her lips with a nice neutral lipstick, her silver-streaked hair neatly combed, before she would even think about departing forever. I was far less certain she would ever reveal what she and Dad were arguing about.

"I'm scared," Barry again interrupted my thoughts.

"So am I."

I tried to convince Barry we might as well go back to our game of Chinese checkers while we waited. He resisted. He wanted to go look for Mom. He didn't seem to realize the presence of a gun made this a different situation from when Mom and Dad had argued over whether Dad should take the exam to become a supervisor at the post office. Other instances of Mom fussing at Dad usually ended with Dad sulking away and bellowing: "Woman, don't you understand, I can't take the pressure!" I told Barry that our leaving the house might further anger Dad, and that Mom might come back while we were out searching for her.

We sat down again at the kitchen table and stared wide-eyed at each other, our bodies frozen into stillness as if a drill sergeant had just shouted "ATTENTION!" My jaw tightened and I pursed my lips to concentrate. Barry's lower lip quivered, but his eyes mimicked my own blank yet focused expression. We were afraid to venture upstairs or leave the kitchen, our sanctuary. So we sat and listened—for footsteps through the ceiling; for the creak of the front storm door opening; for ominous thuds on the stairs—for anything that might signal someone was coming.

Minutes later the screech of the back screen door opening startled us. Our fears had flown out the front door with Mom and walked up the stairs with Dad and his gun. Our collective inner radar had been swirling from the front door to the ceiling, searching simultaneously for approaching missiles and white flags. So it startled us when Mom appeared at the back door—no evidence of glasses or makeup, hair uncombed—clutching her bathrobe around her ample, braless bosom. In a confessional voice, she muttered, "I shouldn't have slapped your father while he was shaving," as she glided past us and disappeared up the stairs without any further explanation. I rose and went into the entrance hallway. I looked up just in time to see her turn at the landing and continue up, heard her quiet "Bud" as she opened and closed their bedroom door.

I listened for other sounds, but heard no further murmurs from the second floor. I said to Barry: "Why don't you come help me collect for my paper route?" He hesitated. Perhaps he hadn't heard or understood that the term of endearment, "Bud," was the white flag we'd been on the lookout for, the reinstatement of—if not peace—at least the normal scope and order of emotional chaos and tension that reigned in our home. The usual family rules were once more in effect, including the one that stipulated I was responsible for taking care of Barry. "Don't worry, I'll leave a note on the kitchen table telling Mom and Dad that you're helping me collect my route. Okay?" He nodded in agreement, and I heard a soft, "Okay."

As we walked to my first customer's house, I was reminded of something that had happened when I was about six and Barry four. I'd been walking through the kitchen on my way out of the house to play when I saw Mom slap Barry really hard. Her left hand hit the right side of his face, causing his head to swivel violently. As Barry stood there with tears pouring down his cheeks, the right side of his face swelled and the imprint of Mom's hand appeared in angry red welts on my brother's light tan skin. His crying eventually broke through the frozen silence, Mom standing stunned. I could hear her mumble to herself, "You should never hit a child in anger," as she drenched a dishtowel with cold water from the sink and put it on Barry's right cheek. My fear turned to envy as she hugged Barry, squeezing him to her body and closing her eyes to whatever had caused her outburst in the first place, and to me, standing there, living through the aftermath with them.

I remembered, too, the time I myself tried to hurt Barry when we were pretending to be television wrestlers. Before beginning our game, we agreed on some rules, such as "no choke holds," to insure we wouldn't hurt each other. As our match progressed, I managed to get Barry on the floor in a pinning position. When I let him go, he still lay on the floor—and suddenly my own capacity for violence erupted within me. I jumped as high as I could and came crashing down with my knees in Barry's stomach. Barry clutched his tummy and began to moan and cry. In my rage I got up and was about to perform another flying knee drop into Barry's midsection, when Louise shouted. "BOY, ARE YOU CRAZY! I'M GOING TO TELL MAMA ON YOU!" Awakened to feelings of wrath that previously I'd hidden even from myself, I mumbled an apology to Barry and begged Louise not to tell Mom. I don't recall what I said that kept Barry and Louise from reporting me.

THE SUMMER BEFORE I went away to Exeter, Dad announced he was taking Barry and me hunting for rabbits. I'd never known Dad to go rabbit hunting, though he and Al had hunted squirrel before, with Dad's brother, Uncle James. On those trips, Dad would leave early, before dawn, and usually return before noon. On this occasion, it was already ten o'clock on a Saturday morning in August. Wherever we were going hunting had to be at least an hour out into the country.

Dad went upstairs, apparently to retrieve his guns. In addition to his shotgun and the .38-caliber pistol, he had a .22-caliber rifle, which Barry and I had been taught to shoot the previous summer, camping in the Ozarks on the only family vacation we had ever taken. When Dad reappeared in the kitchen, he only had his shotgun: He didn't mean for Barry and me to shoot any rabbits. Barry gave me a puzzled look about what our silent father might be planning. All I could do was shrug.

I was flabbergasted when Dad instructed me to get the dog. Jet, a little black mixed breed with a patch of white on his chest, was a fairly recent addition to the family, and, as far as I knew, had never hunted anything. Jet hadn't been around long enough to engender more than polite affection on my part. I don't even remember how he came to live with us. Still, I was concerned about what might happen to him on his—and my—first-ever hunting trip.

By midday, we were tramping through tall grass in an enormous field. Dad cradled his gun in both arms, the barrel angling up and across his left shoulder. Barry and I walked along his right side, avoiding the sight line of the gun.

Dad noticed a grove of trees in the distance and told me to unleash the dog. I hesitated for a moment to reflect upon a few family myths. I certainly had my doubts about Dad's hunting abilities, and I wondered if he'd ever even been rabbit hunting. I'd heard stories about Dad's skills from Uncle James, which always ended with the punch line, "I was a farmer and your Dad was a teacher before we left Arkansas." Yes, Dad had shot some squirrels. But I had the impression Uncle James (and perhaps even Al) were better shots based on the number of squirrels each of them had bagged. In the end, I did as I was told. I unleashed

Jet and followed Dad slowly toward the grove of trees, Barry trailing along some distance behind us.

Jet wandered off a bit to my left. He was so small it was impossible to see him, but the grass swayed as he moved through it. As I tramped through the knee-high stalks, my mind wandered, abstracting me from the rural Missouri landscape we traipsed through to a small, still imaginary New England town. In the eerie silence, I pictured leaving home. I was impatient for answers, for explanations. I puzzled over what exactly I was supposed to be doing. I would have appreciated even the smallest tidbit of information about what wild rabbits looked like or even what signs to look for that might lead me to them, but mostly I was relieved I was not expected to try to shoot a rabbit. As I approached the trees, Dad finally broke the silence with a question of his own: "Where is the dog?"

I spun around to see a large grassy swath of field wavering in the wind. I called out, "Jet!" Dad and Barry took up the refrain. Jet, at least at home, always responded to his name by running toward whoever in the family called him. We spent the better part of two hours searching for him before giving up and returning home without any rabbits, only to report that Jet was lost forever. I didn't wait around to hear how Mom reacted to Dad's tale of the failed hunting trip. I scurried upstairs to the room Barry and I shared. My little brother followed me.

When Mom yelled up the stairs for us to come set the table for dinner, I decided to pretend the hunting trip had never happened. I chatted with Mom about a book I'd been reading as I gathered and placed utensils and plates on the kitchen table. No one mentioned Jet during dinner, my father occupying his usual chair at the head of the table. The only sign that Jet was gone: no discussion of whose turn—Barry's, Louise's, or mine—it was to feed him after dinner.

I was not particularly upset about losing Jet. That night before bed, Barry and I even shared a secret laugh about Dad's ineptitude at hunting. I wasn't concerned about how Dad felt about our dog or what he might have wanted to teach us through our rabbit hunting misadventure. I'm still uncertain what lesson Dad was trying to teach through his botched hunting expedition. Was the trip his non-verbal way of saying he wanted to spend time with me and Barry, his two babies, before I left for Exeter?

More likely than not, the hunting trip was about Dad's desire to hold me close before other men took over my education and ushered me into manhood. I had thought his misgivings about my leaving home were a sign that he opposed my desire for Exeter's more rigorous academic education. Mom was unabashedly enthusiastic about me attending a boarding school a thousand miles away, making her my ally in my imaginary battle with Dad. We won, banishing my father into silence about Exeter, depriving him of any opportunity to explain his misgivings—perhaps fear—about my leaving home: That I would never return to St. Louis.

NOTHING HAPPENED during my prep year at Exeter to change my expectations, or my family's, of what I would do my first summer back at home: find a job like Harold and Mac did when they were fifteen. The job I landed, as a carhop at The Foot Long, a local drive-in restaurant on Kingshighway, was one neither of my older brothers would have been able to get because of the checkerboard pattern of de facto segregation in St. Louis in the 1950s. "We reserve the right to refuse service to anyone" signs were commonplace in the restaurants in our neighborhood. These establishments also wouldn't hire Negroes.

By summer of 1959, things had changed. As early as 1951, years before the *New York Times* gave front page coverage to the student-led sit-ins at lunch counters in Greensboro, North Carolina in 1960, the St. Louis branch of the Congress of Racial Equality (CORE) engaged in sit-ins and protests at restaurants inside department stores and dime stores in downtown St. Louis. By the mid-1950s, many of the eateries downtown had reached agreements with CORE to serve Negroes. Boycotts and negotiations to get some department store restaurants to hire Negroes as waiters and waitresses were part of this movement as well.

By the end of the decade, desegregating the restaurants along Kingshighway was a top priority for CORE. So, by the time I arrived home from Exeter, the manager of the Foot Long had agreed to allow Negroes to eat at the counter (rather than restricting them to service at the take-out window) and to hire some Negro carhops. Mom insisted that both Barry and I apply for these jobs.

There wasn't much of an interview process. As I think back on it, I'm not sure there were any other applicants for the jobs, or any advertisements of openings at the Foot Long, or public announcement of the change in its policy on serving Negro customers. News of these changes had more likely spread through word of mouth after the end of negotiations with CORE. There might have been articles announcing the changes in one or more of the Negro weeklies, or reports on the radio stations whose music catered to Negro audiences, but, since I was at Exeter, I wouldn't have read or heard these.

Mom might have heard directly from CORE members she knew about the Foot Long's change in policy and the availability of the carhop positions for the summer. My mom's friend Mrs. Oldham (formerly Miss O'Fallon, one of my kindergarten teachers) had been a CORE member involved in the early sit-ins and protests in the early 1950s and was undoubtedly part of the grapevine that would have passed along information about new job opportunities available for Negro youth in their own neighborhood—less than a half a block away from our home. Many Negro teenagers lived within walking distance of the Foot Long, so it was not simply a matter of chance that Barry and I walked into the restaurant just as the manager was ready to hire us on the spot.

Had the invisible strands of Palmer DNA engineered an opportunity for Barry and me to work together for the summer after I'd spent the school year in New Hampshire? Had Mom arranged the whole thing? Lela, Harold, and Louise had often brought Barry and me to the Foot Long to spend our allowance (or money I made from my paper route) on their famous twelve-inch hotdogs and milkshakes, so the manager did know us. Whatever his motivation, he hired Barry and me immediately and told us to acquire uniforms—white shirts and pants—and report right away to train for our first weekend shift.

The manager let us work the late evening shift (from about 7:00 P.M. to midnight) because we lived nearby and could safely walk the half block home together late at night. In addition, he told us that evening customers tended to tip more generously than lunch and afternoon crowds. He also taught us how to cover for each other if an order came up for one of us and the other was still occupied with another customer. "Grab the tray and run it over to the waiting car and tell the customer that Barry will be with him in a minute," he told me. "That way, the customer learns your names and gets the message that you want their food to arrive hot."

I don't know if the manager tutored the white carhops with the same care he showed Barry and me. I do know I paid close attention to his instructions because I realized we were his first Negro hires, and our jobs were part of a larger strategy to break down the de facto racial discrimination in employment in the city. As Mom had said to us, we had to be better than white carhops and not make mistakes so these new opportunities wouldn't disappear for other Negroes. While the white carhops often strolled to the waiting cars, Barry and I ran.

During the peak summer period, seldom more than four carhops worked the entire lot. On the weekend, the lot was often filled to capacity, offering plenty of tips to go around. But some weeknights, the flow of cars was slow, the tips meager, and Barry and I would spend a lot of time just chatting with the other two carhops as we all took turns waiting on the few customers who dribbled in. After one particularly slow weeknight, I asked Barry if he thought we could have handled the entire lot by ourselves. His dimpled smile and the gleam in his eyes signaled that his answer was "yes." After the shift, once the other two carhops left, Barry and I went inside to talk to the manager, who was cleaning off the grill. We presented him with the idea of letting us work the entire lot by ourselves one evening. He told us the other carhops had been asking for time off anyway, and agreed to let us try the following week.

We were eager to prove (perhaps only to ourselves) that we were better than the two white carhops. We were convinced that if we ran fast enough we could earn a lot of tips that the white carhops failed to make because they didn't know how to hustle. That night we agreed to pool our tips and divide them equally.

After the last car left the lot, we counted our separate tips to see if our experiment had worked. With four carhops on duty, I earned perhaps seven dollars in tips on a very good weekend night; for a shift during the week, normally two or three dollars. Barry usually garnered about the same amount. But the night we worked the entire lot just the two of us, we earned over twenty dollars in tips! I was exhausted at the end of our shift, but that ten dollars in my pocket felt good. All the resentments I'd harbored against Barry—the twin outfits, the demise of my softball career, my missed trip to the Painted Desert with Willie, and the way he'd displaced me as Mom's baby when I was just sixteen months old, long before I was ready—old bitterness that made me believe I had drifted away from him, seemed to disappear. I felt I was back where I belonged—and glad to be my brother's keeper and companion.

I WAS DISAPPOINTED that Barry didn't even try to follow my eastward path out of St. Louis. He turned down an opportunity to apply to another New England boarding school, Mount Hermon, in western Massachusetts, and when a Negro student from St. Louis who attended Brown University in Rhode Island tried to recruit him he refused to apply there either. Barry had bonded with St. Louis and life on Maple Avenue in a way I never had or, perhaps, could.

Despite our childhood daydream that we would marry sisters, the last time I even mentioned a girl in my life to Barry took place during the unhappy summer of 1964, the one summer I spent in St. Louis while in college. I didn't want to be there, working at a soap factory. But my alternative that Freedom Summer was to join the thousands of white and Negro college students working to register Negro voters in Mississippi, and I was afraid. The Student Non-Violent Coordinating Committee (SNCC) recruiter with whom I'd spoken in Boston told me that SNCC anticipated some of the students would probably be killed. I didn't admit to my fear of dying for the cause of civil rights, or how relieved I was to have the honest excuse of needing to make money that summer because my father had recently become disabled and retired. When the three now-famous civil rights workers disappeared in June, I felt terribly guilty, immediately believing they'd been killed. I could not, or would not, talk to Barry or anyone else in St. Louis about my feelings. Suddenly I was thankful for my many evening and overnight factory shifts that gave me a pretext to spend most of my time at home during the day by myself, sleeping or reading.

One weekend in late July, just before the bodies of the three civil rights workers were discovered, I decided to fly stand-by to Philadelphia to see a former girlfriend, Libby. I needed to talk to someone about what I was experiencing—my disappointment with my recent choices, my confusion about my future. Even though we had broken up around the time of Kennedy's assassination, Libby and I stayed in contact. We'd met during our civil rights activities in Boston our first year at Harvard. Libby didn't know much about my family circumstances, but she knew how distressed I was likely to be amidst all the social and cultural upheavals with which we were all barely coping.

When I mentioned my trip to Barry, he quipped: "Are you going all the way to Philadelphia just for a fuck?" I frowned. It was the first time I'd ever heard him use that word. His question felt tinged with anger, perhaps at me for ignoring him all summer even though we shared a bedroom. I had refused his invitations to join him in any social activities with his friends, never mind to be introduced to any girls he knew. I hadn't gone out with him on double dates the way I had during Exeter vacations. I walked away from Barry without a response and went back to reading *The Brothers Karamazov*. Whatever twin-like empathy might have existed between Barry and me as small children had apparently evaporated.

I hadn't realized how going along with being Barry's twin contributed to my self-imposed isolation within our family. In retrospect, it feels foolish that I thought my younger brother should be interested in the cultural and social upheaval I was living through during the summer of 1964. Among those actually living at Maple Avenue, the person with the wisdom, experience, and intellect to perhaps listen to my ranting about the Civil Rights Movement, Women's Liberation, and the budding antiwar movement was, in fact, Dad. Who knows what might have happened if I had simply talked to him rather than ignored him? But I still held a grudge against him for opposing my going to Exeter, and I assumed he must have still been holding a grudge against me for "disobeying" him. It would take decades for me to realize that true fatherhood isn't a tit-for-tat emotional struggle.

CHAPTER NINE

The Wall

"TWO ROADS DIVERGED in a yellow wood . . . ," recited the white-haired speaker standing at the lectern my upper (eleventh grade) year at a Sunday evening event in Assembly Hall. As he continued, my mind returned to the first time I crossed the small bridge past the track and soccer field to the sun-drenched woods beyond, where I had decided to take one path rather than another. In my imaginary walking, I daydreamed to the rhythm of his voice until he concluded ". . . and that has made all the difference." A moment of silence before the faculty on stage and the boys on long wooden benches erupted into applause. The principal, William Gurdon Saltonstall, "Salty," launched his six-foot-three frame out of his seat and walked to the podium to grasp the hand of the much shorter speaker. Salty took command of the podium and, before dismissing us, said, "I want to thank our distinguished guest, Robert Frost, for inspiring us this evening with his wonderful poetry!"

Who is Robert Frost? I thought as I joined the crush of boys leaving the communal gathering space. Two other boys, as if reading my mind, were engaged in a conversation behind me about the poet. I tuned in to what they were saying and discovered Frost was Poet Laureate of Vermont; he lived nearby and had visited Exeter once before, in 1956. Someone in the English Department knew Frost, according to one of my departing informants. I'd never even heard the term "Poet Laureate" though I knew enough about poetry from my time in Dr. Hyram's class to guess that Frost must be important.

I can still remember hearing Frost read "Good Fences Make Good Neighbors," but I can't recall how I ended up spending an hour and a half on a Sunday evening listening to him read his poetry and talk about the world around us. It's possible a visitor who usually spoke at places such as Harvard or Dartmouth created sufficient buzz that most students simply showed up out of idle curiosity, even if the event was not formally required. In my case, I showed up because I was seriously interested in what was happening in the outside world. Frost's visit on October 23, 1960, near the end of the 1960 presidential election season, had been preceded by Robert Kennedy, who spoke to us about the idea of a "peace corps," less than a year before his brother, President John F. Kennedy, formally launched the program. Frost's talk conveyed an important message about boarding school: pay attention to events in the world outside this pristine New England setting.

"PALMER!" BEDFORD EXCLAIMED, as we almost bumped into each other outside the entrance of the Bancroft dining hall on Prize Day, a few days before my graduation in June 1962. "Congratulations on winning the Williams Cup!" I grinned back at him as he squeezed my hand and shook it. His broad mischievous grin, those playful eyes peering through his brown-rimmed glasses, and those question mark eyebrows brought back memories of my first semester prep year and his "assignment" for me to get a haircut.

His exuberance at the faculty's awarding me the Williams Cup—an honor reserved for "that boy who, having been in the Academy four years, has by his personal qualities and work, brought distinction to Phillips Exeter"—was so evident I was left nearly speechless. I did manage a "thank you" as we entered the dining hall and walked together toward our respective tables for lunch. Just before we parted and he headed for the faculty table in the corner, he gave me another "assignment."

"Palmer, I was thinking this morning about your American history paper on massive resistance to school desegregation," he declared almost pensively, as if the problem of desegregation had some immediate impact on both our lives. I waited for

him to continue, knowing from our many conversations about
my classes and interests, that he'd make a connection for me.
"When you get to Harvard you might want to take a course with
the great social historian, Oscar Handlin, sometime during your
four years there." No stick or carrot with this assignment: if you
want to go with Brink to Jef's home for Thanksgiving, you must
get a haircut. This was simply some guidance, offered because
he thought a history course with Handlin would be good for me
in what I then only vaguely understood was Exeter's meaning
of "good."

Bedford (who was neither my history teacher nor my official
adviser) had peppered me with questions about my history term
paper all spring semester whenever I encountered him in the
dorm or on the path to the gym. He knew I was struggling to
understand the arguments political and civic leaders in the South
were making to resist the United States Supreme Court's order
to end segregation of public schools. He helped me, through his
questioning, to try to distinguish between legal desegregation
and integration, although the popular press conflated the two
terms. His suggestion about Handlin was advice to gain deeper
knowledge about the problem of race relations, a matter he had
surmised concerned me during our haircut discussion. Deeper
knowledge was highly valued at Exeter, as Ted Bedford—Class
of 1948—likely absorbed during his own time in the dorm and
around Harkness tables.

In addition, I knew Bedford didn't believe naively that problems like race were simply matters of ignorance or lack of knowledge about who had the best philosophical, political, or legal
argument. Rather, there were also moral and ethical arguments
to consider that Bedford signaled he understood when, during
our haircut discussion prep year, he stated quietly, but emphat-
ically, "The Academy barber cannot refuse to cut your hair." I
heard underneath his statement: "You and your Negro Hair belong here at Exeter. You will not suffer the indignity of a racially
motivated refusal to cut your hair." But I may not have understood at the time the impact of realizing I could disagree with a
young white faculty member about my Negro hair and yet find
a way to resolve my fears and our disagreement without his em-

barrassing me. Bedford had, by senior year, become one of the adults at Exeter who helped me connect the dots between my ongoing personal transformation and the world beyond.

Earlier my last semester, William Sloane Coffin, the Chaplain at Yale and an annual guest preacher at Phillips Church, said in a sermon, "The image of Americans abroad is Hamlet in the supermarket. To buy or not to buy, that is the question." There was always discussion after the sermon, and during that time it became clear to me what Coffin was selling that morning: he hoped some of us would spend the summer working for a recently formed organization called Crossroads Africa. President Kennedy had described it as the model for the Peace Corps. I already knew about Crossroads Africa because Buechner had invited its founder, the Reverend James H. Robinson, to preach on several occasions. With Crossroads, Coffin had led a group of ten American college students and local residents in building a small cement-block school in a West African country one summer. He hammered home that Crossroads was particularly interested in having Exeter and other prep school students participate alongside the college students being recruited. During his sermon, Coffin boomed over the lectern that raising the fee through fundraising at our local churches and in our communities would be a great way to acquaint people with the needs of post-colonial Africa. In case any of us hadn't immediately decided in our hearts to sign up for Coffin's adventure, he added near the end of his sermon, "Remember, young people, when you win the rat race, you are still a rat."

I translated Coffin's gifted sermon phraseology into language Buechner might have used as: "Listen young men, your big challenge is to find what it means for you to be human at this particular time in history." Our journeys of self-discovery would require us to look beyond the world of Exeter and our families. Buechner seemed to almost whisper to us: Here are some men who have tried to answer that question for themselves with their life's work—William Sloane Coffin, an Andover blue-blood who would soon become a civil rights and peace activist; James H. Robinson, a Negro minister whom Buechner had met in seminary, who saw the resolution of the racial problems in America in global terms; Norman Thomas, a Presbyterian minister and peace activist who had run for president on the Socialist Party of America ticket six times; and William Muehl, a Yale Divinity Professor who was a lawyer active in local New Haven and national politics.

Perhaps Buechner was also holding up his own life as an example and a set of questions for us to consider. What internal feelings led (or drove) this highly successful (by the literary rat race standards) writer—a three-time published novelist with Alfred A. Knopf—to attend Union Seminary and become an ordained Presbyterian minister a few months before coming to Exeter in the fall of 1958 at the age of thirty-two? Why did he, a preppie like us (he attended The Lawrenceville School and Princeton), apparently believe we needed to be entertained by the ethical dilemmas Bergman struggled with in his films such as *The Virgin Spring*?

Even though I couldn't see through the stained glass window at the end of the church's nave, I knew it overlooked the lawn in front of the Academy Building where I attended chapel and studied mathematics and religion in preparation for college. Each Sunday, Buechner and his collaborators at Phillips Church seemed to suggest through the stories they told and the hymns we sang that a dimension of ourselves existed that we could not see, or even know with our minds, a realm of living we would only come to understand and appreciate as we engaged with those human beings beyond our Exeter and college experiences, especially with human beings who were suffering.

I must have internalized those weekly messages without knowing it because throughout my Exeter stay I eagerly attended talks by non-religious speakers in order to gain perspectives on the world. My upper year, following the failed Bay of Pigs Invasion into Cuba in April 1961, I attended two evening discussions, one led by William F. Buckley, Jr., and another by the liberal journalist Max Lerner. Buckley—the epitome, in my mind, of the prep school boy as grown-up—wowed the students, including me, with his erudition and eloquence in his defense of the need to defeat communism.

Max Lerner, a columnist from the *New York Post*, gave a

very different interpretation of the Bay of Pigs a few days later. Lerner used the incident to illuminate the forces changing the geopolitical world. He warned that those forces spelled some-thing "very ominous for the future of America." In Lerner's opinion, the role of the United States military in training and advising the Cuban invaders, which the CIA had recruited, was something new. These military advisors, or Special Forces, were already in Southeast Asia—in Laos (then part of French Indo-China)—helping the anti-communists in a civil war. His tone was very somber as he gazed almost tenderly at the teenagers in the room, and predicted the United States could find itself fighting a war in Southeast Asia, or elsewhere, without a declara-tion of war from Congress. Some alarm-chimes—bells would be too strong a metaphor—went off in my head. There was a world beyond Exeter that could literally destroy me, whatever college I might attend or profession I might pursue. To avert that danger, the world needed to change. I needed to experience and learn about the world beyond St. Louis and Exeter, to participate in creating change.

My French teacher upper year suggested I attend a summer program in France to enhance my proficiency in French. After hearing all the talk about possible wars in Indo-China, I recalled Hyram telling me he'd met many people from the former French colonies while in Paris and other parts of France. A sum-mer in France might do more than improve my French; it might improve my understanding of how much I didn't know about the world. With support from my French teacher, I approached the Director of Scholarship Boys, Hammy Bissell, about financ-ing such a venture. I then approached Mom on the phone about the possibility of my living with a French family for the summer. Her answer, which came so swiftly she couldn't have consulted Dad: "No."

A year later, Coffin's use of the Hamlet-in-the-supermar-ket metaphor to encourage us to spend a summer in Africa still reverberated in my mind. What an adventure before going off to Harvard! Suffering from a case of temporary amnesia about Mom's veto of my plans for France, I dashed off a one page note asking her if I could apply for the Crossroads Africa summer pro-

gram, hoping against hope that—without giving her any background—she could somehow intuit through the Palmer DNA my
excitement about the prospect of really seeing the world, working with others to build a small school in West Africa.

I'd become so accustomed to tamping down my enthusiasm
for so many things while at home, I'm fairly certain Mom and
everyone else in St. Louis had no idea I'd heard Coffin speak
several times, never mind even heard of Crossroads Africa. I
never mentioned Buechner, Coffin, Buckley, Lerner, Thomas,
Frost, Bedford, or Robinson (the only Negro speaker I'd heard
at Exeter). By now, Exeter and my St. Louis family occupied
two separate places in my soul. The wall I'd built internally between these two worlds was so thick, I didn't know on which
side to plant my disappointment when Mom conveyed her expected "No."

CHAPTER TEN

To Kiss or Not to Kiss

I LEFT MY USED VIOLIN at home when I went to Exeter, but brought my voice. I'd started violin at Washington Elementary and progressed far enough for my public-school music teacher to suggest my parents purchase the violin, but when I left I passed it down to my nephew Cornell, Lena's oldest son. I had enjoyed singing in our church's junior choir since I was nine and envisioned myself a member of the Exeter Glee Club. When I joined I told Arthur Landers, director of the Glee Club, I was a tenor. I enjoyed the music, but I didn't last long, most likely because being both a budding photojournalist and a wrestler took so much time. Nonetheless, I saw Landers regularly at Phillips Church where he also conducted its choir.

One day my first fall he stopped me on the path and asked if I wanted to see Leontyne Price, the famous Negro soprano, sing in Boston. In those days, the Metropolitan Opera performed in select cities on its national tour. He must have sensed from Glee Club practices that I'd benefit from hearing great choral music. Although classical music, particularly opera, wasn't part of my family's entertainment menu, I'd attended a dress rehearsal of the St. Louis Symphony Orchestra. The father of one of my classmates during my Hyram days played bass in the orchestra and had arranged a class visit to see the orchestra as part of our ongoing discussion of sound. Furthermore, I knew about some of the racial barriers being erased in opera because another Negro opera singer, Grace Bumbry, was from St. Louis.

A co-winner of the Metropolitan Opera National Council Auditions in 1958, she had attended the segregated Charles Sumner High School with my sister Lela and my brother Mac. Bumbry wasn't a friend of either of my siblings, but she was famous among Sumner High students because she'd won a local radio station music competition by singing an opera aria when she was seventeen—her first prize included a scholarship to a local music conservatory. The conservatory was racially segregated and refused to accept her. The embarrassed sponsors of the contest arranged for her to study instead at Boston University, from which she later transferred to Northwestern. I jumped at the chance to spend a Wednesday afternoon in Boston and grasped the free ticket Landers offered me. I knew Leontyne Price was the first Negro to become a leading artist with the Metropolitan Opera, and was eager to hear and feel a voice that had been described as capable of shattering glass.

I attended enough musical events at Exeter—Glee Club, orchestra, and jazz band concerts—to know, by the spring of senior year, something about Nadia Boulanger, the famed twentieth-century Parisian composer and instructor who had trained the likes of Aaron Copland, Quincy Jones, and Philip Glass. Boulanger came to Exeter to conduct the Glee Clubs of Exeter and Concord Academy (a girls' school near Boston) in a joint concert. The buzz—Exeter students weren't allowed to have telephones in their rooms until the mid-1990s, so verbal communication was truly the way information flowed through the community—spread quickly. To see Boulanger conduct would be a once in a lifetime experience. I'm not sure any of us knew she'd broken gender barriers by being the first woman to conduct many of the world's leading orchestras, such as London's Royal Philharmonic, New York Philharmonic, and the Boston Symphony Orchestra. But when an announcement appeared in the mimeograph Daily Bulletin on corkboards in all the buildings that she would have an open dress rehearsal, I joined the flock of non-Glee Club members who watched and listened to a true musical virtuoso.

After the actual concert, which I didn't attend because of a conflict in my schedule (probably an away varsity lacrosse game), a new idea bubbled up in the student community: if we were exposed to great classical music, why couldn't we be exposed to the greatest American contribution to music, jazz? A group of seniors came up with a plan to ask the principal, Salty, to invite the Modern Jazz Quartet to perform a concert. Several members of Exeter's jazz band were ringleaders and, knowing Exeter, might well have had parents whose contacts included the booking agents for the Quartet. Although I wasn't part of the group who met with Salty in May 1962, Conway, one of my four Negro classmates and a trumpeter in the jazz band, along with some of his fellow band members asked me if I would support the idea. We openly discussed pitching the idea to the administration as another way to break down racial barriers at Exeter. The Modern Jazz Quartet took the stage of the Assembly Hall on a Sunday evening not long after—the first time Negroes performed in a space that could hold the entire community. After the concert, I bought my first jazz album, the Quartet's *Lonely Woman*.

AT EXETER there were no girls for me, lonely or otherwise, not even as occasional visitors. Once or twice a term, the usual Saturday night routine of watching a movie in the gym might be disrupted by an invitation to a mixer. Bancroft Hall would invite a dormitory from a girls' prep school to attend, or the girls' school might invite Bancroft boys to their school. When the first busload of girls pulled up outside of Bancroft, I knew I had two problems.

One, I was very short—in fact, the smallest kid in the dorm. But since Brink, who wasn't much taller, planned to attend the mixer, I thought I might be able to commiserate with him if we were ignored by all the girls who towered over us. But I'd been the shortest boy in Hyram's class and often danced with taller girls who didn't seem to mind. Finding the right height girl might be difficult, but perhaps not an impossible barrier. Maybe prep school girls wouldn't mind my being vertically challenged.

Second, I was Negro; certainly, our guests would all be white. I'd danced with Cynthia, the only white kid in Hyram's class, on many occasions; but Cynthia and I were friends, not strangers. That her family had insisted she attend our predominantly Negro class, and that they lived in a predominantly Negro neighborhood, meant she had grown up in an environment of interracial tolerance. I rationalized that the racial problem with strange white New England girls might be avoided if I only asked Jewish girls to dance with me. I'd heard enough slurs like "kike" and "hooked nose" in reference to some Exeter boys to know the predominantly Christian (or should I say Gentile) boys might shun any Jewish girl. From things I'd heard about the civil rights battles in St. Louis, I believed Jews were more racially tolerant than most other whites.

Despite my overwrought thinking, the first girl I asked to dance was taller than I was, but she said yes anyway. We made small talk and danced around the common room; I never learned if she was Jewish.

Ted Bedford and his wife, the faculty chaperones, danced by us and shot me a wide grin. There was no danger I'd violate the rule the Bedfords were there to enforce about dancing too close. My partner was the most mechanical dancer I'd ever encountered. I felt I could hear her counting one-two as her feet flopped around the linoleum floor. I'd watched my teenager brothers and sisters dance at home from the time I was about nine or ten. I'd also danced at parties with various girls from Hyram's class, some so good they could have been on American Bandstand.

The Bedfords controlled the music, featuring Lester Lanin albums. The music sounded like Glenn Miller's big band from World War II. My heavy-footed partner informed me Lanin was the New England band that played at all the important debutante balls and big parties in Boston. When the music stopped, I noticed a few girls on one side of the room standing around, while most of the guys who'd danced were chatting with their partners. I continued to try small talk with my partner about Glenn Miller's famous song "In the Mood," and then the music started up again. I felt compelled to ask her for another dance rather than walk away—what I wanted to do. After all, she was a guest at Exeter. A few more dances passed before I could graciously move on to the wallflowers. I forgot Dad's fears—that if I danced with white girls their fathers might worry I'd want to "marry" them (the adults' way of saying I'd want to have sex with them). I finally asked one of my new partners, one with a sense of rhythm, what kind of music she liked. "Oh, Rock 'n' Roll, but they would never play anything like that at a prep school mixer!"

It didn't take me long to conclude prep school mixers weren't for me, despite my propensity to embrace everything new at Exeter. I tried one other mixer at a girls' school shortly after the Bancroft mixer, and another during my second year. Talking to a girl I was unlikely to see again unless I went to a New England Debutante Ball didn't meet any need for female companionship I might have been experiencing. I found the girls uninteresting, and I lacked the common experience of summers on Cape Cod or in Maine. Once I got beyond "where are you from?" I didn't feel like talking about sports or photography or world events with any of them.

I BECAME AWARE of how living in an all-male environment might have influenced my view of girls not at a mixer, but around a Harkness Table during my lower (tenth grade) year. It happened during a late afternoon Math 3 class. Most of the students in the class were uppers (eleventh graders)—I was good at math and had tested out of Math 1 my prep year, thanks to my half-year of high school math and Hyram's early tutelage—and Don Dunbar was an effervescent, demanding teacher and assistant varsity soccer coach. He'd gone to Andover, where his father had taught, so Dunbar had grown up as a "faculty brat." He exuded joy at being in a boarding school. This information about his own prep school background came to light that spring day in 1960 when he decided to suspend our planned discussion of the math material and instead engaged us in a Socratic dialogue: How would Exeter change if it admitted girls?

Something extraordinary must have happened for Dunbar to suspend the assigned material for a day. Had our all-male faculty started a discussion about coeducation? Had those old men who met in the Latin Study of the Academy Building—the trustees—raised the issue of planning for a coed Exeter? The only thing I recalled overhearing were plans for some new buildings: a new library, a new gym, among other projects. The question of whether these new buildings should include bathroom facilities for girls had arisen. But those building plans were for the dis-

Larry with his dormmates and their dates, 1962

tant future—at least ten years away—so I'd dismissed the discussions among students about coeducation as irrelevant to my
Exeter experience. Until Dunbar brought up the topic in class.

It's entirely possible Dunbar had already had some conversations about coeducation with boys in his dorm that spurred him
to discuss the matter with a larger sample of the student body.
Whatever motivated him, I don't recall. I have suppressed what
I said during that class conversation. It's hard to believe I was
totally silent, being both a regular contributor in class and very
comfortable talking to Dunbar. His words, just before the bell
tolled in the Academy building signaling the end of class and
time for dinner, still embarrass me. Our inane comments, our
clever banter, our vacuous attempts to express our feelings about
having girls at Exeter, allowed Dunbar to seize the most memorable teachable moment of my early Exeter life. "Don't forget,"
he held forth, "if the Academy decides to admit girls, they will
not be your emotional filling stations, here for you to drive in and
be recharged. They will belong here, just like you!"

AFTER escorting my blind date—
a Negro girl who was a friend
of a classmate—to where she
was staying after the graduation
dance, I strolled back to Bancroft Hall.

I discovered most of the
other seniors standing in front
of the dorm with some girls. I
joined a circle and made small
talk with my classmates and
their dates. Who besides your
parents are coming for the ceremony tomorrow? Brothers, sis-

Exeter graduation photo, 1962

ters, grandparents, aunts, and uncles, were all mentioned. Did
you like the band? I am sick of Lester Lanin-type music but at
least they played a few upbeat Rock 'n' Roll tunes! No twisting
allowed at Exeter, someone joked. After less than fifteen minutes of this idle chatter, it was time to say goodnight to the girls.

Someone suggested each of the girls should give every senior
a graduation kiss. This communal and public kissing wouldn't
violate any boyfriend/girlfriend relationship, assuming any existed. I stood in the circle, painfully aware I had no date. An
awkward momentary silence came over the group. One boy
broke the silence with an additional rule to the newly devised
kissing ritual. "If you don't have a date to offer kisses, you don't
get kissed."

I looked at both of Coach Seabrooke's daughters. Seabrooke's
younger daughter, Phyllis, was Brink's date. Kathy, the older
one (about our age), was also someone's date; I can't remember whose. I stood and watched as the girls kissed all the white
boys in the circle and paid special attention each time Phyllis
kissed a classmate. I had to suppress some feelings that Brink
was somehow more lovable than me even though I was a better wrestler—I had won a New England Championship—and a
better student—I was headed to Harvard, he to Tulane—simply
because his skin was white and mine was brown. Did I have any
idea why any girl would choose to kiss a boy or become his date?

On that night of celebration, I knew if I allowed my sense of emotional deficiency to become visible in my facial expression or audible through my words I would only feel more vulnerable, more out of place. I often wonder if the kissing ritual would ever have been devised if I'd had my Negro blind date with me.

CHAPTER ELEVEN

A Broken Leg

WHEN MY PARENTS ARRIVED for graduation, I didn't mention Cheryl, my new St. Louis girlfriend, or Brenda, who Mom still thought was my girlfriend back home. My blind date for the graduation dance that Saturday night was a decoy, a way of deflecting any unspoken questions they may have had about how I had survived in the all-male environment they were entering for the first time. I introduced her to my parents an hour or so before the dance as Jane from Harlem, figuring her presence would indicate to Mom something was awry between Brenda and me. I offered no explanation of how I'd met a girl from New York. In fact, I hadn't met Jane until a few hours before introducing her to my parents. She was a friend of my classmate Bill's girlfriend in New York and had accompanied Bill's parents and girlfriend to New Hampshire to attend Exeter's pre-graduation dance and ceremony the next day.

Why did I agree to this blind date?

My realization that all the seniors in my dorm—at least the ones I was friendly with, like Brink and Jef—had dates for the graduation dance, persuaded me to avoid going stag. I'd sought out Bill's help arranging a safe blind date, meaning someone who wouldn't upset my parents. Even though Cynthia back home was white and my good friend, I'd never been on a date with her. My fears that my parents would be upset if I had a white date were probably not well-founded. Mom had a brother in Chicago, Uncle Rufus, who'd married a white woman, Aunt Hilda, before

World War II. For all I knew, Mom might have been more upset if I didn't have a date at all, as that might indicate her Harvard-bound Negro son, a member of the graduation committee (noted in the program), hadn't been fully accepted at Exeter.

Jane was someone I could dance with, and nothing more. But to Mom, Jane served as a signal that despite my all-male education at Exeter, I had the knowhow to connect with girls she didn't know. If Mom had asked the anticipated—"who are her people?"—I could have truthfully answered, "I don't know." If Mom wondered why I hadn't invited Brenda to the graduation dance (her parents, assuming they had the money, would have gladly allowed her to accompany Mom and Dad), she may have found solace thinking what happened in Exeter stayed in Exeter.

She also probably assumed my encounters with girls occurred only in St. Louis, under her watchful supervision. I wonder if she axed my plan to spend the summer before my senior year in France because she was afraid of missing an opportunity to hover over my social interactions with the opposite sex. I imagine she trusted the male superintendents at Exeter to keep me busy with academics and athletics, but who knew if European men and women also believed, as she did, that idleness was the devil's workshop. So, despite the allure of places unknown, as I turned seventeen, I resigned myself to another season working as an usher at the outdoor summer musical theater in St. Louis's Forest Park, thereby fostering the family narrative that I would return to St. Louis after I finished my education.

THIS FICTION INCLUDED going out again (and exclusively) with my pre-Hyram-days, fifth grade girlfriend, Brenda—a rising senior at Soldan High School and one of the girls who had been corresponding with me. More important, Mom liked her—she was a good student, and her parents, like Mom, were very involved in school activities. Her brother was friends with Barry. Seeing Brenda was a dependable and safe way to signal that being in St. Louis was just as good as being in France.

Mom bragged to her friends at church that my elementary school ambition to become a doctor remained intact, but I secretly harbored growing uncertainty about what I wanted to be when I grew up. Mom had somehow ascertained from Brenda's parents, or from Brenda herself, that she wanted to be a nurse. Our supposed shared interest in the health professions indicated to Mom that Brenda and I would make a good match. By the end of summer, I felt the pressure mounting. Mom may not have exactly arranged my future marriage, but at the very least she had elected Brenda, a hometown girl, as the leading candidate to become my wife.

Brenda was a cheerleader and invited me to the first football game at Soldan, just a few days before I was scheduled to return to Exeter. As we walked into the stadium together, I realized two things. This was the only time all summer I'd been out with Brenda on a date without Barry around. On double dates my brother and I acted as each other's platonic police: nothing beyond kissing was allowed. Second, I'd be alone amidst strangers once Brenda lined up with the other cheerleaders. I doubt I knew any of the spectators moving toward the Soldan side of the field. The twenty kids I knew from Hyram's class attended a different high school because only a limited number of high schools had classes for "gifted" students.

Brenda, perhaps over solicitously, offered a solution to my impending loneliness as a solitary spectator in the crowded stands. We walked behind the Soldan bench, and Brenda told me she'd introduce me to one of the freshman trying out for cheerleading, someone to sit and chat with. I wasn't particularly concerned about not having a companion during the game, but didn't object. Such passivity was my default posture toward others' attempts to surmise my thoughts or feelings that summer.

"Cheryl, come over here," Brenda shouted in her cheerleader voice toward the girls in the first row of seats in the stands. "I want to introduce you to someone." A girl clad in a light blue sweater leapt to her feet, moved quickly to the aisle, and scampered down the stairs. Her cross-legged lope made her hips sway from side to side under her pleated skirt. She sashayed. As she drew near, my gaze shifted from her thighs and hips to her face. Her skin was the color of ocean-wet sand and her dark, sparkling eyes danced above her dimpled cheeks. She gave me a wide smile, her lips rich and full, with no trace of lipstick. I smiled

back, perhaps to stop myself from staring, before Brenda offered
a few words of introduction. The key phrases in Brenda's verbal sketch: "my boyfriend," "Barry Palmer's brother," and "prep
school." Thus, having established the boundaries, Brenda asked
Cheryl if she would mind watching the game with me in the
stands rather than sitting with the rest of the cheerleader wan-
nabes. Then, without waiting for an affirmative answer, Brenda
left us standing there in silence, facing each other.

I stared at Cheryl's face more intently, Brenda's watchful eyes
no longer present to dampen my enchantment. Cheryl broke
my fixation by looking away. I believe I caught a twinkle in her
eye before she turned back and asked if I wanted to sit up high
or down near the front. It didn't matter where we sat, my eyes
would be glued to Cheryl, not the play on the field. Her casual,
"What's prep school like?" gave me an opportunity to take her on
an extended excursion through my Exeter experience—classes,
dormitory life, extracurricular activities, sports. Although she
was only a freshman, I explained the intricate details of the college application process and shared with her my hopes of attending Harvard or Yale. When she asked if Barry was my only
sibling, I told her about the whole Palmer clan, with special em-
phasis on the other Soldan High School attendees—Harold,
Louise, and my niece, Sandra. I didn't care if her bright eyes and
winning smile were sincerely meant for me or simply her facial
default. But I knew I didn't want those few moments sitting together to be the only contact we'd ever have.

The referee signaled the end of the game and, before Brenda
had a chance to retrieve me from my sitter, I asked Cheryl if I
could write to her when I got back to school. She gave me her
last name and address, which I hurriedly memorized as I spotted
Brenda—or, more precisely, her ivory sweater emblazoned with
a gold and maroon Soldan "S" across the chest and her matching cheerleader's skirt—waiting for us at the bottom of the stairs.
Brenda thanked Cheryl for keeping me company, flashing her
pearly teeth in my direction rather than toward Cheryl. I did my
best to mirror Brenda's delight, my eyes wide in terror and wonder at how dishonest it felt to tell her how much I'd missed her
during the game. She folded her left arm around my right, her

pompons dangling forgotten in her right hand as we exited the stadium.

We meandered down Kingshighway toward her house. I occasionally used my right arm to squeeze her left and pulled her closer to me as she greeted other pedestrians she knew, introducing me with her well-rehearsed litany: my boyfriend, Barry's brother, prep school. Fortunately, her introduction mostly led to questions about me, not about the details of the game, to which I'd paid little attention. I put on my date face and found my most gracious voice for my responses. I have known Brenda since the fifth grade; I am older than Barry; I go to Phillips Exeter Academy, in New Hampshire.

Flying back east (I no longer made the journey from St. Louis to Boston by train), I kept visualizing Cheryl, somewhat afraid of my immediate physical attraction to her. I replayed how she'd walked toward me, the intensity of her eyes looking back at me, and the Cheshire-cat grin that settled on my face as soon as Brenda had left us standing there, alone together in the crowd. My self-doubt quickly overtook my fantasies. I told myself Cheryl was just being nice to Brenda; she had smiled at everyone the way she smiled at me. I was sure Cheryl wouldn't answer my letter, and if she did, we might, at best, become friends, or maybe pen pals. Such was the fate of boys with my nappy hair and dark skin, and much cuter brothers like Barry.

I made a mental note to make sure I wrote to Brenda when I got back to Exeter—before I contacted Cheryl. I needed to hedge my bets until I could be more certain of Cheryl's feelings for me. I didn't know what, if anything, she felt about me, or what she might say to Brenda. After all, I didn't really know anything about Brenda and Cheryl's relationship. But somewhere deep in the end matter of my mind, on a page I reckoned no one would ever read carefully, I scribbled an entry to not mention my correspondence with Cheryl to Brenda, to Mom, or to Barry. Cheryl, at least as I imagined her, was an end-of-summertime secret I took back to Exeter with me. The feelings I was experiencing were important to me and I wanted to enjoy them, to live with them for a little while without worrying about how anyone else might judge them.

I arrived at North Station from Logan Airport a few hours before the train departed for Exeter. I recognized several students milling around as I checked my suitcase. I noticed one Exeter boy holding the latest issue of *Playboy* magazine in his hand. This bold public display of a girlie magazine, and the boy's total lack of furtiveness, meant he was certain no parents or Exeter teachers were around. He suggested we all go to an afternoon burlesque show at the Old Howard Theater nearby, in what was then called Scollay Square. (This "entertainment" district has since become the Government Center.) I, or another of the straight arrows in our group of a dozen boys, mentioned that Exeter's rules probably prohibited us from being in Scollay Square. Someone pointed out we could ride our bikes over ten miles to Rye Beach in New Hampshire, but were prohibited from riding to Hampton Beach about the same distance away because of the casino there. We huddled together as if debating a scholarly issue across the shiny oval of a Harkness table and came up with an interpretation of our situation that satisfied the more punctilious among us, those who needed to follow the Exeter rulebook. Since we had not yet checked-in at Exeter we were technically still under our parents' jurisdiction. Conveniently, no parents were present. En masse, we trekked from North Station to Scollay Square, a clump of curious boys, disguised as young men in sports jackets and ties, at liberty for a few hours to choose between heaven and purgatory, and to make up the rules as we went along.

Seeing the bodies of those scantily clad women fulfilled the version of heaven we prayed for that afternoon. When the first woman danced by us, revealing her breasts, the boy to my right nudged me and whispered, "She must be a thirty-eight!" (This was prep school talk based on the erroneous notion that the larger the number in inches, the bigger the woman's breasts.) I thought of Brenda. Of how underneath that big Soldan "S" on her cheerleader sweater she was probably a twenty-eight—quite flat-chested by *Playboy* standards—although I'd never actually seen her breasts or even touched the clothing covering them. I hadn't actually committed a sin, even if thinking about touching Brenda's breasts was bad. In a split second, as my mind flashed toward Cheryl, I knew I was headed for the hell of the guilt-ridden. I imagined she must be at least a thirty-four in prep school speak. I remembered the tantalizing curves beneath her light blue cardigan that day at the game. I pictured myself unbuttoning her sweater, undoing her bra, caressing her breasts. Wasn't it Brenda's fault I was even thinking such a thing?

I quashed my inner musings and looked at the heavily mascaraed, barely clothed plump human being with lipstick smeared across her lips on the center of the stage. My sexual fantasies about Cheryl made me ashamed. Cheryl was, after all, Brenda's friend, or at least trying out for cheerleader and the possibility of becoming part of Brenda's high school in-group. Brenda epitomized a good girl, and I had the distinct impression this was one of the reasons Mom selected her as a leading candidate for my future wife. I didn't think about hips or breasts when I saw Brenda walk toward me. Did I want to have sex with Cheryl? I told myself, "no," having absorbed Mom's implicit rule that "the right kind of sex" came only after marriage, marriage to a good girl, a girl who was a virgin.

Later that evening, as the train neared school, I dog-eared the page in my head containing the striptease dancers, Brenda, and Cheryl, and closed that entire book. By then, Exeter for me had become a de facto girl-free zone. Once back on campus, the comforting dynamics of the world I navigated so adroitly as a scholarship boy settled me down. Time for intensive study and my senior history paper; football instead of soccer (I'd gained sixty pounds since freshman year); conversations about Saturday night movies—like Ingmar Bergman's *The Seventh Seal*; exposure to world events presented by a host of visiting speakers, whose words and ideas would later be considered and reconsidered during the twenty-minute chapel talks held each morning. In this world, girls were distant correspondents. A few square inches of lovely handwriting. As two-dimensional as the sheets of paper onto which we projected our images of them.

With no homework assignments the first night back, I wrote to Brenda and Cheryl. About what, I'm not sure. I corresponded with them all fall with short and increasingly infrequent notes filled with superficial news items—my junior varsity football team's victory in which I scored two touchdowns; a particularly vexing exam or test on my calendar. My short notes reflected two limitations of life at Exeter. Time for writing of any sort was extremely limited thanks to the school's underlying operating principle: idle minds are the devil's workshop. A more benign interpretation of the intense schedule might suggest it was simply an antidote to homesickness. More important, I assumed any letter I wrote to either Brenda or Cheryl (or anyone else, for that matter) would be shared with any number of adults at the receiver's end.

Maybe I projected my experience of the total lack of private space at my own home onto Brenda's and Cheryl's day-to-day lives. In the Palmer household a teenager would be questioned about the contents of any letter received and expected to give detailed responses, or even to hand over the letter. I imagined Brenda's mother or father saying, "You got a letter from Larry," followed by, "What does he say?" Brenda wouldn't dare respond with anything resembling "none of your business." Having expended so much effort to keep my Exeter and St. Louis worlds separate, I had no idea just how busy or direct the lines of communication between my house and Brenda's might be, or who I could trust in St. Louis not to be an informant and successfully keep to herself whatever information I gave.

My self-censoring led me to give Brenda only snippets of any information I'd already given Mom. Before I'd drop Brenda a note about the JV football game, for example, I would have already sent Mom a clipping about the game from the school newspaper. I knew almost nothing about Cheryl's parents, but assumed writing to her, too, was like writing to a prisoner. The warden-parent had the right to open all mail and determine what was appropriate for the various inmates of the household. I knew my parents could revoke my parole to Exeter in a heartbeat if I broke any of the unspoken rules about how a teenage son accustomed to being away from home was supposed to behave while away.

At Christmas break, my suspicions about ongoing communications between my family and Brenda's were partially confirmed. Before I escorted Brenda to her winter formal, Mom offered me unsolicited advice on what color corsage to pick. How did Mom already know the color of Brenda's dress? She'd obviously talked to Brenda's mother (or Brenda herself) about the event before I'd even arrived home. At the time, I didn't find it at all disconcerting that the precise hue of a daughter's prom dress and a young boy's fifth grade Harvard dream were details Mom and Brenda's mother might have shared.

DAD AND I had never discussed sex, so I was surprised when, that same Christmas break, in a rare private moment, he handed me some dollar bills and told me to buy some protection. I chuckled to myself, but didn't say what I was thinking: There was no chance I'd have sex with Brenda before we were married. I did tell Barry, then sixteen, about Dad's rough acknowledgment of my developing sexuality. I assumed Barry shared my fear of the consequences of getting a girl pregnant, and even though he laughed at my story of Dad's fumbling sex-ed lesson, I knew he shared the family's stance that sexual intercourse, whatever you might be feeling in the moment, mustn't take place before marriage.

I didn't want anyone—especially Brenda, Mom, or Barry—to know I'd written to Cheryl. Between family activities and carving out time to do things with Brenda, there wasn't much of a chance for me to see Cheryl. I found it easier to keep my thoughts about Cheryl folded between the same seldom-visited pages in my mind where those lustful fantasies from the burlesque show remained. I didn't want to risk slipping up and mentioning her name. I had no idea if Cheryl had mentioned the letters we had exchanged to Brenda. I didn't hear Cheryl's name during the entire Christmas break and so assumed she had kept our correspondence a secret.

Once I returned to school after Christmas break, I became a bit bolder in my letters to Cheryl. I hinted at my interest in her by sharing more information about what I was doing in my studies and discussing some of my plans for college (after I was sure I was going to Harvard). She responded in turn with more questions about my prep school life. My letters became longer, energized by my sexual fantasies. I did my best to convince Cheryl (and possibly myself) that I was a very interesting teenager, someone concerned about the world around him. I hadn't overcome my nagging feeling that Cheryl might not find me physically attractive, but I was putting forward my best efforts to make sure she (and any other readers or listeners), would see me in the best possible light.

In a letter I received just before spring break, Cheryl informed me she'd broken her leg at cheerleader practice and was home recovering while everyone else was at school. She invited me to visit her when I got home. I re-read the letter several times on the plane, pulling Cheryl and Brenda into focus, trying to sort out my conflicted desires and loyalties. My strong attraction to Cheryl, and an unexpected opportunity to explore it, was more than a bit terrifying.

I arrived at the St. Louis airport around noon. The airport shuttle service had a drop-off at the Chase Park Plaza Hotel, only a mile down Kingshighway from our house. The house felt eerily empty with only Mom and me at home. Barry was still at school, Harold in class at the teachers college, and Dad at work. Louise had moved to Rhode Island and was busy taking care of her first-born child, now six months old. When Mom left the house to go shopping, I took out Cheryl's letter and called the number in the postscript.

Temporarily free from classes, homework, and wrestling practice, I had lots of mental energy to devise a means to visit Cheryl without anyone—Brenda, Mom, or Barry—knowing. As my mind raced through the various possibilities, I became enthralled with the idea of a secret meeting. I glamorized each eventuality. At that point she still only existed as the tenuous voice I'd imagined while reading, and re-reading, her letters. She was the sweatered goddess of those all-too fleeting moments on the sidelines of a football field. I imagine my French teacher at Exeter might have described my plotting for my rendezvous with Cheryl as an *idée fixe*. But what a fix.

I lied to Mom the afternoon I walked to Cheryl's house, saying I was going to the library. I took a deep breath before I rang the doorbell. When Cheryl opened the door, my body started to tremble. I stared at her just as I had at the game back in September. Hoping my mouth wasn't hanging open, I scanned her body from head to toe. I quit trembling when I took in the large white cast on her left leg. She must have noticed me staring at her broken leg, yet she flashed me a wide smile as I looked up at her face. She didn't seem nervous at all as she hobbled toward the living room sofa like a peg-legged pirate.

As we sat side by side on the sofa, I became agitated by the realization that Cheryl's mother was at work. *We are alone in the house. This is the first time I've ever been alone with a girl.* My mind raced through the possibilities of how far we might go. *Can I get my hands underneath that sweater and feel her breasts?*

I immediately asked about the cartwheel that led to her injury, feigning interest to alleviate my own tension. After Cheryl recounted her accident, I launched into a monologue about the New England Wrestling Championship tournament, my classes, and my plans for college, grinning broadly at her all the while. The drone of our chitchat distracted me from what I really wanted, at least for a short while. I desperately imagined kissing her, holding her in my arms. Weighing all the possible consequences of my hormone-fueled behavior became the biggest obstacle standing between me and the object of my desire. I held back, fearing Cheryl's rejection. Or betraying Brenda. What if I tried to kiss Cheryl and she felt compelled to tell Brenda? I had no idea what being cheerleaders together meant in a public high school. Was being a cheerleader like joining a high school sorority? What if I tried to kiss Cheryl and she simply refused, insisting we were just friends? Would that be a nice way to tell me she wasn't attracted to me?

Flipping off the switch on my doubts and fears, I slid closer to Cheryl on the couch. She closed her eyes as I wrapped my arms around her shoulders and kissed her tentatively, my entire body electrified. I held her, gazing at her face until she opened her eyes. I kissed her again with more confidence, pushing my tongue into her mouth. My brain clicked back in. Neither one of us had even mentioned Brenda's name. One light kiss and one French kiss didn't mean Cheryl and I were going steady. Besides, I was leaving for Exeter in a few days.

After our short make out session I managed to steal a few more hours alone with Cheryl before her mother returned from work. I mumbled something about having to stop by the library before going home. I had no prior experience with such raw physical attraction. No standard by which to measure how honest I was being with myself about what I was feeling. As I left, I promised I'd write to her when I got back to Exeter.

As soon as I was back on campus for my last term, I realized how deeply I had bifurcated my feelings. Brenda, Mom, Barry, the rest of my family, and the few friends I'd kept in touch with, like Cynthia, became books I carried around but had no time to read and enjoy once I returned to Exeter. My clandestine meeting with Cheryl gave me the impression she might understand the conflicting demands and tension that existed for me when it came to the two worlds I inhabited. She seemed excited when I told her I wanted to travel and live in either Europe or Africa before I settled into a career. She shared her dream of wanting to live in California. When I asked her where, thinking for sure she would say Los Angeles, she surprised me by answering that San Francisco was more interesting than anything Hollywood might have to offer. It felt like the world beyond St. Louis was beckoning her to leave as well, and this comforted me.

I wrote Cheryl about my plans. Short term, I wanted to go to Africa for the summer as part of the Crossroads Africa program. Longer term, I'd admitted to her and myself that I had no interest in becoming a doctor. I wanted to help change the world, but not necessarily from St. Louis. I just didn't know what career bore the hidden label: change maker. I thought about going into social work because one of the Urban League officials who had connected me to Exeter had a master's degree in that field. I was full of ideas and ideals. But I had no plan.

Mom vetoed my trip to Africa sometime in early May. When I resigned myself to the fact that I was going to spend the summer in St. Louis, it dawned on me that I really had to figure out what to do about Brenda, whom I'd managed to ignore most of spring semester. I was at least honest enough with myself to realize I'd only gotten back together with her the previous summer to reassure my family I was still rooted in St. Louis. I'd thought I could finesse a summer away as long as I acted as if I was going to return . . . eventually. Looking back, I'm ashamed of my attempts to manipulate the people in my family who were trying their best to love and support me. I probably harmed myself as much as I did my family or Brenda. Sick of jumping through emotional hoops and frustrated by my own lack of resolve, I did a very rash thing.

A month before graduation, I sent Brenda a Dear Jane letter informing her our relationship was over. No explanation of why I was breaking up with her. No thought about the cruelty of not waiting until I could speak to her in person. No consideration of the fact we'd known each other nearly half of our young lives. I didn't stop to consider if she'd been waiting for an invitation to my graduation (and the dance the night before). I didn't think about how intertwined our families were and the awkwardness she might feel when she encountered Barry in the hallways at school, or my mother or simply strolling the neighborhood. True to my cold-hearted M.O., I didn't inform a soul in St. Louis that I'd dumped her.

I also threw caution to the wind in my next letter to Cheryl, telling her I'd broken up with Brenda. I wasn't totally crazy. I left out the part about my sexual fantasies toward her and simply asked if she would be my girlfriend. But I never stopped to ask myself if Cheryl, who I'd talked to twice, kissed once, and to whom I'd written less than a dozen letters, would turn out to be simply an imaginary girlfriend. In one of my previous letters, I'd assumed she was sufficiently fluent in French after only one semester of study to understand my confusion about a passage in Camus's *L'Étranger*, which I'd read in third year French. In another letter, I presumed Cheryl would share my interest in learning the different views of conservative columnist William F. Buckley, Jr. and liberal journalist Max Lerner concerning the implications of the failed Bay of Pigs invasion. I failed to notice that Cheryl didn't comment on my question about Camus or even mention anything about Cuba in her replies.

But I waited anxiously for her reply to my proposal to go steady, hoping against hope she would say yes so I could surprise Mom with an introduction to my new girlfriend when I got home in June. Cheryl agreed to be my girlfriend a week before graduation. I started to reimagine not only our first kiss, but also a future in which Cheryl and I strolled arm in arm along the Charles River in Cambridge, admiring the Harvard campus. I'd written to her about my excitement about going to Harvard as if it was a place she would also see eventually. I assumed we would spend the summer figuring out how she could get to an eastern women's college close enough to Harvard to make my fantasy a reality in a few years, after she graduated from high school.

I hadn't told anyone in my family how I'd met Cheryl. Nor had I shared with anyone how she became my steady girlfriend, or how we exchanged letters about a life beyond St. Louis. My secretiveness about Cheryl no doubt added fuel to the fire of general suspicion on Maple Avenue that I'd lost my teenage mind. I didn't consider that Mom might have already found out about Cheryl from Brenda, Brenda's mother, Barry, or someone else. Soldan may have been a large desegregated high school, but many of the Negro parents, particularly those whose children had attended Washington Elementary together, formed a tight community.

The first time I mentioned going to see my new girlfriend, Cheryl, Mom was less surprised than I expected. Instead, she immediately went on the attack. My mother's major concern was that Cheryl's parents were divorced. I countered with a technical correction, "separated," and a quip that I didn't see the relevance of the state of Cheryl's parents' marriage to the matter of our dating. Mom next attacked Cheryl's alleged lack of academic distinction. I tried to deflect these remarks by snapping back something about not wanting to spend my time examining her report card. Mom's last strike: Cheryl was too young for me, only a sophomore in high school. I refused to counter, fearing anything I said might clue Mom in to my sexual attraction to her. Cheryl looked more like a woman to me than Brenda, two years her senior, did.

I resisted the temptation to ask Mom how she'd gathered intelligence on Cheryl. I tried hard to avoid even the appearance of defensiveness during these summer sparring matches. I was afraid to say flat out I wasn't having sex with Cheryl, knowing this would lead to follow-up questions that probed exactly what I was doing with Cheryl. If I'd simply answered, "kissing," Mom might well have prodded further, asking if I wanted to have sex with Cheryl. I wasn't sure I could lie my way out of that question, so I ignored Mom's invitations to confirm or deny any sexual relationship.

Mom was wise enough to know that constantly belittling Cheryl only increased her attractiveness to my teenage heart. But Mom remained distressed by the relationship, and grew desperate after I invited Cheryl to a family picnic in Forest Park late that summer without informing her ahead of time. My act of defiance drove Mom to call in reinforcements, asking Willie and Al to have separate conversations with me about the facts of life. And that's just how Willie described it. His paternal tone, his occasional use of his annoying schoolteacher voice, and his inability to make eye contact as we talked stood in stark contrast to Al's straightforward approach. He repeated what I already knew—that Mom was worried about my relationship with Cheryl. But he didn't presume to tell me what to do about Cheryl. Al's tone and the gentleness of his manner reflected the kindness and humility I so admired about him.

Willie, despite his lecturing, was clearly embarrassed by Mom's assignment. He talked about how my feelings might run away from me when I was alone with Cheryl and handed me a packet of condoms. I wasn't inclined to tell Willie I was still a virgin, or affirm that I had the will power not to go too far with Cheryl. Nor did I reveal that I'd talked to Cheryl's mother about inviting her to attend the Harvard-Yale game in November, never mind tell him that Cheryl had started to investigate colleges near Cambridge so we could be together. As far as I was concerned, Willie was Mom's agent. I also didn't want to provide him with any information that might alleviate Mom's anxiety— such as pointing out that Cheryl was even more Victorian in her sexual attitudes than Mom. I refused to hear any genuine concern in Willie's awkward attempts at parental advice about my romantic involvements.

I still adhered to our family's implicit no sex before marriage message that Mom had badgered me with all summer. Cheryl was, indeed, voluptuous and alluring, but I managed to stay the course. I took sinister pleasure in watching Mom suffer over the sex she imagined I was having with Cheryl—a battle between Mom and me about control and boundaries. I fought to avoid sharing my emerging sexual feelings and my insecurities about my attractiveness. My feelings about Cheryl might have been only hormones kicking into high gear, but they were my own. My feelings. My desires. Not my mother's. But that didn't stop Mom from warning me repeatedly, all summer long, that a shotgun wedding would ruin my chances of going to Harvard.

WHEN I ARRIVED at Harvard in the fall of 1962, the coeducational setting of Cambridge and Boston was so different from Exeter, brimming with possibilities. My pledge to Cheryl of eternal faithfulness would prove to be more of a challenge there than it had been at Exeter, with no girls to offer any temptation. Girls I danced with at the Harvard-Radcliffe Freshman Mixer during orientation week might be in some of my courses. Those dance floor chitchats quick-stepped from "where are you from" to matters of substance: "what are you planning to take for your humanities requirement?" Most of all, little adult supervision oversaw any post-mixer encounters, except Radcliffe's rules about check-in and parietal hours at Harvard. Female visitors were allowed in the Harvard dorms weekdays from 4:00 to 7:00 P.M. and until midnight on Saturdays. Radcliffe girls were required to check in by midnight unless they had permission from the housemother to stay out later. Cambridge also provided many opportunities for informal interaction with girls: coffee houses with cheap coffee, movie theaters, small eateries, and the local tradition of study dates at the Radcliffe Library (which Harvard boys could use, even though Radcliffe girls didn't have the same privileges at Harvard's undergraduate library) followed by coffee at the Hayes-Bickford in Harvard Square.

Before I could even explore all Radcliffe offered, invitations to mixers at womens' colleges in Boston, only a subway ride away, appeared on our dorm bulletin boards. The first Saturday offered mixers at Simmons, Wheelock, and Emanuel College! I chose Simmons, met a girl, and invited her on a date to go to dinner at the Freshman Union and a movie in Harvard Square the next Friday night. As I said goodnight, she replied, "I'll meet you under the clock at Harvard Square at 6:00 P.M.," taking the lead before I could offer to take the subway and pick her up at her dorm. I quickly realized Harvard Square sat at the hub of the Boston/Cambridge student culture—a girl-magnet, a meet-up place for dates, a place to hang out, in today's terms, before inviting a girl to sign-in for parietal hours. The Negro upperclassmen at Harvard also made sure I received invitations to parties sponsored by Negro fraternities and sororities in Boston, where I could meet freshman Negro girls at Boston University, Northeastern, and other more distant schools like Wheaton College. During my first month, I had dates with girls from Simmons, Boston University, Wheaton, and Radcliffe and several "coffees" with Radcliffe classmates.

By mid-October, without Mom's constant reiteration of Cheryl's alleged character defects goading my rebellious passion, I'd all but forgotten about Cheryl. It happened so fast even I was surprised when I learned Cheryl had left a message with one of my roommates, Rob. Her mother had agreed she could come to the Harvard-Yale game in late November. She and I had discussed many times during the previous summer how much fun it would be for her to come to Cambridge for the big rivalry game (referred to locally as The Game), and to see what college life was like. Suddenly I wasn't the least bit excited by the prospect of Cheryl's arrival in Cambridge. I hadn't given any further thought to our conversation about lobbying her mother to let her come to Cambridge. My mind had already shifted to inviting a girl I'd met at Boston University to the Harvard-Yale game. We were enjoying a movie date in Boston when my roommate took Cheryl's call. I stood, staring blankly into space, trying to remember the exact page and paragraph in the busy chapter of those few weeks that led me to believe Cheryl's mother would never allow her to come for a visit, thereby giving myself permission to forget about those secondary characters back in St. Louis until Christmas vacation rolled around.

Rob looked at me with a puzzled expression, as if to say, "Aren't you going to call her back?" I looked over at the black rotary dial phone and announced it was too late to call back. "Do you want Cheryl to come to The Game?" Rob asked bluntly.

"I don't know," I fumbled. I hedged that I needed to think about it, even though I was fairly certain what I wanted to do. Disinvite her.

CHAPTER TWELVE

Dancing with My Sister

I ALWAYS LIKED slow dancing with Lela to bluesy crooning from the "hi-fi," the high-fidelity record player in the far corner of our living room. When my impromptu lessons in the fine art of rhythmic motion began, Lela was seventeen. Rouged cheeks. Penciled eyebrows. Glamorous! I was nine, skinny, and nearly bald from a recent haircut—the cliché of a pesky little brother in my striped pullover shirt and brown corduroy pants. As I gazed up at my sister's coffee-and-cream face, suddenly aware of the scrawny curve of my arms around her, I recall thinking wistfully how she always looked ready for a party.

Lela would lead me across the carpet, around the speckled round pool of the black marble coffee table, toward the hi-fi cabinet. If my foot bumped into one of hers, or I stepped on her toe, our dancing would stop and she'd release me. Repeating her instructions about which beat to move on, almost whispering out the slow rhythm . . . one . . . two . . . one . . . two . . . Lela would take my right hand, pull it around her waist, and place it once more on the small of her back. She'd hold my left hand and bend my arm into the shape of an L, releasing it to float, suddenly, in the empty space just above my head until she replaced her right hand in the opening, dropping her left hand onto my shoulder to tap out the beat. I'd tilt my head back and look up to see if her face showed any sign of disapproval over my missteps, but her eyes only flashed reminders—don't look down; don't look up either; keep your eyes level; stare straight ahead at the midsection of my body; feel the music.

Finally, we'd start moving again. Lela would push slightly on my left arm and I would step backward on the beat; sensing her slight pull to the left, I would move in that direction. A slight pull on my right hand and I followed as she stepped backwards, toward the hallway. All her pushes and pulls moved us in small circles or intersecting triangles that never extended beyond our out-of-the-way corner of the living room. There we danced until the music faded into scratchy static. Once Lela let go, I'd stand flat-footed in my Buster Brown shoes on the well-worn patch of carpet of our small dance floor and wait for her to float over and restart, again and again, whatever 45 or 78 rpm record happened to mesmerize us.

The wailing lyrics of the song, its swirl of clarinets, piano, and saxophones sounded like something we'd listened to before, on the radio. "Am I blue . . . You'll be too." Lela would retrace her steps until she stood in front of me again, her wide-checked skirt whispering softly against me as, through an apple-red smile, she commanded, "Let's try that again, but this time you lead." As she closed her eyes and hummed a familiar tune she could sense my intended direction before my body had a chance to signal where I was going. I didn't feel like I was leading. Rather, we were two fish floating side by side through the wavering tide of music that filled the living room. "If your dreams like your schemes done fell through."

Our lessons continued all through the spring of 1954, Lela's senior year, right up until she graduated from Sumner High in June and left our home on Maple Avenue to attend nursing school. Since Mom didn't allow any fast dancing on the living room carpet, Lela showed me the boogie and the jitterbug in the front hallway. I loved the feeling of skating over the linoleum, holding onto one of Lela's hands as we quick-stepped to the music, our free arms flapping like bird wings behind our heads. But slow dancing with Lela was my favorite. Eventually, I advanced enough in these languid grooves to lead all the time, until one day Lela surprised me, mid-record, with a sudden compliment: "You're really good! I'm gonna tell Momma to let you take ballet lessons."

We immediately stopped dancing and Lela cut off the record player and led me by the hand into the kitchen where Mom was making dinner. Lela had told me about various dance styles— modern, jazz, and ballet—she'd learned as part of the high school dance group she belonged to, but I hadn't made any connection between the kind of dancing Lela and I did and these other forms. I'm sure I'd never even seen ballet performed, except maybe in the movies. But I suddenly wanted to take ballet lessons because I trusted Lela's instincts about dancing, and I enjoyed how I felt as we traced the infinite curves of our lessons together. I was curious to hear how Lela would make the connection between our living room studio and the exotic world of ballet in a way that would convince Mom to agree.

Lela started by describing how well I could sense the rhythm of any song we danced to, even a new one. Mom peered at us over her glasses and stopped stirring whatever she was tending to in the pot on the stove. I was unable to hide my delight in Lela's acknowledgment of my accomplishment as a dancer and beamed my approval as I looked up at Mom. I resisted the temptation to compliment Lela in return. I knew I should remain silent because decisions about spending money, be it for piano lessons for Harold, new shoes, or the presents we received at Christmas, were clearly a matter for adults. Lela herself avoided any mention of money, instead continuing to praise my talent: how light I was on my feet, how smoothly I led her. I noticed she didn't mention the boogie or the jitterbug, wisely avoiding any reference to the sort of music that Mom didn't like and the wild hallway dances it inspired.

Lela did mention how I could capture the feelings of a blues song when I danced. I didn't grasp what she meant at the time, but wondered if Mom understood. She said nothing, and I couldn't read the blank, emotionless surface of her listening face. Mom's steady, piercing eyes looked through or past my sister, and she turned her back on us, Lela still talking, to continue her dinner preparations. Mom's silence made me uneasy.

When Lela quit talking, Mom turned back toward both of us and said, "No," adding an explanation that confused me. "Boy ballet dancers are funny." Puzzled though I was, I knew from Mom's expression that she didn't mean they were comical. And I remembered Mom had once used "funny" to describe disapprovingly a high school boy in the dance club with Lela at Sumner—he lived just around the corner, on Aubert Avenue, and wore his long hair chemically processed in the conk style popular with some Negro entertainers. Lela turned quickly away, retreating down the hallway, dashing out the screen door, onto the front porch where she plopped down in one of our metal, all-weather chairs. I followed her outside, stood in front of her for a long while, searching through the signs of disappointment in her sad face and slouched body, hoping she'd explain what Mom had meant.

Lela volunteered nothing. I pestered. Lela shifted in her seat, her eyes turned from mine, as if to give herself time to compose an answer. When she finally claimed she didn't know, I knew she was telling a white lie. Lela knew what Mom meant, and her denial was just a way to suggest Mom shouldn't have said anything beyond her initial refusal. As I continued to bug my sister, wondering out loud what was so funny about the word "funny," Lela rose from her chair laughing quietly and, if only to stop my nagging, asked me if I wanted to go back inside and dance some more. I smiled and nodded my emphatic silent of course.

LELA CONTINUED to introduce me to the dances she was learning in her teenage world, always eager to show me the new moves she'd seen in dance clubs or at some party, but she never mentioned ballet to me again. During this same period, perhaps as a way of apologizing for getting my hopes up about being *en pointe*, Lela initiated me into a secret part of her world, a secret I came to realize she guarded carefully, at least from Mom and Dad. Lela loved comic books. Though our parents thought they were a bad influence and banned them from the house, Lela used some of the money she earned working part-time at an ice cream store to clandestinely amass a small, impressive collection. She hid the contraband under her mattress.

Tucked high up in the attic, which Al had divided into three small spaces before he married and left Maple Avenue, Lela's room beneath the front eaves of the house was barely large enough to accommodate her double bed. With our heads almost bumping up against the slanted ceiling, my sister and I would sit together reading her favorite titles, which always included the latest installment of Blondie. Our family didn't live the suburban lifestyle of Blondie and her husband, Dagwood, but I had a strong sense this was the life Lela dreamed of having someday.

My sister's collection also included many Archie Comics, but the antics of the teenage characters in this series made her laugh in an odd way. When I asked her why, she told me it was because their lives seemed so unreal to her, even as comic book characters. Archie and his friends didn't have to work part-time jobs like she and my brother Mac did. Archie and his gang drove in their own cars to whatever movies or drive-in restaurants they wanted to. I remember Lela once reeling off the names of a bunch of restaurants along Kingshighway (within walking distance of our house) that refused to serve Negroes. Not with any sense of anger, but with nervous little chuckles. I didn't realize at the time the deep irony in my older sister's laughter. But I remember what a big deal it was when she and Mac left the house one Saturday to attend a matinee showing of a film at a whites-only movie theater downtown that Negroes could attend only on that particular day. Perhaps Lela shared the Archie characters' sense that being a teenager required some measure of rebelliousness—against parental control, against the arbitrary boundaries the world puts in a young person's way. Before I realized it, the secret stash of my sister's comics and the conspiracy of our secret attic reading had transformed me.

LELA WAS THE first member of my family to notice I could read at the age of four and a half—before I entered kindergarten. I can't recall exactly how she discovered I could decipher written words, but I know it wasn't in the process of reading to me. I do recall reading *Humpty Dumpty* to Barry many times, especially after my own plunge from the front porch banister had landed me in Children's Hospital. Lela might have overheard some of these intense readings, which often took place at the foot of the staircase leading up to the second floor. Barry and I liked to puzzle over just how all the King's horses (nurses?) managed to put my head back together.

When I managed to escape from Barry (and everyone else in our crowded house) into rare pockets of solitude, I could spend hours by myself, in the basement, in what had once been the coal bin, poring over old newspapers, using the light from the small windows above my head to see how many of the words I recognized in the dated headlines, the stories, and even the ads. These activities may have led, indirectly, to becoming the subject in a little experiment involving Lela and Mac and a bottle of milk—an experiment that ended up convincing my brother I could indeed read well enough to enter kindergarten.

One day Barry and I were playing with Tinkertoys under the kitchen table when Lela and Mac, in the throes of an animated conversation, walked in and stopped right next to us. I couldn't tell whether they'd noticed Barry and me there, or simply didn't feel any need to acknowledge us with a greeting because we were, in their eyes, the babies. I didn't pay much attention to what either of them was saying until I heard Lela tell Mac that the principal of Washington Elementary had asked all the students to see if any of their younger sisters or brothers (even those under five) were ready to start school. Lela's explanation confused me: if enough students didn't enroll at Washington Elementary, the school board might close it, forcing her to ride a public transit bus to another grade school. (At that time, there were no middle schools in St. Louis, so children remained in elementary school through the eighth grade.) She pleaded with Mac to help her convince Mom to let me start school in January, a half-year early. Mac, who had entered Sumner High the year before, claimed, in his usual mocking voice, that he had no interest in grade school affairs. In his typically sardonic way, he asked what made Lela think I was ready for school.

When she declared, "He can read!" Mac demanded proof. Though I'd been eavesdropping carefully, the conversation sounded more like a big sister/big brother battle of wits than anything that might require input from me. But there was Lela, beckoning me with an impatient fluttering of her hand to come out from under the table. So I crawled out, got up, and stood obediently in front of her and Mac, leaving Barry to amuse himself under the table.

Mac walked over to the window next to the sink and picked up one of the milk bottles lined up on the sill, then walked back to where Lela and I stood in front of the refrigerator. He thrust the glass bottle in front of me and pointed to the large red letters printed across it. He asked what the letters said. I glanced up at Lela and caught the twinkle in her eye that I took as a sign it was okay to answer, despite whatever seemed to be making Mac so mad, and spoke the brand name of our local milk company: Peverly. With a spark of wonder in his voice, Mac asked me to spell the word, which I did without even glancing at my older sister. She and Mac went back to talking as if I wasn't standing right in front of them. Mac, suddenly excited, asked Lela how I'd learned to read. She wasn't sure, but pointed out that I asked her all the time what words in the newspaper meant. Mac reluctantly agreed to go with Lela to talk to Mom, handing me the milk container as they walked out of the kitchen. I put it back where it belonged and crawled back under the table where Barry was still sprawled, playing quietly.

LELA WAS THE first member of my family to label me a reader, but she did have an additional incentive to get me into Washington Elementary early. We were all caught in the web of St. Louis-style segregation. If Washington closed, there would be no school for "colored children" within a fifteen-minute walk of Maple Avenue. I was too young to assess if Lela's fear of Washington's possible closure was realistic. I can still recall the mixture of anxiety and pride in her voice as she talked to Mac. She was clearly worried about remaining at Washington Elementary until she could join Mac at Sumner High. Her concern and persistence motivated Mac to help gather evidence to convince Mom (and Washington's principal) to admit me to kindergarten in January 1949—at the mid-year.

LELA WASN'T ALWAYS pleased I developed verbal skills so early. I believe that's why, before she left for Los Angeles, she gave me my nickname: LIP. It was, she explained coyly, just a play on the initials of my name, Larry Isaac Palmer. But I got the real message.

My nicknaming ceremony took place at the kitchen table one night at dinner when I was in second grade (Lela was then in high school). After Dad said grace, he looked around the table and asked his assemblage of children—Lela, Harold, Louise, Barry, and me—what had happened at school that day. I immediately started to tell a story about the arithmetic my class worked on and how, as soon as we were finished, my teacher, Miss Lewis, asked me to read out loud to the entire class. I was all set to talk about what happened during recess, when Lela, frowning, snapped at me: "You talk too much, LIP!" Her insult hung in the air for a few seconds like a yellow jacket before it pushed its stinger inside me. My childish ego throbbed as Barry, Louise, and Harold all laughed in apparent agreement with Lela's new name for me. I immediately stopped talking. Mom smiled. Did she think the hurt inside me was funny? Deserved? Dad just pretended he hadn't heard Lela's declaration, looking around the table expectantly to see who might offer up the next report.

I kept myself from crying by imagining I was back at school. Miss Lewis had invited me to speak in class. She acted like I had something important to say and important for the other members of my class to hear. She punished kids who talked too much with a rap of her ruler. She never punished me. I was usually the first child she asked to read or answer an arithmetic problem. I tried to console myself by thinking that school had changed me. I was important. I didn't have to wait my turn to speak. I liked that!

The next time I heard "LIP" it came from Harold, at the dinner table a few evenings later. I'd launched into an animated tale about Miss Lewis and the story she'd read to us that day, but before I could finish, Harold giggled. "Stop, LIP! I've heard enough." I glanced over at Mom and Dad observing the sibling squabble without comment. Nothing in their facial expressions indicated disapproval. I decided to ignore Harold and finish my tale. I even prolonged it a bit to see if he'd interrupt me again. Of course he did, muttering another "Okay, LIP," as I described a painting we'd done at school that day. But he got the same message I did from our parents' silence: I could express myself as much as I wanted, and he could express his irritation at my verbosity. We went back and forth—my school-day tale punctuated with four more of his slightly irritating "LIP!" wisecracks.

Lela, Harold, and occasionally Louise used "LIP" at the dinner table whenever my dinnertime recitations tried their patience or perhaps violated the unspoken rule that our speaking order at the table started with the oldest and descended to Barry (who only occasionally piled on a "LIP!" of his own). Our conversations usually operated without much parental intervention. Dad's "Amen" at the end of grace marked the beginning of our overlapping, competing storytelling. Despite my new nickname, I usually managed to defend my own right to free speech at the dinner table.

By the time I was in fourth grade, Lela found another way to shut me up: by making fun of the way I looked once I lost my baby teeth. One evening, as I chattered away, Lela turned to me and pronounced, "You look like a snaggletooth baboon!" right in the middle of one of my sentences. I tried to hold back my tears, to erect a floodwall of good memories of my best day at school, but nothing could counter the sharp stab of Lela's remark. The thought that she—my sweet, glamorous dancing partner—found me ugly, disgusting, and painful to look at brought tears to my eyes. I glanced toward Mom and Dad, but they seemed not to have heard Lela's hurtful words, or perhaps considered them harmless. Did they agree with her? I longed to ask them for help, but I couldn't speak. And so, my sister managed to achieve what she wanted: momentary silence around the table. Until Harold and Louise, suddenly a duet, took up the refrain of "snaggletooth, snaggletooth" that brought on even more tears. Barry sat in silence next to me as I looked to our father again, wishing he would see my heaving chest and stop my hurt with a stern word directed at Harold or Louise. But Dad just looked down at his plate, my crying reaching a crescendo of heaving sniffles, my upper body shaking, as I peered through squinted eyes toward my mother.

Mom glanced my way, rolling her eyes and pursing her lips as she hissed through clenched teeth: "Larry, don't be such a crybaby. You're too sensitive!" These words at least stopped the obnoxious refrain from Harold and Louise. I wiped my nose on my sleeve, still searching inwardly for some image that might offer momentary reprieve from the idea that Lela saw me as loathsome. What had I done to make her want to hurt me? I had no answer, but from that day forward she referred to me as snaggletooth—not just at the dinner table, but anytime I (apparently) got on her nerves. I would cry every time she taunted me, though I tried to take comfort in the fact she had dropped "baboon" from my moniker.

Lela's teasing stopped well before I had my full set of permanent teeth, when she won a scholarship to attend nursing school and moved into the students' residence at Homer G. Phillips Hospital—until the 1960s, one of the few teaching hospitals in the nation for Negro physicians seeking residency training. As time went by, Lela sometimes came home for Sunday dinner, but perhaps because my geeky performances at the table were no longer part of her daily experience, she never called me "LIP" again. And happily I was no longer "snaggletoothed." But the joy of my dance lessons with Lela ended as well.

DURING ONE OF her infrequent visits to Maple Avenue for a Sunday family dinner, Lela revealed she had a new boyfriend, James. She described him as brilliant, and announced she wanted all of us to meet him. Mom suggested Lela bring him to dinner the next Sunday she had free.

I knew the moment Mom told me to set the dining room table for James's first visit that something important was happening in Lela's life. None of her high school boyfriends had ever made it past the front porch or the living room couch. I'd watched those relationships come and go and, on one occasion, even helped Lela entertain two boys at the same time by engaging one in conversation on the front porch while she talked to the other on the living room sofa. After the suitors left, I told

Lela I liked the front porch boy. Porch Boy was a "nice guy," she said, but Sofa Boy—the one I didn't get to talk to—was more "exciting." As I set the dining room table for James, I wondered which character he would most closely resemble.

As James and Lela entered the front door, I noticed how slender he was. And how much taller than anyone in my family. Once we sat down at the dining room table, no one needed to tell me the usual family dinner rules were suspended. James wasn't simply a guest; he was at Maple Avenue for a family inspection. This was one dinner gathering where I understood quite clearly I should keep my LIP(s) zipped until someone asked me a direct question. I watched my parents' reaction to James as they engaged him in conversation. He had strong opinions about everything, which he expressed freely and often. He spoke quickly, almost snarling. A question from one of my parents revealed he was about nine years older than Lela, roughly the same age as our oldest brother, Al. I later learned James worked as a draftsman for a company making charts for an aeronautical firm, and he had attended Stowe Teachers College for two years, though he hadn't graduated. He also mentioned (several times) his plans to move to California, which he claimed offered greater opportunity for Negroes.

As James became a regular Sunday presence and accompanied Lela at larger family gatherings like Easter Dinner, I sensed Mom didn't like him. After Lela and James left one Sunday, Mom mentioned that James hadn't finished college—in her mind, one strike against him. She didn't like his explanation for why he quit either: He claimed he discovered he didn't want to be a teacher even though he'd earned top grades. Although James had secure employment, I felt our mother had very different (read higher) aspirations for Lela's married life. Maybe Mom hoped Lela would meet and marry one of the up and coming medical residents at Homer G. Phillips.

The second strike against James was his tendency to interrupt others, including Lela. I couldn't quite understand why Mom objected to this. When there were no guests, conversations in our house were always crowded affairs, and interrupting others was the norm. Although we were instructed to follow Emily

Post's rules on conversation in public, all bets were off within the family. I thought to myself that James might fit right in with the Palmer clan, which, after all, had more than its share of smart alecks.

The third strike against James was his misfortune, in my mother's estimation, to be HBD: "handsome but dark," her label both objective and subjective. Slender and muscular, with chiseled features, sharp eyes, thin lips, and a Harry Belafonte crew cut, James was strikingly handsome, whether dressed in slacks and a short-sleeved shirt or in a well-tailored suit. But James's complexion was dark brown, darker than my own skin, though not "jet black" as Mom described some Negroes. Mom, lighter-skinned than my father, didn't see James's skin tone as complementary with Lela's light complexion. I assumed my mother worried about having dark-skinned grandchildren.

After Lela graduated from nursing school and took a job at Homer G. Phillips, James moved to Los Angeles. Lela announced that as soon as he found a job she'd be leaving for Los Angeles too, to marry him. Mom, as usual, worried about "who his people were." She hadn't met James's sisters, brothers, or parents and wondered out loud whether his family even valued education since James didn't finish college. Dad, on the other hand, was more concerned that James should come back and marry Lela in St. Louis before she moved to Los Angeles. Dad looked worried whenever Mom mentioned the wedding plans, fearing James might not marry Lela once he had her all to himself in California with no family nearby to look out for her.

My parents always discussed their misgivings about my sister's prospects in muted tones—and I never heard them say anything to Lela about her plans. In fact, they knew very little about Lela's relationship with James, which had developed under the scrutiny of the housemothers at the nurses' residence, not on our front porch or living room sofa. Mom and Dad must have realized they couldn't stop Lela, so they adopted the practice of silence. A short time after her announcement, Lela booked a flight to Los Angeles and quit her job. She married James on New Year's Eve, 1957.

Lela returned to St. Louis for a visit late in the summer of the following year. She regaled me with stories of Los Angeles life. When she described the landscapes full of palm trees, I wasn't surprised that it was different from anything I'd seen in St. Louis. From movies, I'd surmised Los Angeles was basically an irrigated desert. Lela's stories about how people lived there intrigued me. I couldn't imagine why the grocery stores were open all night and on Sunday—unless people there didn't go to church and shopped after they finished late shifts at hospitals or factories.

Lela spoke as if she'd seen the future with her stories of roads with no traffic lights that allowed her to drive from her house in South Central Los Angeles to any place, even Hollywood, in a matter of minutes. As she painted a picture of bustling around in her car from the San Gabriel Mountains to the city's east, then back west to the Pacific beaches, I couldn't understand why the roads she described were called "freeways." But I could feel the wind blowing through the rolled down windows of her car as her animated voice took me on a spin through Beverly Hills.

The gleam in Lela's eyes disappeared, though, when I asked anxiously, "How long are you staying?" She looked away, and took a long time to formulate her answer, eventually saying in a measured, flat voice, "I don't know." But after two weeks passed and she was still with us, I wasn't shocked to learn Lela had found a job in St. Louis. Though the words "separation" or "divorce" were never spoken, I worried that Lela's marriage might be in trouble. She assured us that she'd found a job as a nurse in St. Louis because she'd missed her family and just wanted to spend a few months at home. As if to squelch any questions about the future of her marriage, she also pointed out she could easily find another job back in L.A.

I can't say why I assumed there was a rift in Lela's less-than-a-year-old marriage. It's entirely possible James simply had no reason to return to St. Louis with her on that occasion. Lela was pregnant with her first child, Kim. Maybe Lela's impending motherhood drew her to St. Louis for an extended visit, the Palmer DNA creating some deep need for face-to-face contact

with our parents (and the rest of us) before she gave birth. Whatever the real reason for her extended visit, Lela was still at Maple
Avenue the Sunday morning I left for Exeter in the fall of 1958.

She sat across the kitchen table from me and watched me
eat breakfast. After everyone else left the table, she asked, with
a mixture of sadness and excitement, "Larry, are you nervous
about going away?"

"Nope," I answered casually.

"Then why didn't you eat all your breakfast?" she queried
seriously, studying my face.

Before I could stutter something about not being hungry she
went on: "I've never seen you not eat all your breakfast." She
looked tenderly at me and dropped into silence. She rose from
her chair, walked around to where I was sitting, and stood beside
me for a moment, then slowly put her arm across my back and
squeezed my shoulder. "It's okay to feel scared about leaving
home. Don't ignore your feelings."

Lela returned to St. Louis the following summer for another
extended visit, this time with Kim, who'd been born in December—but again without James. I was home after my first year at
Exeter, with plenty of time to lounge around the backyard with
them during the day. My carhop job at the Foot Long drive-in
was evening work. As we sat out back, enjoying the relative pri-
vacy of the lawn chairs, I felt I could speak from my heart when
she asked me about my East Coast experiences. Lela giggled
easily at my stories about prep school mixers and faculty characters such as the German-teaching Dean of Students, Kessler,
who'd stopped me on the path one day to inform me that in German, Dad's name, Arglister, meant something along the lines of
"a mean person."

One sunny afternoon as we sat on the back lawn, laughing
and talking while my newest niece crawled around on her blan-
ket, Lela started to comb through the clover absently, worrying
it with her slim fingers. As I watched her, it occurred to me Lela
was no longer part of the daily life of Maple Avenue, and thus,
like me, an outsider to the ongoing struggles for emotional prominence and attention that so defined us during my childhood
and her teenage years. Within a few seconds, or so it seemed,

Lela managed to find a four-leaf clover. She plucked it from the ground and handed it to me, smiling.

"May your life continue to be a lucky one."

DECADES LATER, Lela and I now speak frequently by phone. After a recent call, I hung up the phone and noticed I'd picked up an earworm. Suddenly "Just for a Thrill" from *The Genius of Ray Charles* began playing in my head. I first remember hearing the tune my second year at Exeter. My inner Ray Charles raspy voice brought back memories of slow dancing with Lela as a kid, and of the way, through our dancing, she somehow gave me permission to feel the amazing rhythms of good music in my young body. She was a good teacher.

I recognize today how my long-winded descriptions of unremarkable school days at the dinner table might have tested Lela's nerves. I adored her, but couldn't understand how my smart aleck antics could drive her to distraction or how her teasing me to the point of tears was, for her, a type of self-defense. I couldn't count the number of times I interrupted Lela with one of my ebullient second grader's yarns about what I'd learned that day, just as she was about to share something important of her own. I acted as if Lela, a teenager, should hang on every word I said because my grade school teacher did. Perhaps she and my other siblings were trying to teach me that if I ignored the feelings of those trying to love me—like Lela—my ignorance and cluelessness would eventually make them angry and lead them to strike out at me in some way, or worse, ignore me completely.

In retrospect, Lela's period of hurtful teasing was short-lived, though it didn't seem that way at the time. I can't recall hearing a cross word from her once she left home. I guess that makes it oddly appropriate that Lela was the only member of my family to say anything at all to me on that fateful morning in September 1958. I believe I was telling her the truth when I said I wasn't nervous about leaving. But Lela's gentle squeeze of my shoulder cautioned me not to ignore my feelings. To let their music guide my steps.

In some ways, it feels as if Lela and I will be floating above those few square feet of carpeting on Maple Avenue forever.

Those moments blur and blend in my memory. I know it wasn't Ray Charles singing "Am I Blue" that afternoon in 1953; he didn't record his version until he released *The Genius of Ray Charles* in 1959. I was at Exeter by that time, and Lela was in Los Angeles. I have no idea who was singing the blues the day Lela began teaching me to dance. It could have been any number of Negro artists featured by St. Louis rhythm and blues stations like KATZ or KXLW.

I remembered the first time I heard *Genius* at Exeter. I instantly recognized the words of "Am I Blue" and purchased the album. I listened to it often at school and when I was home on break. Once, as I sat in the living room listening to other tracks from the album, Mom asked me why I liked blues music so much. At the time, I had no answer for her. But I now see it wasn't because I was unhappy or blue as a teenager. Rather, when I heard Ray Charles, I was reminded of a time when whatever might have been bothering me, trapped as I was in my large, emotionally complex family, I could absorb myself for a few minutes inside the music. I was whole, not blue, slow dancing with my sister.

PART III

Grief in Slow Motion

CHAPTER THIRTEEN

Our Wayward Black Sheep

LOOKING BACK, I realize it was Louise who always reminded me of things I had forgotten. She's always seen herself as our family historian, as the keeper of Palmer memories. It was Louise who greeted me with a lingering hug as I entered the house on Maple Avenue the day before Dad's funeral. I'd come directly from the airport, and was disoriented by being in St. Louis instead of in New Haven, registering for my second-year classes at Yale Law School. I kissed Louise on her cheek, untangled myself from her embrace, and put my suitcase in an alcove by the stairway in a swift, nearly singular motion. She put her hand on my arm, stopping me to make sure I listened carefully to what she was about to say.

"Guess who's here?" she asked, as I looked over her toward the crowd gathered in the kitchen. Not waiting for my answer, she blurted, "Urshel!"

I hadn't heard my brother Urshel's name mentioned in years, at least not since I'd left Exeter. I had always had the impression my parents simply didn't know how to get in touch with our itinerant sibling as he moved around the Los Angeles area. I wasn't sure how the communication chain between my mom and my other seven siblings had been assembled after Dad died. Mom had probably called Al to make Dad's funeral arrangements. He likely went to see my oldest sister, Lena, to deliver the upsetting news in person, before soliciting her help in calling the rest of my brothers and sisters, our out-of-town relatives, and the members of my parents' church. Lela called me to say Dad had died while visiting her in Los Angeles. I was fairly certain no one had Urshel's number. Maybe Lela had tracked our wayward black sheep down.

Standing there deadlocked with Louise in the hallway, I started to mutter something to the effect that Urshel was the last person I expected (or cared) to see. He hadn't been home since I was four years old, and I hadn't thought of him very much, if at all, over the intervening years. But Louise was grinning and anxious to tell me how Urshel, who'd run away from St. Louis so long ago, managed to make it home for our father's funeral. I forced myself to put on my listening face.

"Boy, it's a miracle!" she beamed. "God works in mysterious ways! Al called Kansas City to tell Uncle James about the funeral and Urshel walked into Uncle James's house at that very moment! Can you believe that?"

"What was Urshel doing in Kansas City?" I asked.

"Okay, get this. Urshel and Uncle James's son, Junior, have kept in touch. They used to be running buddies when they lived in Arkansas. Lord, all these years wondering where Urshel was, and Junior always knew!"

"So, did Junior also come to St. Louis for the funeral?" I again interrupted, trying to get at the facts, without getting caught up in Louise's jubilance at Urshel's unexpected arrival. Three years older than I was, Louise might have experienced a more visceral sense of loss when Urshel ran away, whereas I only recall puzzling momentarily over the possible reasons for his sudden disappearance. Her revved-up emotions in the hallway made me feel exposed. *I've got to get her to calm down. She's about to start shouting like one of those women in church when we were kids!*

"Nope. Junior didn't want to come," she replied more quietly, a bit of disappointment seeping into her voice. "But," her ebullience returned, "Junior loaned Urshel a black suit, shirt, and tie! So, he hitched a ride, just like he did when he left for California, and he showed up here with Uncle James and Aunt LaVerta. Praise the Lord!"

"That's quite a coincidence," I ventured, eyeing the crowd in the kitchen.

"Larry, no. It's God's hand in the life of this family."

I let Louise have this last word. I didn't want to invite any inquiries about my own lack of regular church attendance since my graduation from Exeter. I told Louise I should go let everybody know I made it home and left her standing near the front door as if she were the official greeter for some Baptist revival meeting, waiting in the vestibule to welcome in all true believers.

In order to avoid the boisterous mob at the kitchen end of the hallway, I walked through the living room and entered the kitchen through the dining room door, searching for a spot where I could observe the crowd of my relatives, many of whom I didn't really know, and where I could eavesdrop on conversations as I had done as a child.

I squeezed past several relatives standing between the door to the back porch and the kitchen table, then maneuvered behind several others clumped in front of the refrigerator to perch myself in the well of the window between them and the kitchen sink. This placed me directly across from the clogged hallway entrance I'd just avoided using, offering a clear view of my sister Lela standing in front of the stove with all eyes focused upon her.

She was recounting for the assemblage of relatives her efforts to revive Dad after he suffered a heart attack in her house in Los Angeles. She had painted the scene for me in a relatively calm manner when she'd called me on the phone with the news of Dad's passing. But her retelling of the story, the way she described our father lying on the floor, and how she'd pounded on his chest and grabbed his face, pulling open his mouth to receive her crying breath, elicited a palpable hush as if we'd been gathered by her voice into the immediate aftermath of my father's dying breaths.

She paused to wipe away a tear, not perceiving that Urshel had entered the crowded kitchen from the hallway behind her. All eyes moved from Lela's tears to his figure looming in the doorway and several audible gasps pierced the quiet. Urshel, an open beer bottle in his right hand, seemed to suck more and more of the oxygen from the crowded room with each forward step.

I was so totally taken with Urshel's charismatic entrance that my mouth involuntarily dropped open. *He is the most beautiful*

man I've ever seen! Every woman in the kitchen seemed to flash
momentary weak smiles in his direction. His penetrating eyes
seemed to freeze anyone they landed on. His high cheekbones
and nearly Roman nose floated softly above those easy-going lips.
Urshel wandered into Lela's tale of grief, gathering up our fascination. All broad shoulders and chest, sipping beer from a bottle,
it was obvious he worked out. He looked like he was about my
age, but I knew he was thirty-five.

Suddenly Urshel's eyes and nostrils flared with anger as he
shouted, "Man, what the fuck are you looking at me that way
for?" at Harvey, a cousin from Chicago who happened to be
standing in Urshel's line of sight. Rumblings rippled through the
embarrassed crowd of Urshel-gawkers. Everyone in the kitchen
knew Cousin Harvey had been randomly selected as the object
of Urshel's epithet-laced question. Harvey (and the rest of us)
stood suspended in the silence that reasserted itself in the wake
of Urshel's outburst. I clung to my perch, wondering . . . Who's
going to stop Urshel from fighting with poor old Cousin Harvey?

"That's the sixth beer he's had today," Al's calm voice proposed, part accusation, part explanation regarding the distur-
bance Urshel was creating. His voice growing more forceful, Al
offered the solution: "Willie, get Urshel out of here!"

Willie moved from behind Lela and grabbed Urshel's arm,
apparently intent on escorting him back through the hallway
door, but Urshel, still gripping the neck of his brown glass bottle, refused to move. Willie's eyes circled the room, searching
for reinforcements. He shot a glance at me and ordered, "Larry,
help me take Urshel to my house!"

I felt the crowd's eyes following me as I made my way in a
straight line from my hiding place in the corner to where Willie stood holding Urshel's right elbow. Standing in front of them
both, I realized for the first time that I was taller than at least
two of my older brothers. I suspected Willie chose me as his
assistant for this very reason. As I slipped my hand gently under
Urshel's forearm, he smiled at me, his face relaxing into a wist-
ful stare. The tension in the room dissipated as if someone had
punctured a balloon with a pin. We turned around to leave the
kitchen and made our way through the hallway. Willie was on

one side of Urshel and I was on the other. Urshel babbled like a happy drunk being escorted home by two more sober buddies, then I heard him mutter "Larry . . . Larry . . . Larry."

Once we were on the front porch, I loosened my grip in response to cooperative signals from Urshel's body. He eased into the passenger side of Willie's car as if we were just three brothers on an outing. As the youngest Palmer present, I knew I was expected to take the back seat.

The ten-minute ride gave Willie the opportunity to lecture Urshel on the evils of too much alcohol. But he would occasionally turn off his public-school-teacher diction and revert to his excited, stunned big brother mode to glance at Urshel and exclaim, "Boy . . . you sure look good!"

I wanted to interject that Urshel, muscles bulging in his Lacoste polo shirt, didn't look like someone who lived on the edge, but I refrained. Willie seemed as dumbfounded by Urshel's presence as I was and, perhaps trying to sweep past the barriers that distance and time had created between them, asked him, as casually as he might have asked me: "Who cut your hair?"

Urshel didn't respond, instead falling into his refrain from before, in the kitchen: "Larry, Larry . . . Larry." He twisted his body around to stare at me in the back seat. There was no flash of anger in his eyes; instead they reflected his soft smile. He seemed as amazed to see me as I was to see him. I tried to keep my face neutral. But something about those easy-going lips made me smile in return. Urshel turned back around and looked out the window. Willie, ever the wise schoolteacher, abandoned his lecture for the remainder of the ride.

"Nice house," Urshel remarked, as we entered Willie's living room. Willie waved his arm around the room, motioning for us to sit in the overstuffed chairs or on the ample couch. I waited until Urshel chose his spot in the middle of the sofa and Willie plopped into the chair opposite him to slump myself into a chair on Willie's left. Willie's wife, Irma, also a schoolteacher, wasn't at home. We sat staring at one another across the small coffee table, wondering who would break the silence of the otherwise empty house.

"Do you have any scotch?" Urshel finally asked.

"You've had enough to drink," Willie barked, then glanced at me as if to cue the beginning of a new conversation.

"Larry, how is school?" he queried, eyebrows arching.

"Fine. Classes start tomorrow, but a friend is taking notes for me."

Turning to look directly at Urshel, Willie proclaimed, "Did you know Larry is at Yale Law School?"

"Wow, that's really great, man," Urshel slurred, shooting me a squint. Willie's interrogation proceeded on to my post law school plans. A series of questions and answers allowed Urshel to hear that I'd worked as an intern in the Mayor's Office in New York City the previous summer, and that I planned to interview for summer jobs with law firms at the end of my second year. I volunteered that I intended to sign up for interviews with the St. Louis firms that came to campus (as well as firms from a variety of other cities, including New York).

Urshel rolled his eyes and shook his head from side to side, repeating, "Larry, Larry . . . Larry" after each of my responses. At first I thought Urshel's refrain mimicked the way folks shouted, "Amen, Amen, Amen," in the Baptist church we attended when I was younger. But after Urshel had chained together the brief syllables of my name this way several times, it dawned on me that there was a kind of dreamy affection in his voice, perhaps even some pleasant remembrance of me. Despite Urshel's drunken state, he seemed to understand that Willie's chatter was just his older brother's way of proselytizing him with a sermon on our "family values," and of chastising him for his long absence.

If Willie thought Urshel was ready to offer an apology to either him or me—"I am sorry, Larry, for missing your growing up"—Willie totally misjudged the impact of his sermon. Urshel offered no explanation of what he'd been doing the previous eighteen years, and, rather than apologizing for rarely letting anyone in the family even know where he was, simply ignored Willie's rebuke and began to reminisce about their boyhood together in Arkansas.

I could feel the altered tone in the room but couldn't grasp the meaningful substance of the conversation that followed, because everything my older brothers were discussing happened long before I was born. Urshel's story started with an accusation. He claimed Willie had wronged him somehow, back in their past. I sensed the story would end with Urshel demanding an apology from Willie, even though I didn't understand what the original disagreement was all about.

It had something to do with Willie claiming that Urshel, long before, had misused some piece of farm equipment. Back when they were kids. Back when Mom and Dad still had the farm that Grandpa Palmer left them, and when the older Palmer children were still expected to spend their summers helping the man my parents hired to work it. The gist of the matter seemed to be that Urshel believed Willie had reported the broken tool to Mom and Dad, bringing down a beating with Dad's leather strap upon Urshel's back. As a familiar, mutual anger flared between them, Willie denied any wrongdoing. Eventually Urshel paused and gazed at me and said, "Larry, you have the power."

I had no idea what he meant. Either I had not been paying close enough attention to their dialogue, or they'd been speaking in a coded language I couldn't decipher. I didn't ask Urshel to explain. I just attributed his attempts to involve me in this intrigue as further evidence of how drunk he was.

Urshel soon shifted his focus back to Willie, hitting him up for money. I tuned in to the drift of the conversation with my ears, but mostly just watched it with my eyes. Urshel made his request for cash as if it would be compensation for past wrongs. He reasoned that Willie could easily afford whatever the requested amount was because Willie and his wife both had well-paid jobs as teachers. Willie became defensive (again) and denied that he owed Urshel any money. Urshel (again) turned to me and repeated, "Larry, you have the power."

Now I had a better inkling of what Urshel wanted me to do: referee, judge the validity of his new claim against Willie. I was accustomed to role-playing a hypothetical judge from my first-year law school classes. "Mr. Palmer," a professor would ask, "if you were the judge in this case, how would you decide?" But this was a matter of real life, my life—and my connections to two of my brothers. If it came down to Urshel's version of what hap-

pened or Willie's, there was no way I would side with the black
sheep of the family.

On the other hand, taking Willie's side could really anger
Urshel. I thought he'd seemed eager for a fight with Cousin Harvey back on Maple Avenue. It occurred to me that my admittedly
dim memories of Urshel were all laced with violence. I looked
first at Urshel, then Willie. Then Urshel repeated his refrain,
"Larry, you have the power."

I didn't want to admit I hadn't been paying close attention
to their conversation, and so retreated once more into my own
silence. After another half hour of slurring babble, Urshel fell
asleep on the couch. He was still laid out there when Irma came
home. Willie told her he'd be right back and drove me back to
Maple Avenue. We rode in silence. He didn't seem interested in
drawing me out of my private musings about Urshel's volatility.
I sighed as I walked up the front stairs, emotionally exhausted,
glad that keeping Urshel in line for the funeral would be Willie's
job, not mine.

THE LAST TIME I remembered seeing Urshel, he and Al were fighting in the kitchen. From my perch in the window well I watched
fists fly until Al grabbed Urshel and wrestled him to the floor in
front of the icebox. As Al straddled Urshel and punched him in
his face and chest, I moved out of the well and stood near the
stove. I could see the muscles in Al's shoulders through his white
tank undershirt, the arteries in his neck bulge with each blow he
delivered. "Don't you ever wear any of my clothes," Al screamed
at Urshel between punches, "without asking me first!"

Urshel didn't fight back or speak. He did cry. Al let him up.
Urshel took off the white tank undershirt he was wearing and
gave it to Al, then stood there for a moment wearing just his blue
jeans. Suddenly Urshel grabbed a plaid flannel shirt (presumably
his own; perhaps a hand-me-down) hanging from the back of a
kitchen chair, and slipped into it without buttoning it up. Al just
turned and stalked out of the kitchen.

As soon as Al was out of sight, Urshel opened the back door,
squinted at me through his tear-reddened eyes, and bounded
down the porch steps, two at a time. I rushed to the door to see

him sprinting down the cement sidewalk, the tail of that plaid shirt flying above his jeans. He turned quickly to his left at the corner of our garage, and then turned on a dime to his right onto the brick path toward the covered brick ash pit and the garden patch. Without breaking his stride, he leaped onto the wooden cover of the pit then jumped down into the graveled back alley.

WITH HINDSIGHT, I realize I'd become skittish of Urshel even before he ran away. One day I overheard Mom talking to someone on the phone in the hallway. She called up the stairs for Al to come down, not seeming to notice me as I stood there in the entrance of the kitchen. She ordered Al to call Lena, adding that she wanted them both to go get Urshel out of jail. I wondered what had happened, but didn't want to ask. Mom appeared more perturbed than upset, as if Urshel having trouble with the police was simply part of a familiar pattern. I figured if I waited, Al and Lena would soon be back and I could eavesdrop on whatever they reported to Mom.

I went back in the kitchen to my favorite spot for listening in on adult conversations (especially those not intended for my ears): the well under the window. I pretended to be looking out at the backyard as I waited for the doorbell to ring. When it did, Al and Lena escorted Urshel into the silent kitchen. He wore a long tan raincoat and a gray Homburg hat like Dad's. I stood still as Urshel rolled up his right pant leg to show Mom his bandage. He uncovered the dark red spot of his wound, explaining to Mom that a small bullet from a policeman's gun had penetrated his calf without shattering the bone. *A policeman shot Urshel!*

I couldn't hear anything Al or Lena said as Mom roared questions at them all. What was Urshel doing with that gang of boys? Where did the police say this happened? Why didn't that fool of a boy stop when the policeman told him to? Was he charged with anything? Does he have to go back to juvenile court?

I could make out Urshel's pleading: "I didn't do anything wrong enough for that fucking cop to shoot me in the leg!" But Mom, Al, and Lena all ignored Urshel as they discussed the next steps he'd have to take to deal with this situation. Mom's frustration and disgust seemed to permeate the air in the kitchen. As I

*Urshel, about 17 years old,
before he ran away from home*

eavesdropped, I extracted some
lessons for my own behavior:
shun boys in gangs; avoid all
contacts with the police; be a
"good citizen." It felt as if Urshel was being condemned for
dishonoring our family, as if his
misbehavior might infect us.
Did Urshel's cross-examination
somehow make him feel he deserved the bullet?

To this day, I'm struck by how the adults in that kitchen paid
no attention to his protestations of innocence.

My parents (and Al) reacted to Urshel's sudden departure
from Maple Avenue as if he certainly would be back soon. He'd
taken nothing from his room, not even a jacket to protect him
from the cool fall air. I suspect Al was assigned the task of inves-
tigating Urshel's usual hangouts—his job, his high school, whatever friends he had—to see if anyone had seen or heard from
him. Al or Lena probably checked with the jail to make sure he
wasn't back there. Without anyone saying it, I realized Urshel
had simply vanished.

Several weeks passed before I heard someone, probably Dad,
give Urshel the label "runaway." Some months later (perhaps
as long as a year), we received news of his whereabouts. Mom
announced one evening at supper that a long-distance truck
driver, apparently at Urshel's request, had stopped by the house.
This white man had told her he gave Urshel a ride from Okla-
homa to California some months before.

When I was in grade school, Urshel sent infrequent letters to
Mom. Sometimes years passed between these messages. Mom
never let me read this correspondence, but, occasionally, at the
supper table, she would report on a new letter and provide us
with an edited summary of its contents. Just before I went off to

Exeter, a letter reported that Urshel was living in Venice Beach working as an extra in Hollywood movies.

I'd hear tidbits about Urshel during my Exeter vacations. He lived in many different parts of Los Angeles, preferring its beach communities. But, as far as I knew, no one in our family, not even our sister Lela, who also lived in Los Angeles, had laid eyes on Urshel since that day he leaped over the ash pit. Not until the very moment he strode back into our kitchen on Maple Avenue in the middle of Lela's tale of Dad's death.

THE MORNING of Dad's funeral, Urshel was sober. He was dressed in his black mourning attire like the rest of us, and able to perform his duties as pallbearer without offending Mom's sense of propriety. Later, at the repast on Maple Avenue, I nonetheless kept my distance from him; there was something both mysterious and disturbing about his refrain from the previous afternoon. Larry, you have the power.

I exchanged pleasantries with neighbors, distant relatives, and members of my parents' church who prepared the meal. I politely acknowledged their sympathies. Before the buffet began, someone suggested a family picture. As I looked to see who had mentioned posing for a photograph, my mind swam back in time to some photographs of Urshel I'd seen before he ran away.

WHENEVER WE played house, Louise assumed the roles of director and scriptwriter for our playhouse in the basement. She played the mother in our make-believe family. I portrayed the father. Barry was our child. I went off to my pretend job somewhere in that cavernous space and returned home with my paycheck. Louise took my check, went to the corner grocer to cash it, and gave me back my weekly allowance and an allotment for a pint of whiskey. Mom was the model for her character. Louise insisted I act like Dad and accept her management of our finances.

Mother Louise and Father Larry never had any disagreements about who cooked, since Louise's script dealt only with ordinary days at Maple Avenue. If Barry misbehaved while I was at my make-believe work site, I could overhear Louise scold him that she would report his misdeeds to me.

On the day I went off-script, Louise and I had thrown a few quilts over some chairs to create an imaginary room in our pretend house. Our quilt-rooms were usually erected near, but never in, the hand-me-down makeshift bedroom where Urshel and a succession of older brothers slept—a single-occupant window-less space in the far corner, enclosed by two limestone walls and single sheets of plaster board attached to two-by-fours. A curtain covered its entrance, five or six giant steps away from the water drain that our teenage brothers, or even Barry and me, used to pee into. When I went off to my "job" that day, I made Urshel's bedroom, rather than my usual spot near what had been the coal bin, my place of employment.

Despite Urshel's warning to stay out of his room, I knew he wasn't home and I was curious about this forbidden place. I thought I'd use the time in Louise's script for me to be at work to explore Urshel's sanctuary. The cramped room contained an unmade double bed, a small wardrobe with underwear on the shelf and shirts, slacks, and jackets hanging, and a dresser with two sets of drawers on each side of a mirror.

What's in those drawers?

I forgot I was supposed to be working at the bread factory like Dad did at his real job (before he obtained his civil service job at the post office) and moved toward the dresser. When I opened the narrow top drawer on the left side, I saw coins and bills scattered about. I was tempted to take a few coins, but resisted, thinking he would know I'd been in his room if I took any money. The other, deeper drawer on the left side contained socks.

I moved over to the drawers on the right side, opened the top one and discovered paper, pencils, and paperclips in a heap. I didn't bother to try to read any of the papers. I was still fighting the temptation to take maybe a dime from the coins in the left top drawer as I opened the second, deeper drawer on the bottom right. It was half full with a stack of black and white photographs.

The photo on top of the stack pictured Urshel, naked, with two white women. One of the women, dressed in what looked like a swimming suit, was on her knees in front of him, holding Urshel's penis in her hand near her mouth. The other woman stood behind him, her naked white body pressed against Urshel's muscular, mahogany back and buttocks. I was curious about who the women in the photograph might be. With only one bathroom in the house and a rigged-up shower over the water drain in the basement, I'd seen Urshel and my older brothers naked many times. I flipped through the stack of photographs noticing that Urshel, sometimes clothed but usually unclad, was in all of them. I went back through the stack slowly and paused to stare at a picture of a white man and Urshel together, both naked. They smiled and faced the camera with their arms stretched across each other's shoulders. Their penises, crowned with pubic hair, dangled between their legs. I wondered if the photographs could be part of some game Urshel and those white men and women were playing. I thought about how Urshel was seldom at home. How he had a job shining shoes at a hotel downtown. *What does he do besides shine shoes when he's at that hotel?*

I put the pictures back in the drawer, left the room, and went back to my imaginary house and wife. I picked up an old newspaper to read as Dad might do after work. I didn't share with Louise—or anyone—what I'd discovered about our older brother. I felt going through Urshel's stuff was somehow wrong. Even though "dirty pictures" wasn't yet a part of my vocabulary, I intuited that Urshel would be in big trouble (and mad at me) if Mom and Dad knew about those pictures. Neither of our parents talked easily about the human body and used euphemisms to describe my own uncircumcised penis. Make sure you pull back the skin and wash your thing.

I CAN'T RECALL how I felt about my first encounter with pornography. I was too young to understand what the images might imply. I remained concerned about my association of violence with memories of my seventeen-year-old beautiful brother. Were he still alive, I wouldn't want to ask him about the logistics of appearing in pornographic images. I would, however, want to know what made him take off with literally just the shirt on his back when I was about four years old. It couldn't have been the fight with Al. After all, brothers fight. Did it have something to do with events that took place in Arkansas, before I was born? A psychologist once told me that children who run away from home often feel pushed or even propelled out of their home environments. The migration from rural central Arkansas to St. Louis may have reshaped my tight-knit family into a configuration that made Urshel want to flee and often left me feeling uncomfortable, unwanted, and alone.

Urshel's answers might have helped me understand why, some years later, when I was nine or ten, I tried to run away myself. I don't remember what set me off, but something happened inside me one day as I was sitting on the front stoop. Something that made me bolt. I didn't get very far. I wandered around the neighborhood for nearly an hour before I returned home, prepared for a good whipping for my unsanctioned absence. I was shocked when I walked in the front door and realized nobody had even noticed I'd gone AWOL. I never even got a verbal thrashing for my attempted escape. I wondered how long it would have taken Mom or Dad to realize I had either run away or been stolen by some passerby desperate for a child.

Experiences like this made me feel our parents neglected me or, at the very least, saw fit to simply put my older siblings in charge of my care. Did Mom and Dad have too many mouths to feed, too many hearts to nurture, too many bodies in need of hugging, too many questions that they had already answered thousands of times? Did this lead to the suppressed anger that always floated in the atmosphere on Maple Avenue, a resentment that could, at any moment, flare up in beatings like the one Al gave Urshel? Did the fear of becoming a perpetrator of that kind of violence frighten Urshel away?

By some odd grace I got my last beating around the age of twelve, even though I was physically very small for my age and, unlike my older and much larger brothers Mac and Harold, easily overpowered by my parents. They outgrew their beatings, but I spent a lot of time watching how our parents (mis)treated Urshel and perhaps internalized some negative messages about him. He was so clearly the black sheep, especially in Mom's eyes.

I can't imagine how Urshel managed to go nearly twenty years without seeing any of us. I realized, once I was an adult, that all my siblings are too much a part of the person I am to leave them completely behind. I understand how Urshel's experiences growing up might have left him with very conflicted feelings about each of us. But wasn't there one of us he'd missed and longed to see?

I never saw Urshel again. I heard though, through the Palmer grapevine, that he came back to St. Louis and stayed with Mom for a few months after Dad's funeral. But she eventually asked him to leave Maple Avenue and he complied, never to be seen again by anyone in the family.

The circumstances of Urshel's death may contain the best answer possible to all my persistent curiosities, and shed some light on how Palmer DNA informed and failed to inform our lives. Brother, how could you be dead without a single other Palmer being there as your body was lowered into the ground or your ashes scattered? There was no announcement of his death, only Louise's premonition that he must be dead. She told me at a family reunion that she'd dreamt he died. I didn't believe her, stubbornly holding onto the notion that he might meander back into our lives again as he did at Dad's funeral. I was nearly seventy when I searched the death records in California and found some proof (there I go being the lawyer) that Urshel died in 1994, at age sixty-three. Childless, as far as I know. I was finally able to accept that he was never coming back into my life. But that none of us was there for him haunts me. Perhaps that's why I sometimes feel he's still with us.

I take some comfort in the realization that I'm likely to be around to help memorialize and bury Al, now in his early nineties, as I was for Willie, Mac, and Lena. Whether any of my other siblings—Lela, Harold, Louise, and Barry—will be there to help send me to the other side doesn't bother me because I suspect my own children and grandchildren will be there. I also live with the hope that, when I die, there will be friends I've not met yet to mourn my dying and remember my footsteps on the earth.

My wish for Urshel, the first runaway from our chaotic but loving family, is that when he died at least one friend he hadn't yet met the day he left home was with him. One with whom he shared the story of how he jumped over the ash pit in our backyard. One who shed a tear for him in that precise moment. Because he had lost you. Because he knew right away that you were gone.

CHAPTER FOURTEEN

A Tour of Headstones

ARKANSAS WAS, and remains, Upper Hill, the cemetery outside Biscoe where my parents buried Herschel, their infant son, in 1931. Barry and I were about eight and ten when Dad drove us through fields worn out by cotton and overgrown with long grass, along reddish brown dusty roads, to visit Herschel's grave, over twenty years after his toddler's body had been laid to rest. It had probably been many months since the last funeral vehicles—car, truck, or mule-driven wagon—rolled up to the grove of trees surrounded by an iron fence.

Dad stopped his 1948 black Chevrolet in front of the gate and nodded for us to get out. Barry and I stood knee-deep in grass next to the car. It was coated with a film of dust that had turned its side a dark chocolate. Dad looked back down the slope for a few seconds, as if he was catching his breath after climbing a steep mountain. But Upper Hill was barely a hill, more a slight rise in the otherwise flat landscape.

Dad opened the gate and told us the cemetery had been placed on Upper Hill, so flooding from the White River wouldn't wash away the graves. I'd never heard of the White River, but Dad had taken us on streetcar rides to see the flooding from the Mississippi and Missouri Rivers in St. Louis. I wanted to extend Dad's geography lesson and ask him if the White River connected to the Mississippi River. But he moved silently through the grass toward the far corner of the enclosed space, no bigger than our backyard on Maple Avenue. We followed him, ignor-

ing the gravestones and wooden markers, and stopped where he
stood in front of a small tombstone. I followed his stare and saw
what he saw: Herschel L. Palmer. *My brother!*

I'D HEARD his name many times, mostly from Mom, in relationship to Urshel, especially after he disappeared. I can't count the
times she told me if Herschel had lived, Urshel would have never
run away. He would have had an older brother to play with and
protect him from the bad influences of the world. Herschel's
death had broken Mom's most effective way of raising sons. Al
and Willie were the first brother pairing; Mac and Harold, second; Barry and I, third. In Mom's view, Herschel's death left the
teenage Urshel untethered to our family.

Mom's strategy for raising sons in the city may have reflected
her dual struggles over Urshel's departure and the loss of baby
Herschel. She blamed herself for Herschel's death. The few times
I'd seen Mom about to cry took place whenever she mentioned
how Herschel had probably caught a chill on the porch, leading to the pneumonia that killed him. She never explained how
she could have prevented Herschel from falling ill. Her beliefs
contained such strong emotion, I never questioned her account,
even after I learned pneumonia was most frequently caused by a
bacterium, and penicillin, the earliest antibiotic used to treat the
disease, wasn't widely available until the 1940s, and a vaccine to
prevent pneumonia in infants wasn't generally used until 2000.
There was no rational balm for her guilt-ridden heart.

I'd never done the arithmetic until I was a father myself;
only then could I imagine what other pressures Mom faced as
a parent when Herschel, her fourth child and third son, died.
She was already pregnant with Urshel at the time of Baby Herschel's demise. Lena had just turned six, Al was four, and Willie
was two. She and Dad both worked as school teachers, raising the question I would never have asked as a child: who took
care of my sisters and brothers while Mom and Dad worked? I
don't remember babysitters other than our older siblings for any
of us. But unless six-year-old Lena wasn't in school, there must
have been some other person, unknown to me, who helped with
childcare that spring of 1931 when Herschel died. I wonder if

Mom had much time or space to grieve Herschel's death as she tried to balance her work, her duties as a wife and mother of three small children, and a baby. Without understanding what I know now, even then I surmised Mom had a backstory whenever she invoked his death as a justification for dressing Barry and me as twins.

As I stood with Dad and Barry in front of Herschel's gravestone, Herschel seemed to speak parental, or at least Mom's, wisdom from the grave: take care of Barry, your younger brother.

DAD BROKE the standing silence with a slight movement of his eyes toward a larger tombstone with the inscription: "Isaac Palmer." "That's my brother, your Uncle Ike," Dad almost whispered. I'd seen Uncle Ike's chocolate ice cream colored face with splashes of pink on his neck and cheeks (the skin disease vitiligo, I would later learn) in a casket at the funeral home in St. Louis before Aunt Lillie brought his body back "home" to this hillside resting spot. Dad led us on a tour of the headstones in that corner of the grassy patch of a cemetery and pointed out other relatives. That's my sister he told us. Over here is my daddy. That's my momma. I interrupted Dad to ask how to pronounce her name: Adarlier Switchlor Palmer. He explained her parents had been born slaves in Missouri to people from Germany, so her name before she married was German.

We moved into a ring of headstones outside of the Palmer circle. Dad stopped in front of one inscribed with the last name "Hall." The family history lesson continued as he described how the Halls were related to the McNeelys, "Your Momma's people," as he called them. The details exceeded my ten-year-old understanding of family relationships, which was limited to brothers, sisters, uncles, aunts, nieces, and nephews. Dad's conclusion got my attention: Uncle James's wife, Aunt LaVerta, was a Hall and that made Aunt LaVerta and Mom some type of cousins.

Cousins. I had heard Dad's nieces and nephews (about the ages of Lena, Al, and Willie) referred to as my cousins, but I hadn't associated them as family until I remembered how Mom and Dad once lived in Arkansas. Before taking us out to Upper Hill, Dad had shown Barry and me where he and Mom lived when they first married. He drove us through the center of Biscoe, where four dilapidated wooden clapboard houses, whose whitewash had long ago faded into a grayish hue, defined the intersection of two nameless dusty roads.

On one side of the street, from the mid-1920s until the late 1930s, Dad and Mom had lived next door to Uncle James and Aunt LaVerta; Uncle Ike and Aunt Lillie Belle shared the third adjacent house. Grandma Palmer lived across the dirt road in the fourth house. Dad described with glee in his eyes how sharing adjacent fenceless backyards with his two brothers, their wives and children, and his mother across the way, created a close-knit family. Back in St. Louis, Mom had always described these living arrangements, with her mother-in-law across the street, as nothing but trouble—at least when Dad wasn't around. But seeing the actual houses with Dad, I sensed the comfort he drew from living in such close proximity to his brothers and his mother.

As Dad stood in the road, probably imagining the houses in their original, newly white-washed glory, a pickup truck emerged from a cloud of dust and stopped as we moved out of its way. A dark-skinned Negro man got out of the truck and rushed over to us. "Profess' Palmer, you back!" the man gushed. Dad shook hands with the man and explained that we'd only come to visit his Aunt Melinda for a few days. The stranger chewed on his gums the way Grandma Lela did when she didn't have her dentures in and looked admiringly at Barry and me as if he knew us because he knew Dad. Then he burst out, ". . . taught me everything!" He paused to rearrange his gums to speak, directed his attention back to Dad and said with a bellyful of affection, "We sho' miss you!" Dad let go of the stranger's hand, patted him on the shoulder, and told him we were on our way to Upper Hill to visit Herschel's grave.

I noticed Dad didn't say he missed teaching, or anything else about Arkansas. Maybe he was reluctant to express any longing for Arkansas in front of Barry and me, the only Palmer children without any Arkansas roots. This was our first visit to Dad's homeland. Biscoe was a storyland, a place Dad, my aunts and uncles, and some of my older brothers and sisters reminisced about. Whenever any of those Arkansas-born relatives detected that I had no idea what they were talking about, they'd remind me that Dad gave up on Arkansas so that my siblings and I could have better educational opportunities. Underneath this family narrative lay a message: be grateful for Dad's sacrifice and for growing up "up North."

We got back into the car and continued slowly along the dirt road Dad said would take us to the highway to Upper Hill. Few of the weather-beaten frame houses adjacent to the road, their doors shut and shades lowered, appeared occupied on that sunny late summer day. A stout woman in a calico dress stood outside a house with curtains flapping in the breeze and a screen door casting a shadow inwards. She waved us down. Dad stopped. The woman leaned through the open passenger-side window and we heard Dad greeted again as "professor." She seemed even more ebullient in her greeting than the truck driver had been. Word must have spread through town that Dad was back! She also asked if he was coming back. Dad repeated his tale about our visit. She seemed disappointed and gave Barry and me, seated in the back of the two-door Chevy, a parting glance, as Dad sped up. I asked Dad how many people lived in Biscoe. Less than four hundred. I wondered how many of them remembered Dad, who'd left just before I was born. I tried to sort out my feelings about the greeters we encountered along this brief journey.

As the houses disappeared and became fields of cornstalks, we turned onto the paved highway. A man and woman, standing at the edge of the dirt road, waved at the car as Dad turned. Dad nodded and smiled at the roadside greeters. I suspected that if we'd driven through Biscoe longer or stopped along any of the small wooden houses along the highway, more folks would have come out and hailed Dad as "Profess' Palmer."

The professor title confused me. I knew enough about the educational hierarchy to realize that people who taught at colleges were sometimes called "professor" or "doctor." The people who taught Willie were professors. John Dewey, who Dad told me taught at a college in New York City, and George Washington Carver, who probably taught Dad at Tuskegee when he left Biscoe to train for his job with the Farm Security Administration, were professors. But the people who taught me and the other

Palmer kids in elementary and high school were simply "teachers." So why did people call Dad, who'd been a teacher at a high school that ended at the tenth grade, a professor?

I'd almost broken out laughing when I heard people in the town call Dad "Profess' Palmer"—a very nervous laughter, because I thought of Dad as "just" a mail handler at the post office who'd refused Mom's many entreaties to take the civil service exam to become a supervisor. As the folks in Biscoe greeted Dad with the utmost affection and respect in their voices, I was painfully aware of his economic insufficiency in the urban environment where Christmas toys were shared between me and Barry, and where an older brother, Mac, couldn't borrow money to attend the college of his choice because of the economic risks to his younger siblings, including me. I was seeing the hardships of rural life in central Arkansas for the first time, and my inner nervous laughter served to mask my emotions as I realized what Dad had done to give my siblings and me a chance to flourish.

I realized only later how bleak the educational opportunities were when Dad graduated from Arkansas Baptist College in 1920. After World War I, only about forty-five percent of school-age children in Arkansas, Negro or white, attended school on a regular basis. In many rural areas, a "split term" was used, with children attending school only in the winter, July, and early August, so they could be available for the planting and harvesting seasons. Fewer than two percent of high school age Negro children attended school as local white officials diverted money earmarked for Negro education to white schools. It's easy to see now how Dad's (and his parents') perseverance to obtain a college education made him some sort of hero to the Negroes in Biscoe and its surrounding farming plots.

We rode in silence, afraid to ask Dad why the people called him professor. I didn't want to laugh out loud, or hear an answer from Dad that might make me so sad I would cry. I wasn't old enough to fully understand Dad's past rural life. Dad put his arm out the driver's window to signal he was turning left onto another dirt road, interrupting our silence to tell us this was the road to Upper Hill.

During the final part of our cemetery tour, as we moved away from the Hall section of tombstones and glided through the high grass toward the gate, I noticed what looked like a garden plot of worn wooden crosses. I assumed from what I'd seen in movies that these were gravesite markers, and expected to see names carved on them. There were marks on some of the crosses, but I couldn't make out any names. I asked Dad whose graves lay under those worn wooden markers. He stopped and gazed down at one of them, before glancing back toward the headstones in the Palmer and Hall sections of the cemetery. When he didn't answer immediately, I wondered if his hesitation gave him time to make up an answer. Surely he knows. If everyone living in the town knows Dad, he must have known these people before they died. He looked down at me before saying, again quietly, "I don't know." Perhaps sensing I wanted more, he continued in a muted, sad voice: "Those are the graves of folks whose families didn't have money for headstones."

CHAPTER FIFTEEN

Uncle Larry

I BECAME AN UNCLE before I knew what the word meant. Lena's first child, Sandra, was born when I was barely eighteen months old. To Sandra and her two younger brothers, Cornell and Frank (whom we all called Butch), I was simply "Larry." After Sandra's birth, it would be a decade before Al's or Willie's children would refer to me as Uncle Larry, and, with that designation, reveal to me my inchoate brotherhood with their own fathers. Even then, it wasn't until I was old enough to hear about the birth of Willie's daughter, Pam, and she began to talk and call me Uncle Larry that the word's significance clicked in my head. My uncles, James and Ike, were Dad's brothers. To be Pam's uncle, I was her father's brother. And since I was also Lena's brother, I was uncle to Sandra, Cornell, and Butch, even though they never added that title to my name.

Sandra, Cornell, Butch, Barry, and I were so close in age I assumed we were all siblings. After all, Sandra and her brothers called my mother "Mom" or "Momma," and my father was "Dad" to them just as he was to Barry and me. This custom may have resulted from my mother and Lena experiencing pregnancy, and all the amazing chaos of having a new child, together—Mom gave birth to Barry in October and Lena gave birth to Sandra the following January. I don't recall ever having seen Sandra, Cornell, or Butch as diapered or nursing babies. Not only were they close in age to Barry and me; we were about the same size.

But Barry and I were, in fact, the youngest children of a different Palmer generation. When Lena and her husband first arrived in St. Louis from Arkansas, they lived downtown in an apartment, a streetcar ride away from my parents' house on Maple Avenue. But by the time Sandra entered school, Lena and her family had moved into a small one-story house with a basement on Cote Brilliante Avenue, one block east and about four long city blocks north, across two busy boulevards from our Maple Avenue house. By 1956, two years before I would go off to Exeter, Lena's house had become my summertime refuge from the frigid emotional atmosphere that surrounded my mother. I wasn't simply running toward a warmer climate, I was running away from my fear that I was becoming too much like my mother.

I always had to ask Mom for permission to go over to Lena's house, and gradually learned how to increase the odds that her answer would be yes. I would finish all my chores: cut the backyard grass, sweep the kitchen floor, and clean up my room. And I would include Barry in my request (usually without asking him if he even wanted to go along), telling Mom, who seemed always to need a reason for our leaving, that we wanted to play with Sandra, Cornell, and Butch. Not that we didn't have plenty of time to play with them at Maple Avenue. During the summers, Mom, and to some degree, Barry and I, babysat Lena's children on the five or six days she worked at the dress factory. Some nights, Sandra, Cornell, and Butch would even spend the night with us and we'd all sleep on quilts on the living room floor, the oscillating fan swishing around to cool the air.

I barely sensed why I was so drawn, even on the hottest and most humid afternoons of the summer I turned twelve, to Lena's house. I was afraid to confront the way I felt at home, even when I could name the disturbing emotions I was experiencing. My impulse on any given day was simply to escape my mother's troubling emotional detachment. One morning, excited by something I'd read or some new idea that had stirred the surface of my imagination, I went to the kitchen where Mom was cooking to share my excitement. As I nattered on about my most recent intellectual discovery, I could tell my mother's thoughts were elsewhere. The hollow, unfocused cast of her light brown eyes communicated that I had interrupted her deep in thought. It took her a few seconds to focus on me, peer over her eyeglasses, and parse what I was trying to tell her.

Something in the emptiness of her gaze repelled me. I couldn't ignore the familiar warning in her flat expression, one that caught me up short and usually meant I shouldn't close the physical distance between us, that I should stay at arm's length. I always imagined she looked this way the afternoon in Forest Park years earlier when she had pushed me off her lap for no good reason, and I had run downhill to find my sister Louise so I could lean into her shoulder.

But I didn't need to sit on my mother's lap anymore; I needed to find rest in her heart, in her tender regard. I wanted desperately for her to echo whatever childish awe I was experiencing with a simple smile, a glistening of her eyes. I blamed myself for the vacancy in her pursed, slightly turned-up lips, assuming I hadn't brought home enough "prizes" that the summer—prizes in the form of daily retellings of some brilliant thing I'd done at school, or good report cards, or a list of compliments from my teachers. At first the way she slammed the door to her heart only hurt a little, but gradually it made me want to flee, to run away. The unspoken rule in this situation dictated that I could leave, but I couldn't acknowledge what was driving me away. Walking the five long city blocks in the heat was a small price to pay for Lena's eye-popping, glad-to-see-you-smile and warm greeting that offered a welcome balm for Mom's cool indifference.

Lena always welcomed us eagerly, teasingly referring to Barry and me as "the rest of her little rascals"—a good-humored reference to a then-popular television series. She never seemed annoyed when we showed up at her doorstop, or too busy to tell us at least one funny story about our family's life back in Arkansas. The mischievous lilt of her "I remember one day when . . ." was a dependable signal that we'd all be laughing soon enough. But not before she'd call us back down to earth with more serious tones, describing a hot, dusty Saturday when Mom woke her and Al very early to help the hired farmhand with some chores. The hired hand actually ran the farm day to day while Mom and Dad both taught school, Lena explained, admitting how scared she'd been that something must be seriously awry because Saturday was usually her day off from milking the cow, the one day of the week she was allowed to sleep in. And because Mom hadn't even mentioned the word breakfast.

As Lena painted a picture of herself dressing quickly and rushing dutifully out of the silent house, right behind Al, she transported all five of us—Barry, Sandra, Cornell, Butch, and me—to that distant farmyard where we imagined a ten or eleven-year-old, overall-clad version of her, standing ready to help with whatever emergency awaited. Had the cow escaped from the fenced pasture? Was there some valuable crop in need of harvesting quickly, before a tornado or hailstorm could strike? As her laughter overcame any attempt to be serious or mysterious, we all asked in unison What happened!? And we all giggled as Lena confessed that nothing had happened. Mom and Dad had promised the farmhand they would help him do some routine weeding that Saturday, but then decided to sleep in instead. Nothing indeed. Not even breakfast. Still, from her tall tales of childhood hardships working on the farm to her offhanded gossip about her co-workers or her white bosses at the dress factory, Lena's stories nearly always ended in comic relief rather than anger or resentment. She was a natural-born tease and storyteller. She still was, at ninety-plus.

Any story I tell about Lena must include a set of Chinese checkers. I remember sitting alone with her at the Formica oval of her small kitchen table as we deployed our white and black marbles at opposing vertices of the sturdy wooden game board. At first I'd insist loudly that I wanted to move first, not volunteering to my sister that I believed the reason I couldn't beat Mom or Dad in a one-on-one game was that they always made the first move. If I couldn't beat my parents, maybe I could beat my oldest sister. But, after a few games, I figured out that Lena had no interest in beating me. She even cautioned me from time to time against what would have turned out to be very bad moves. Perhaps she guessed how disappointed I'd be if I lost and so, unlike my parents, found a way to let me win most of the time. And on the rare occasion when I lost a game, if I showed the smallest sign of pique—a frown, a sigh of self-disgust—she'd suggest we play Crazy Eights or learn a new card game.

I often wonder what Lena thought about my frequent (and sometimes unplanned) flights from Maple Avenue to her haven on Cote Brilliante. Lena and Mom both seemed to understand there was always a chance these afternoon visits would evolve into requests to spend the night. On the lucky days we were allowed to stay, Barry, Cornell, Butch, and I would sleep huddled tight together in the basement double bed, while Sandra slept in the second small bedroom on the first floor. Lena and Mom always handled the negotiations about whether we could stay for dinner or have a sleepover by telephone. When Mom said no, I wondered if she simply felt guilty about having chased us away in the first place with her aloofness. It never occurred to me that her periodic refusals might mean she missed me. Barry? Maybe. But not me. In Mom's eyes, Barry had better hair. It wasn't as kinky as mine. He also had lighter skin and dimpled cheeks that she liked to squeeze. More important, Barry didn't badger Mom with questions or comments about what he'd read, imagined, or thought.

After one of our sleepovers, Lena let me try to make pancakes for all the rascals—something I'd never done before. I'd watched Mom make pancakes from a mix, and brown them in her cast iron skillet, but she never offered to teach me. If I asked her how to make something, she usually replied that the recipe was all in her head and the steps simply came to her as she went along. I'd noticed the directions on the side of the Aunt Jemima box though, and deduced that the biggest trick was flipping the cakes when they were just the perfect color so as not to burn them.

My first batch turned out to be an undercooked disaster. I blamed my failure on changing technology—Lena had an electric skillet instead of a cast iron one like Mom's. But this first attempt at making breakfast led to loads of teasing and good-natured laughter at my expense—and years later continues to be a favorite excuse among my nieces and nephews to rib me. At the time, I accepted Lena's humorous taunts, knowing instinctively she believed I was trying to be helpful. I knew I would get a second, third, or even fourth try to experiment with making pancakes at Cote Brilliante. Lena's kitchen-lab was always open.

One of Mom's explicit prerequisites for approving our summertime visits to Lena's was that Barry and I complete our two hours of daily reading before we left. Mom offered any number of rationalizations for the non-negotiability of this requirement, starting with the weather. Like many mothers in the 1950s, she had latched onto the popular belief that too much perspiration and lack of rest could bring the onset of polio. It was, thus, too hot and humid in St. Louis for us to be running around in the heat of the afternoon. The dog days of summer were a real threat. I didn't question Mom's reasoning, but I suspected her true motivation for enforcing this regime was her desire that we earn the certificates awarded by the Vacation Reading Club for reading fifteen books during the summer, adorned as they were with bright gold St. Louis Public Library emblems. Technically, the library handed out the certificates with our names emblazoned on them once we checked out fifteen books. Nobody at the library inquired whether we'd actually read the books we returned. No tests or book reports were necessary to earn the certificates. But bringing one home before the end of July not only brought a smile to Mom's face, it prompted a challenge to see if we could read another fifteen books before Labor Day. As acting big brother, one of my duties was to organize our frequent trips to the public library and, since Maple Avenue and Cote Brilliante were so inextricably enmeshed during the summer months, those junkets included Sandra and her younger brothers who were also drafted into the library's summer reading program.

I enjoyed going to the library and the assigned reading time at home. The quietness of the house and my flights of imagination into the stories and biographies of famous men, which were my staple in those days, came as a welcome diversion. No one on Maple Avenue supervised or commented on what I read. I can't remember a single book Barry read, nor do I recall if we ever discussed any book that I read, or if Louise was even involved in the summer reading program. Reading at Maple Avenue was a solitary activity that allowed me to forget, albeit momentarily, the responsibilities of being a big brother, an uncle, and a son. But this solitary engagement with ideas also created a longing (never expressed) for someone with whom I could converse.

I was at Lena's house (around the time I entered Hyram's gifted class) when I had my first real discussions about literature. I remember sitting with Sandra in Lena's small living room and reading out loud from *Little Women*. One passage about how the girls missed their father who had left home to fight in the Civil War moved her to tears. When I finished reading and looked up to see Sandra crying, I started crying too. It was also the first time a scene in a novel had ever made me cry. Reading with Sandra must have somehow put me in touch with my own buried sadness.

At the time, I didn't grasp that my empathy with fictional children missing their father resonated with my own experience as a preteen. If Mom was having a bad day, I couldn't say to myself, "things will be better when Dad gets home." Dad was unfulfilled and physically exhausted from his work as a mail handler. Often in a bad mood, he was either unavailable when he arrived home or fussed at me for some minor infraction, like chewing food with my mouth open. Not until I graduated from college did I grasp that the only time I felt his presence in the summers growing up was when he took Barry and me away from Maple Avenue to go fishing in the park after supper.

Margaret Mitchell's *Gone with the Wind* proved to be the bane of our two-person reading circle. Sandra's summary of the novel's perspective on the Civil War, along with its various romantic subplots, didn't appeal to me. The passionate melodramas my niece invested in so fully, grafting the novel's depictions of male-female relationships with her own childish thoughts, fancying herself a matchmaker for Barry and me and two fair-skinned girls named Betty and Jane who lived across the street from her, resonated too uncomfortably with my preteen anxieties about love and sex—anxieties that I was trying desperately to hide from everyone—including myself.

Sandra had casually observed, and I'd agreed, that Jane, with her dark, wavy hair and hazel eyes was the prettier of the pair, but, based on her insights from Margaret Mitchell, assigned

Betty to be my "girlfriend." Sandra explained that Barry—the dashing Rhett Butler character—got the prettier girl, Jane. Then, in her sweetest voice, consoled, "Girls like Barry because he's cuter than you. But girls like you, Larry, because you're a really nice guy." Did this mean I was the unexciting and dutiful Ashley Wilkes? Sandra's feeble attempt at a compliment missed the mark. Nice? Our two-person salon ended as I lingered over how much it stung that even Sandra thought Barry was more attractive than me.

Once I immersed myself in the all-male environment at Exeter, I forgot about Sandra's unwitting assault on my fragile ego and concentrated on winning new prizes—like an admission slip to an Ivy League college—I could bring home for Mom's admiration. Still, all during my Exeter years, the first place I would visit, after settling back into the routines of Maple Avenue, was the brilliant coast of Lena's house. As I approached her front gate, I'd glance across the street at Betty's porch where I'd rehearsed my entrance into teenagerdom. Or I'd pause on Lena's porch and recall the sounds of Mr. Banks, a school teacher and friend of Dr. Hyram's, who happened to live next door to my sister, practicing a piece of classical music on his piano. Almost before I'd ring the bell, I found myself sitting at the kitchen table with Lena playing Chinese checkers, the smell of breakfast filling my nostrils: my pancakes finally perfected.

LENA MARRIED an older man when she was eighteen years old, a year before the Palmers migrated to St. Louis. Though married, she seemed unable to escape (or perhaps didn't completely want to be free of?) her childcare duties inside the Palmer family. Our mother, Mattie, never acknowledged the instrumental role Lena played in making the move north possible.

Apparently, there were too many Palmers to fit into the vehicles my parents used when they left central Arkansas, so they left six-year-old Harold behind with big sister Lena, still a childless young bride. Just for a few months. Just until Lena and her husband could join the rest of the migrating Palmers in St. Louis. She and her husband would relocate their own family operation to St. Louis within the year to join Mattie Palmer's conglomerate.

Mom, who was pregnant with me in March 1944, probably departed central Arkansas with three-year-old Louise perched in her lap in the front seat of the truck, as Dad shifted into first gear for the trek north. I imagine Lena standing there in the warm spring sunlight holding Harold's hand as a little wind devil picks up a swirl of dust and hurls it halfheartedly in the wake of the departing truck. My father honks the horn and waves a haphazard goodbye through his open window. Mattie never once looks back.

CHAPTER SIXTEEN

Promise and Potential

A PERSON WITH "promise and potential"—my girlfriend Marian's label for me at her first encounter with the Palmer clan. I introduced her to the Maple Avenue assemblage one Sunday evening in December 1965, during Christmas break of my senior year at Harvard. On the previous evening, I had endured Mom's disappointment at my failure to bring home a Rhodes Scholarship to Oxford.

I had two concerns on the flight home from the regional interviews in Des Moines, Iowa. How to deal with Mom's unhappiness about the Rhodes outcome, a distress I'd already sensed in her voice when I called with the results of the competition before boarding my flight. And how to break the news that Marian would be arriving in St. Louis the next day with the intention of meeting my family. I didn't talk about my college social life with anyone in my family, and none of them knew anything about Marian.

As I came through the front door, fresh from a taxi, Mom couldn't hide her anguish. As she looked around me (I assume to avoid having to look at me), I could read the silent reproach in her eyes. Surprisingly, I felt sorry for her: she'd have to tell her friends and neighbors that her academic star had "failed" to win a Rhodes. Both local daily newspapers had reported, with photographs, that I was the first Negro ever nominated as a finalist by the Missouri Committee. I wanted to assure her in some way— with a slight hug, or a kiss—that I had a bright future without a Rhodes Scholarship on my résumé. But my failure was unacceptable in her eyes and she moved away as I approached, as if I'd committed a crime.

Brother Al was there when I arrived, but no sign of his wife and kids. I wondered why he would be at Maple Avenue so late on a Saturday night. It occurred to me that Mom or Dad might have asked him to be there when I got home because they didn't believe they were up to the task of helping me sort out my feelings about the outcome of the competition, and they knew how close I felt to my eldest brother. They also knew how much Al cherished me and my education. When my parents had disagreed about whether I should accept the Exeter scholarship, Al had appealed to our father's heart and beseeched him in tears to relent and allow me to attend Exeter. Seeing how Mom turned away from me, Al grabbed me, gave me a hug, and asked in the gentlest of voices, "Let me ask you just one thing? Do you think you didn't win because of race?"

"God no!" I exclaimed. "The other finalists were outstanding and very interesting guys."

"Good. Don't ever think that. It could destroy you," he replied earnestly.

I DID WONDER though, without sharing my inklings with Al, if some of the questions I'd been asked had something to do with my being Negro. A member of the regional committee—white, side-burned, and pinstriped—began with the flattering remark, "Mr. Palmer, your lacrosse coach says you are one of the finest athletes he has seen at Harvard in many years," followed by a biting inquisition: "Why, then, did you refuse, not one, but two invitations to try out for the varsity football team your junior and senior years? Apparently, the football coaches all felt your speed and physical toughness would have really helped Harvard out at the defensive cornerback position."

This was obviously not going to be like my state-level interview, where all the questions seemed to flow from a sense of respect (awe, even) on the part of the Rhodes interviewers for the things I had accomplished—athletically, academically, and outside of the classroom. *This man has doubts about my ability to face difficult challenges. I'll disarm him with candor and be ready for the same question later in a different form.*

My response began with a bold, pointed critique of Harvard's football coaching staff. I asserted that the coaches had in fact made a few players, some I'd known since freshman year, worse. I thought of Harvard's first Negro quarterback, John. I'd seen him throw both left- and right-handed my freshman year. I'd also caught passes from him. They were like bullets—decisive, forceful—and required real hand-strength on the part of the receiver. John, a high school All-American from Ohio, threw more like a professional quarterback than most college players I'd seen. Over his sophomore and junior years, as the Harvard coaches attempted to "lighten up" his speed, John seemed, at least to me, to throw with less and less confidence.

Of course, I didn't mention John specifically, or call attention to the fact that my experiences as an athlete at Exeter had given me the opportunity to work with men like Ted Seabrooke—who epitomized good, effective coaching. Picturing Seabrooke's shock of wavy black hair and his penetrating gaze and friendly smile, I realized I could have reeled off twenty Seabrooke stories if anyone had challenged my stance on the Harvard football coaches. Instead, I explained that the main reason I'd opted out of football was my burgeoning desire to devote a portion of my college years to social activism. If I'd wanted to devote my college years solely to studies and sports, I told them, I would have gone to a small liberal arts college, like Swarthmore, where I could have played three varsity sports—football, wrestling, and lacrosse.

I also chose not to point out that I needed to work part-time during my fall semesters to feel more financially secure, since my parents had withdrawn all financial support my sophomore year. I did receive a Harvard National Scholarship in my senior year (one purpose of which was to eliminate the need for part-time work so recipients could participate fully in academics and other leadership activities). But I actually enjoyed my part-time job at the furniture store and didn't need to take any student loans my senior year. I'm not sure anyone at Harvard, other than a few folks in the financial aid office, knew that during my junior year I was receiving monthly Social Security payments as a minor child of a disabled worker. I wasn't about to explore my mixed-up feelings about my family's inability to provide financial support for my school expenses with a bunch of total strangers on the regional Rhodes Scholarship Committee.

I thought my list of accomplishments—Harvard National Scholar, All-Ivy Lacrosse Team, and president of a student organization—adequately conveyed my identity. But neglecting to talk about my family's economic situation and how I responded to it hid a major part of who I was. The financial struggles of my parents, and the burdens they imposed on my siblings and me, remained a family secret, not fully shared with even my Harvard classmates. I didn't want those white men to see me as a victim or as a mere symbol of Negro progress.

When the same committee member later asked why I hadn't majored in what he viewed as a more substantive major, like history, I spoke about my senior thesis advisor in Social Relations, George Goethals, who had guided me through my sophomore tutorial and encouraged me to explore other interests such as history (I'd taken both American Political History and American Social History my freshman and sophomore years) and Russian literature. When I decided to pursue the interdisciplinary major that made forays into sociology, psychology, and anthropology, I already knew Goethals would support me with my honors thesis. He had offered to act as my thesis adviser at the end of our sophomore tutorial. He told me he enjoyed working with scholar/athletes and my sophomore papers had shown great promise.

It appeared the first committee member to question me was, at best, skeptical about my candidacy, or he'd been assigned the bad cop role of asking the questions that might rattle a candidate and lead to his self-elimination. I resolved at that moment to adopt my own strategy for any encounters of this sort in the future. Intellectually, I could accept the doubts or negative views of a person who wanted to test my inner mettle, but I couldn't afford to cede emotional control. The doubts and negativity were the interviewer's problems, not mine.

I DESCRIBED to Al the academic and leadership qualifications of the four Rhodes winners, one of whom was a Harvard classmate. I told him that when I wasn't being interviewed, I'd passed the time mingling and discussing world events with the other finalists. I surmised it was okay to move beyond the Rhodes chitchat and break the other news to my mother. I wanted to get through what I anticipated would be another thorough and strenuous interview, this one about Marian, before retiring for the night.

I found Mom in the kitchen. She finally looked me in the eye as I told her Marian—I added the prefix, "my friend," rather than "my girlfriend"—was coming to St. Louis for a few days to visit one of her dormmates from Radcliffe, before flying to Minneapolis for Christmas with her family. I explained that Marian wanted to meet my family while she was here. "Could she drop by tomorrow evening after she arrives?" I asked. I felt certain the answer would be yes, but I also knew there'd be a preliminary vetting process. I predicted Mom would have questions about Marian and that everything I said would eventually be conveyed to other members of my family, so I answered all her questions in the flat, matter-of-fact prose I had adopted for all family inquiries into my college life, just as I had during my years at Exeter.

Mom started with the simple question of what year of study Marian was completing. I gave a more elaborate answer than I'd rehearsed, saying Marian was a senior at Radcliffe, majoring in American history, and adding that she was thinking about going to law school. I was trying to keep Mom away from more probing questions, such as "Why does she want to meet your family?" so I followed the same strategy in response to the next question, which I'd also anticipated: "Who are her people?"

I led with information about Marian's father, suspecting Mom would be impressed with his professional achievements. I told her he was the first Negro judge in Minnesota, then hastened to add he was no longer a judge, explaining that he had practiced law in Minneapolis before President Kennedy appointed him head of the civil rights division in the Department of Defense. Mom interrupted to ask if Marian's father had attended President Kennedy's inauguration. I told Mom he had, adding that

Marian had accompanied him to the inaugural ball because her mother was unable to attend. Knowing Mom's own interest in politics, I expected she'd be impressed by Marian's family's political connections.

Mom asked me what fraternity Marian's father had belonged to in college. I wasn't certain, although I thought it was Alpha Phi Alpha. A mistake on this question would be significant, at least to Willie, whom I believed Mom would fill in, along with everyone else in the Palmer network. I fibbed, claiming I didn't know whether or not her father had been in a fraternity.

I paused nervously. I didn't want to appear too anxious to impress Mom, fearing she might see any display of emotion as an opportunity to explore the more intimate details of my relationship with Marian, as she had tried to do with Cheryl. Mom peered over her glasses at me as if to say, "Continue," so I talked about how Marian's father had gone to Fisk University before enrolling at the University of Chicago Law School. I knew Mom would be well acquainted with Fisk (a private Negro university in Nashville) because she herself had attended Lane College, another private college for Negroes, in Jackson, Tennessee. I thought Mom's next comment would reflect her awe that Marian's father had graduated from a prestigious white university's law school, but she surprised me with a question about Marian: Was she applying to Chicago for law school?

Sensing Mom's curiosity shift definitively toward Marian and so, perhaps, to my own post-graduation plans, I grew a bit leery and defensive. I wanted to steer Mom away from asking me how serious I was about Marian, partially because, as with my post-Harvard plans in general, I was still unsure. I answered as calmly as I could that I didn't believe Marian was applying to the University of Chicago, hoping this simple explanation would suffice. *She's a friend. She's in St. Louis to visit a dormmate from Radcliffe. She just happens to be making a stop in St. Louis on her way home to Minneapolis for Christ's sake!* I could feel my irritation growing. After all, it wasn't the first time a friend from Harvard had come to visit me in St. Louis. Michael, my roommate, had hitchhiked to St. Louis from upstate New York during the summer of 1964 and stayed a few days at our house. At that

moment, in my cluelessness, I didn't perceive the distinct implications of a girl from college asking to meet my parents in the
wild hinterlands of St. Louis.

I was emotionally hung over and exhausted from the long day
of interviews and stimulating conversations with my competitors
for the Rhodes. I wanted nothing more than for Mom's precision
drilling about my relationship with Marian to cease. I answered
her next question about where Marian's dad was born with more
information than requested. I not only said he was born in South
Carolina; I added that her mother was born in Florida, graduated from Fisk, and didn't work outside the home, spending
most of her time in Minneapolis, rather than at their apartment
in Washington, D.C. I don't know if Mom might have sensed my
exhaustion as she analyzed my face, but she finally answered my
original question with an appeased, "Tomorrow evening would
be fine for Marian to come over."

I announced I was going to bed and leaned over to give
Mom a kiss on her cheek. After I planted a light peck, she pulled
away—now twice in one evening—staring at me as if some new
thought had just hit her, and casually asked about the color of
Marian's skin. *Oh my God, she is hoping I'll say "high yellow"
or "light tan."* Fortunately, my brain was still functioning, even
though my emotions were spent. I recalled my anger at Mom's
cold shoulder as I entered the house. She deprived me of any
opportunity to converse about my disappointment, as if her disappointment was enough for both of us.

I certainly didn't want to get into a conversation about Mom's
unswerving faith in the ideals of the black bourgeoisie when it
came to skin color. Marian had the same brown complexion I
did, and I already knew I was too dark to be bougie. I avoided
answering Mom's question, promising cryptically: "You'll find
out when you meet her."

AFTER I INTRODUCED Marian to the gathering seated in the living
room, Willie, the family spokesman (either by self-appointment
or at Mom's request), peppered her with some preliminary small
talk about her plane trip. No, not peppered, this was classic but-
tering up. But he quickly got down to what he viewed as the real

business of the visit. Looking directly at Marian, he grinned and
asked, as if they were the only people in the room, "Why would
you be interested in marrying my little brother? Why wouldn't
you want to marry a banker's son, or someone important?"

I felt my body stiffen. My embarrassment at the imperti-
nence of his first question totally engaged my mental defenses as
I numbed myself to the emotional pain Willie inflicted. His second question stung even more. Did Willie truly feel I wasn't wor-
thy of marrying Marian? What had Mom told him? I'd always
believed that beneath Willie's clumsiness with me—all his goofy
enthusiasms, his frat-boy intrigues—lay some authentic feelings of affection and respect. But I began to wonder what else
was hidden underneath his desire to mold me into a chip off his
block, rather than Dad's or Al's. When Dad didn't want me to go
to Exeter, Willie had offered to adopt me in order to relieve Dad
of any economic obligation for me, such as my required coats and
ties. Willie's offer felt both generous and, in retrospect, controlling. Had my parents accepted his proposal, I could have gone
to Exeter despite's Dad opposition. But would I have been exiled
from my childhood home, my parents and other siblings? In the
end, I suspect Al's tears did more to soothe Dad's deepest fear—
that I would never return to St. Louis—than Willie's plan could
have done. Was Willie, who had been ready to assume full legal
responsibility for all my childhood economic needs, angry because I'd ignored his advice about my major, fraternities, and my
career path? Was he jealous of my success now that the scholarship boy was a Harvard man? Something had changed between
us. Deeply. And it hurt.

Maybe because in all my twenty-one years I hadn't fit into any
of the frames Willie had chosen for me, he sought to punish me
by demeaning me in front of a total stranger, a person he knew
only as a friend of mine. He seemed to be violating all the rules
of Palmer solidarity by which we'd been raised. I'd expected that
the intent of the interrogation would be to determine if Marian
was good enough for me, not the other way around. I recoiled
from the reference to me as his little brother.

I was afraid to look at Marian or anyone else in the room. In
those days, I could still freeze tears welling up in me. But when

I finally looked at Marian to see how she was handling the stress questions the Palmer committee assailed her with, I realized she wasn't the least bit flustered. The ice forming in my heart melted away as Marian flashed her pretty smile at Willie and, almost singing in that clear soprano voice of hers, a voice that reminded me of moonlit strolls by the Charles River and her quiet serenades as we walked back to her dorm, "Oh, Willie, you don't understand how much promise and potential Larry has!"

Willie's sly smile dissolved into a sudden, puckered silence, as if he'd lost an important debate. I smiled inwardly at Marian's adroit comeback, which rendered my brother mute and answered the question I knew was still lingering in the minds of all the Palmers in attendance: Did her visit to St. Louis mean she was to be my future wife? Although she and I had not discussed marriage, her response to Willie's baiting indicated she wanted to marry me. She ignored Willie's innuendo that she might make a better match. In that precise moment, I was relieved that Marian had managed the awkwardness of her very first encounter with my complex family.

I don't remember who besides Willie and Mom were present at Marian's interrogation, but the living room was crowded. I suspect all my other siblings living in St. Louis—Lena, Al, Harold, and Barry—and Dad were in the audience. Though they did not contribute to the conversation, they bolstered the emotional atmosphere of a Palmer assault across personal boundaries and gave Willie's questions to Marian a context in which they appeared normal. I never told Willie how much his questions had hurt me.

MARIAN'S CHARACTERIZATION of me as a Harvard senior with promise and potential became my key to unlocking a mystery about Mom: why had she embraced, without any hesitation as far as I could see, my spending my high school years over a thousand miles away from home living in the company of white boys and men, strangers? It's a question I didn't even ask myself until after her death, at eighty-two, and my becoming a father of three sons. Dad's initial resistance to my leaving home felt more natural. My inheritance from Mom—a box of stuff she gave me after she was diagnosed with terminal cancer and a few months before her death—contained a spotlight to help me glimpse, through the shadows of her death, a younger version of herself: a résumé she had prepared in her mid-to-late seventies.

I didn't look at the contents of the box until after she died, assuming it was full of photo albums, scrapbooks, and papers related to me. Giving me the box was her way of lessening the possibility of any disputes about the mementos she wanted me to have. My preliminary explorations confirmed my first assumption: here were Mom's keepsakes of my childhood academic achievements including my Vacation Reading Club certificates. Those certificates, earned over several sweaty summers, reminded me that a dyed-in-the-wool Library Mom raised me.

But, buried under several scrapbooks and photo albums, I discovered her résumé. I wondered if Mom had deliberately put her résumé in my box, or if this had simply been an accident while sorting through her possessions in the waning weeks of her life. The inclusion of some things related to Willie, such as a letter he'd written Mom in the 1970s, tucked into a scrapbook of letters I'd written her, support the accidental hypothesis: She didn't have the time (or energy?) to thoroughly search the contents and excise the non-Larry materials. On the other hand, she might have thought I would preserve the contents, including her résumé, or pass the contents on to an appropriate relative. At the time, I didn't think of myself in that role even though Al had already given me his box of Mom's mementos. Whether her bequest of her résumé was deliberate or accidental, I did what I imagined she'd want me to do: I studied it.

I was nagged by a question: Why would she need a résumé at all at her age? At first I thought Mom might have written it prior to moving to the senior living facility in 1971, a document she could hand to her new neighbors in case there were positions of leadership for her to assume. It may also have served as a way to maintain her desired distance from any curious new acquaintances. No doubt she meant for it to impress folks with all her achievements in civic and political spheres. A careful reading of the "Community Involvement" section of her résumé indicated that Mom had already served as President of the Senior Citizens Club at her new residence as well as secretary of a senior citizens' council group that worked to coordinate several Senior Centers in four wards of the city. Such details indicated Mom had developed this résumé sometime after 1977, but I couldn't be sure exactly when.

I'd never thought about how Mom presented herself to the world through her writing, especially her life before I was born. Like most résumés, after the usual demographic information (including her date of birth) she stated her current volunteer position as "Presently serving . . ." as a member of the advisory board of a small college in Missouri (Culver-Stockton) run by the Disciples of Christ Church. I didn't know what the board did, but discovered from her annotation that it searched for prospective scholarship applicants to the college, noting the budget for scholarships at the time as $70,000.

As I dug into the Education section, I was surprised to find myself on the far side of a dramatic shift in the tone and voice of the document, a shift from implicit first person phrasing, to an unfamiliar third person narration: "Mattie B. McNeely Palmer, the eldest of five children attended school in a small rural town in Arkansas." All of a sudden, my mother had cast herself as the main character of an educational drama about a Negro girl born in 1903 in the South who had attended college just after World War I. Before I could continue with her story, my mind hung on two words.

Five children? I knew Mom had two brothers who lived in Chicago, and a sister who died of tuberculosis sometime after the family moved to St. Louis. I don't ever remember seeing Mom's sister before she died, and I'd only seen her brothers once or twice in my entire life. Except for Mom's mother, Grandma Lela, I realized how little contact I had with Mom's immediate biological family. Mom's dad died when she was twelve. Grandma Lela sent Mom to live with her father's aunts, schoolteachers who made sure Mom received the same education as her cousin. This cousin was a frequent visitor from Arkansas as I grew up. I knew what no stranger could know—that underneath the dramatic educational civil rights narrative of her résumé lay the heartbreak of losing a father (and possibly a sibling) early in life, and separation from her brothers and sister during her teenage and young adult years.

As I continued reading, I discovered details about her early education. Prior to college, Mattie served as secretary to a youth organization that developed "leadership, pride, and citizenship." She was also a member of both a literary society and the "School Improvement Association," groups she claimed "supported programs and parades commemorating the great leaders who were influential in the stride for freedom of blacks from the state of human bondage." At age sixteen she left Arkansas to attend the Negroes-only Lane College in Tennessee, where she remained for three and a half years, from 1919–1923, earning a scholastic award for high academic achievement. She offers no explanation of why she didn't graduate.

Instead, the next paragraph begins: "Mattie married Arglister L. Palmer, a graduate of Arkansas Baptist College . . . ," and tells how their marriage produced "ten happy healthy children." It then declares that "Marriage did not stop Mattie from searching for more education," taking "extension courses" from the University of Arkansas (I assume these were by correspondence because public education was subject to legal segregation), and obtaining certification in elementary teaching in 1927. She ends by stating she taught elementary school for ten years in rural Arkansas.

I paused at this point to speculate on whether Lena's birth impeded Mom's pursuit of education and whether marriage for a woman after World War I inevitably meant "marriage and children." Apparently Mom didn't need a college degree to teach elementary school in Arkansas, as a lesser certification sufficed. But in rapid succession, Mom married Dad and, just a month before her twenty-second birthday, gave birth to Lena in 1925. By the time Mom had earned her certification in 1926, she had also given birth to Al. At the completion of ten years of teaching, she had given birth to Willie (1928), Herschel (1930, who died at age 9 months), Urshel (1931), Mac (1934), and Lela (1936).

Lena's birth may have delayed Mom's teacher certification, but my sister's often-aired complaints about the number of diapers she'd changed by the time she was ten rang another peculiar but obvious truth: She was older sister to five by the time she was eleven! I could imagine Lena babysitting her younger siblings, but it never occurred to me how early her role as eldest sister became a defining part of her life. Mom's résumé implies that having one, two, however many children, wasn't going to stop Mattie from her pursuit of education in the face of all the obstacles for Negro women in the rural South. Did my mother pursue this ambition at Lena's expense, depriving her of any semblance of a carefree childhood?

The résumé goes on to assert, succinctly: "The Palmer Family moved to Saint Louis in 1944 for better educational and economic opportunities." This remark understates, by quite a bit, the limited educational options available to my parents' then eight children. After World War I, only ten public high schools for Negroes, and perhaps five other private high schools for Negroes (probably sponsored by church groups) existed in the entire state of Arkansas. The available secondary education focused on "training" Negroes for service jobs—"the help" for white families; farming as tenants or sharecroppers; and some industrial occupations. Dad had attended one of the private boarding schools before college, and when Al was a teenager in the early 1940s Mom and Dad sent him to Fargo Agricultural School, a private boarding school in central Arkansas which offered a combined academic and vocational curriculum. Lena remained in southeastern Arkansas, where Dad was working at the time, and graduated from the Desha County Training School in 1942.

When I first learned that Al had attended a boarding school, I assumed, because of my own New England single-sex boarding school experience, that Fargo was an all-boys school. I also surmised there were no comparable boarding school opportunities in Arkansas for Negro girls during World War II. But a little digging online in *The Arkansas Encyclopedia of Education and Culture* revealed that Fargo, from its founding in 1920 until it closed in 1949, was a coeducational institution. During the first half of the day, boys and girls studied English, music, history, mathematics, and natural sciences together. But during the second half of the day, the boys and the girls had separate vocational tracks, with boys learning things such as carpentry, electrical wiring, and livestock care while the girls learned things like childcare, home economics, food preparation and serving, and sewing. I often wonder why Al received this broader high school educational experience and Lena did not. Did my parents view Al as having more promise and potential than Lena? Did they make this judgment based on what they saw as the difference between the barriers faced by boys and girls, never mind Negro boys and girls?

With Willie, Urshel, Mac, Lela, and Harold (1938) all in school, I wonder if the precarious nature of Palmer family finances during the early 1940s forced my parents to migrate north. By 1942, Dad's position as an assistant manager in the Farm Security Bureau in southeastern Arkansas was eliminated through a Congressional budget cut. The family farm in Biscoe had been lost in the economic upheaval of the 1930s, and both of Dad's brothers had left Biscoe for St. Louis and Kansas City before I was born. The presence of a large Japanese internment camp, the Rohwer War Relocation Center, in Desha County, where the family had lived since the late 1930s, served as a constant reminder of the possibility of war swallowing up the oldest son, Al.

Over the years I've found endless fascination in the outline in my mother's résumé of her extensive community involvements. I already knew that while I was at Exeter and Harvard, Mom had received two Mother of the Year Awards: one from the undergraduate chapter of Willie's fraternity, Omega Psi Phi, in 1960; the other from the St. Louis Negro weekly newspaper, *St. Louis American*, in 1963. The latter recognized her school and community activities, the former, "her concern and support" of the fraternity's activities.

Although middle-aged Mattie started with leadership roles in activities usually assigned to women—church, school, and volunteer work like the National Foundation for Infantile Paralysis (The Mothers' March Against Polio)—she became involved in politics more generally by 1948, shortly after arriving on Maple Avenue. I notice how carefully she uses the word "black" rather than "Negro" or "colored," which were the terms of art she would have acquired in childhood. Such terms, by the time she compiled her résumé, were viewed with growing disfavor within the

Negro community due to the rise of Black Nationalism in the late 1960s and 1970s. In describing her leadership roles in organizing events for the neighborhood association, raising money for the predecessor of United Way, and serving as the head of the committee charged with writing the history of her church, my mother even uses the politically correct term "chairperson," coming into vogue in the 1970s.

Sometimes I wonder if Mom prepared her résumé in hopes of obtaining some political appointment later in life, to serve as a document she might hand to the transition team for a newly elected mayor, for example. Her description of her church committee work as a "difficult task," whose goals she believed "can be accomplished with the support of the committee and . . . faith, patience, and prayer," sounds like the draft of a stump speech.

As I read on, I learned three things I didn't know about what had happened to Mattie in 1969. She became involved in a Colored Women's Club; she was accepted into a social club; and she was "very much intrigued by the motto of the National Association of Colored Women's Clubs—'Lifting As We Climb.'" She leaves it to her intended audience to understand the significance of each of these, providing no description of either the social club (its degree of social prominence) or the Colored Women's Club movement. As Mattie's son, reading these final notations made me feel as if she were shouting out to me from beyond the grave. They helped me realize my mother understood her own life as one of racial triumph for herself and for those she lifted up—her children.

As a Negro girl who entered college with Jim Crow firmly entrenched and the women's suffrage movement just morphing into a campaign for passage of the 19th Amendment, she and other educated Negro women realized they faced numerous obstacles to full participation in social, economic, and political life. Still, Mattie counted herself as middle class because of her education, regardless of the economic status of her birth family, or even her own family of ten children. I don't doubt my mother was aware that in order to gain southern support some segments of the women's suffrage movement argued Negro women shouldn't receive the vote—a tacit endorsement of the practice of deny-

LEFT:
Larry's mother, Mattie,
in her backyard, early
1950s

BELOW:
Mattie, 1967

ing all Negroes political participation through poll taxes, literacy tests, and all-white primaries. In 1920, Tennessee's vote completed the three-quarter majority of states necessary for ratification of the 19th Amendment, but did not provide a path for full citizenship for Negro women. Through Colored Women's Clubs, the women raised money for kindergartens, summer camps, and retirement homes while they worked to oppose segregated transportation and advocated for anti-lynching laws. Mattie was a climber, a rung or two ahead of those she sought to bring up to her level. The invitation she received to join one of the social clubs for middle class blacks as she entered her mid-sixties surely served as validation of the leadership skills and racial pride she sought to develop, even before she entered college.

But all this raised a large question for me. Why had none of my sisters ever attended college when our mother had managed to do so in the 1920s when few women, and even fewer Negro women, embarked on such a journey? My sisters seemed to be situated at very different nodes in the rural-southern-Negro-urban-migrant-post-Great Depression culture in which their 1950s lives were all suspended. In that post-World War II era of suburbanization, my sisters may still have viewed a woman's power arena as the home, their rural upbringing reinforcing the predominant cultural norm that the goal for a woman was to enter a good marriage, live in a ranch-style house, and assume a managerial position overseeing a nascent work force (her children) and dabbling in commodities futures (coupon clipping). It's equally possible our mother encouraged my sisters' aspirations to more traditional gender roles, not because she believed in their validity, but because of her cynical assessment (based on her own experience) of the many obstacles Negro women faced should they choose less conventional paths through life. My mother was both defined and limited by the prevailing socio-cultural constructs of women, but her life itself was a critique of them, the embodiment of one possible different future for women and for people of color in general. I don't know whether my mother encouraged my sisters to attend college. If so, was the teachers college in St. Louis the only option? Four of my brothers have college degrees, all but one from that teachers college. Was Mom so preoccupied with my possible leap into the Ivy League, once I got to Exeter, that she ignored Louise's educational needs?

Yet, I've always sensed Mom failed to insist upon higher education for her daughters because of something deeper within her than the cultural and racial ethos surrounding gender roles that she faced as she raised children over the forty-plus years of her marriage to Dad. Mom was extremely realistic, almost to the point of despair, about the possibilities for women, not just because of societal gender roles, but also because of biology. I never asked her why she had so many children, but family lore in the form of nicknaming informed my speculation by the time I was a teenager.

Our Arkansas relatives called Mac, born in 1934, "Baby Brother," and Lela, born in 1936, "Baby Sis." As a small child, these Arkansas nicknames for Lela and Mac always confused me, until I was old enough to realize the innuendo: Had Mom planned to stop having children after her sixth? Mom probably had limited or no access to contraception in rural Arkansas, or other reproductive health services such as physician-assisted childbirth in hospitals. (All her children were born at home with the assistance of midwives in Arkansas and of the mobile gynecological service of St. Louis University Medical School in St. Louis.) If Mom tried any forms of contraception after Lela's birth, they obviously weren't effective.

The four of us—Harold, Louise, me, and Barry—born post Baby Brother and Baby Sis no doubt were living reminders of the constrictions on Mom's ambitions. She projected those restrictions onto her own daughters and perhaps believed that even with college degrees, they would end up in professions dominated by women: teachers at the elementary or secondary schools, librarians, and nurses. That even in the best of all possible worlds, they would remain in support roles or serve merely as stepping stones for boys who would occupy male dominated professions such as ministers, lawyers, and physicians.

I surmised Mom harbored ambitions for a more powerful role in the larger society, based not only on what is revealed or left unsaid in her résumé, but also because her desire to be a mover and shaker in her world was so pervasive throughout her entire life. I suspect also that her view of women's possibilities may have changed in the 1960s when women's reproductive choices changed. I always remember that when I was trying to give Marian's pedigree before introducing her to the family, Mom stopped me to ask if Marian was applying to the University of Chicago's law school. Maybe her question hid a deeply held desire to have had such an option for herself. Her own promise and potential?

CHAPTER SEVENTEEN

Dad's Cane

I PAID LITTLE ATTENTION to Dad's cane as I met my parents at Boston's South Station, a few days before my Harvard graduation. I hadn't seen them since Christmas vacation and wondered if the cane was new, or a stage of Dad's progressive decline, which I'd ignored since freshman year. In the last four years, I'd only spent the summer of 1964 in St. Louis, working either the late shift (4:00 P.M. to midnight) or the graveyard shift (midnight to 8:00 A.M.) at a detergent factory. I slept through most of the day, and during my waking hours I read novels and occasionally talked long distance to one of the girls I dated in college. I don't remember any conversations with Dad; I was too busy still nursing my double grudge—his initial opposition to my going to Exeter and his abrupt withdrawal of economic support at the beginning of my sophomore year in college.

I remember Mom calling to tell me Dad was retiring—he would turn sixty-five in January 1964. More significant—at least to me—she informed me they could no longer afford to send me $500 toward college expenses as they had done my freshman year. At nineteen, with no savings from my low-wage civil rights job the previous summer, I was unexpectedly on my own economically. I felt abandoned by my parents. In the same conversation, in her familiar detached tone, Mom also mentioned that Dad had suffered a mild stroke. I was so absorbed in my feelings of dismissal by my parents I didn't even ask how Dad was doing.

I spent the summer after my freshman year working in Bos-

ton for the Northern Student Movement, a newly formed organization that helped raise funds for SNCC. I also attended the
March on Washington in August 1963. The tepid response of
political leaders to the March on Washington for Jobs and Freedom crushed my interracial idealism. I heard Malcolm X speak
at the Black Muslims' Boston mosque in early September and
began channeling his fiery style on campus and at Boston civil
rights meetings. Whites were not allowed in the mosque, so I
was able to hear Malcolm's critique of the March without any
white media filter. The day after the September 1963 bombing
of the 16th Street Baptist Church in Birmingham, Alabama that
killed four Negro Sunday School children, I encountered a white
Radcliffe student, the girlfriend of someone I knew, in Harvard
Square. She accompanied her cheerful white liberal New England, "Good morning," with an expansive smile. I picked up a
copy of the *New York Times* from the newsstand, thrust the
front-page picture of the bombed church into her face, nearly
grazing her nose, and sneered, "It will be a good morning when
you white people stop doing this!" I strode away before a word
could emerge from her gaping mouth.

My attempts to embody black rage didn't last long. Two
weeks later I had calmed down—or at least I'd calmed my rhet-
oric down—enough to figure out how to respond to the parental budget cut. Five hundred dollars represented more than ten
percent of my annual college expenses. I replaced my dining hall
financial aid job with a higher paying part-time job at a furniture
store in Harvard Square. I also took out my first student loan for
several hundred dollars, which would supplement the scholarship that covered the bulk of my tuition, room, and board. More
important, I became conscious of how I spent money on dates,
entertainment, and snacks.

Standing with Mom and Dad in the grand hall of Boston
South's station, I buried my hard feelings toward Dad, and instead used my voice to reflect the kindness, concern, and confidence of a patrician docent. As we made our way toward the
taxi stand, I provided a synopsis of my plan for their visit. "Your
hotel, the Parker House, is a short distance from here, near Park
Street. It's also on the Red Line . . . oh, that's the subway line

that runs straight to Harvard Square . . ." Both Mom and Dad stopped to stare up at the walls before I could finish my summary. What's so arresting about those walls? The docent-within-me said to the soon-to-be-Harvard-graduate standing next to his parents, "Let them soak it all in," as if they'd never seen a grand hall of a train station before. It may well have been their first time in South Station. On their previous trip through Boston, for my Exeter graduation, they may have received the same advice I had from a conductor: Get off the train at Back Bay Station and take a taxi to North Station in order to catch a train to New Hampshire.

On the taxi ride to the Parker House, I continued my rendition of their itinerary from the front seat, twisting my torso so I could watch their reactions to my litany: Rest for the afternoon after your long train ride. The hotel has a good restaurant if you're hungry. Get a good night's rest because we'll start early in the morning with a tour of Harvard. I added, boastfully, "Tomorrow afternoon is Class Day at Radcliffe. Marian's godfather, John Hope Franklin, is speaking. And then, there's a dinner tomorrow night at Marian's dorm where you'll meet both Marian's father and Professor Franklin, who by the way, got his Ph.D. from Harvard in 1944." Dad flashed a tired smile at my tenuous connection through Harvard to the famous Negro historian from the University of Chicago. The taxi stopped at the Parker House before I stopped talking.

Even Mom, the more physically energetic of the two, looked like she could use a nap after the twenty-four-plus-hour train ride in coach. I pivoted from docent to bellhop and took their bags from the taxi—saving a tip by taking their bags to their room after they checked in. I told them I'd be back a little after nine the next morning and said goodbye with soft kisses on each of their cheeks.

The next morning, we took the subway from near their hotel and exited at Harvard Square. I whisked them down to Lowell House, my dormitory residence after freshman year, pausing in the entryway under the blue dome bell tower to allow them to admire the manicured grassy courtyard. Workmen were setting up tables and chairs for the luncheon for Lowell House's

150 graduates and their guests after the morning ceremony in Harvard Yard the following day. "Here's where," I told them, "the House Master of Lowell House—a classics professor, by the way—will present each graduate with his diploma and say something about his Harvard experience and post-graduate plans."

I pointed out the nearby buildings as we meandered toward the Yard. That's a private club (one of the "Final Clubs"); even John Kennedy couldn't get into one of them because he was Catholic. That's Adams House. That newer building is part of Quincy House. The furniture store where I worked is just two blocks up this street, Mount Auburn. My rapid-fire tour guide chatter kept in rhythm with my quick stride as I headed up a side street toward the Yard.

Mid-sentence, Mom's hand seized my right shoulder. She pulled me out of the middle of the sidewalk sloping up toward the Yard to allow some undergraduates and their parents and guests to pass us. She pierced my exuberant eyes, then glanced over my shoulder to Dad, causing me to turn and see him moving gingerly up the sidewalk behind us. She dropped her hand to my forearm and squeezed it. Her eyes exuded both pleading and determination. "Larry," she hissed through her teeth, "your father has waited his entire life to see you graduate from Harvard and you are going to slow down!"

I looked back at Dad, his cane suddenly appearing as a third leg hinged to his right hip. He limped toward us. His thick gray-black eyelashes curved down toward the crow's feet at the sides of his twinkling eyes. His Clark Gable mustache arched above his wide grin when he noticed me looking at him. His Panama hat cast a slight shadow, graying his brown forehead. A dark charcoal gray suit encased his white shirt and his striped gray and red tie. His compact five-foot six-inch body looked less rotund than I remembered; he'd lost some weight since I entered college.

For a moment, I didn't see my father, but a handsome old man—he was sixty-seven years old at the time—whose eyes brimmed with pleasure and pain. Walking was very difficult, but like a toddler he did his best to catch up to us in the June heat of a sunny Cambridge day. As he approached, the joy in his eyes became more visible. I thought to myself: the contentment

beaming from his face has something to do with me, not only—
as Mom had implied—with my graduation from Harvard. All
the resentment I'd stored up against him for his resistance to my
going to Exeter and his failure to fully support me economically
melted away. I walked back down the sidewalk to where Dad
had stopped, perhaps to catch his breath, and hooked my right
arm through his left. My breathing slowed. Our pace synchro-
nized into whatever was flowing between our bodies.

Walking, as opposed to my normal quick-paced loping, allowed events or feelings I'd suppressed to resurface in my consciousness. I suddenly remembered the Social Security checks
I'd received as the child of a disabled worker. Along with my
part-time job at the furniture store, my savings from my summer
factory job in 1964, my well-paid Boston corporate internship in
the summer of 1965, savings on room and board expenses by living off campus my senior year, and the Harvard National Scholarship I was awarded for my senior year, those checks allowed
me to avoid any student loans my junior and senior years. Maybe,
just maybe, I thought to myself, Dad had done all he could financially for me in college. For the first time, I asked myself where
that $500 my parents gave me freshman year had come from. It
was the equivalent of ten percent of Dad's salary. Had they saved
that money? Borrowed it from the savings and loan association
where they had gone for home improvement loans? Asked my
older siblings for contributions? Whatever the source, someone
in my family sacrificed for me.

As if dream-walking into our shared past before Exeter had
ever been mentioned, I relived one of Dad's lessons, my two-
handed hammer swing landing on the edge of a number eight
nail, bending it into a steel giraffe's neck with its body stuck in
sandy-colored wood. "Use one hand and don't choke up on the
handle!" he barked.

But it's too heavy.

"Nails are expensive!"

But I can't pull the nail out.

"Put a piece of wood under the claw as a lever to get the nail
out. Pay attention!"

It's hot out here and sweat is getting into my eyes.

"Straighten out the nail!"

Can't I use number six finishing nails instead?

"They aren't strong enough for this part!"

My mind then drifted back to house projects in the mid-1950s during Dad's two weeks of summer vacation from his job at the post office, such as the time Barry and I helped Dad build a barbecue pit chimney. Those projects often started with Dad's fussing, "Fools, get to work," until he realized we weren't our older brothers whom he'd already taught how to mix cement. I remembered the weary frustration in his eyes when he came home from work, ready to growl ferociously at any little miscue. I knew to offer cautiously my explanation of what he perceived as our idleness. I turned my eyes downward and mumbled that we didn't know how to mix cement. When I looked up, I didn't see the flash of anger in his eyes that I'd learned to expect when he vented his frustrations on me or my brothers or sisters. Instead I saw a slight twinkle in his eye, as though he was seeing Barry and me for the first time. We weren't Mac and Harold or Al and Willie. We were little boys who also happened to be his sons. He proceeded to show us how to measure out the right amount of cement and sand and how to gradually add water until the mixture formed just the right consistency for spreading. It reminded me of making mud pies with Louise and Barry, or of watching Mom mix cakes.

Sometimes, standing there in the nearly noonday summer sun, I'd glance longingly back at the house and imagine myself curled up in a cool shaded spot reading a book from the library. I was only partially interested in Dad's endless commentary about the engineering of the chimney and his efforts to teach me and Barry how cement somehow tied the bricks together and prevented the chimney from collapsing like a tower of kindergarten blocks. But these explanations, interspersed with stories about his life in Arkansas, helped me overcome my mental and physical resistance to the work. As did his backyard philosophizing. I can't remember how many times he'd mutter, while showing me how to hammer a nail straight or determine whether the cement was ready, a phrase he told me he'd learned from John Dewey: "We must learn by doing." John Dewey was a professor at Colum-

Larry and Barry mixing cement with their father, 1950/51

bia University in New York City, he'd said, but when and where he'd encountered Dewey's ideas seemed of little importance to me. What I gathered from repeated references to his name was that Dad's life had been influenced by Dewey's ideas regarding the ways people learned. I wondered if Dad ever wished to be doing the kind of work Dewey was known for, rather than sorting mail all day and then working around the house during vacations. I also wondered if he wished a different kind of life for Barry and me and expressed this desire in his repeated retellings of Dewey stories.

That summer, while I mixed and hauled cement with Barry, Dad also told us stories about the work of George Washington Carver, the applied scientist who discovered many uses for peanuts. He'd met Carver during the Great Depression, at what was then the Tuskegee Institute. Dad had returned to Tuskegee for additional training in the late 1930s when he left teaching to work for the Farm Security Administration (FSA). That short-lived program of the New Deal aimed at rural rehabilitation by relocating poor tenant farmers and sharecroppers from their worn-out farming areas to large, government-owned productive land where they would be taught modern farming methods. I assume Dad was hired for his teaching ability, but he also had to become an expert in modern farming techniques and so attended several courses at Tuskegee.

Dad talked often, almost dreamily, about his job at the FSA teaching Negro tenant farmers and sharecroppers about the more effective farming techniques he learned at Tuskegee. I imagined the time my father spent at the bureau as assistant manager of a project in southern Arkansas must have been the apex of his working life. Our backyard garden was full of reminders of that rural past: mustard, collard, and turnip greens were staples, along with tomatoes and okra. Trellises built along the concrete fence held wisteria and roses, while an apple tree replaced one of the tall maples at the back of the yard, near the garage and the barbecue pit.

But Dad seldom mentioned to Barry or to me his work as a teacher at a small rural school for Negroes in central Arkansas. Dad also never discussed the fact—which I would not discover until much later—that he was laid off from his job with the FSA because conservatives in Congress saw the work as a form of socialism. If its projects had ever been fully funded, poor farmers, both Negro and white, would have worked in cooperatives and on government-owned farms rather than as tenants or sharecroppers on marginal land rented from (mostly) white landowners. Dad's FSA project was defunded around 1942, two years before the Palmer migration to St. Louis.

SOMETIME IN THE EARLY 1950s, I wrote a letter to Santa Claus that indicates I understood, even at an early age, why our fishing trips went no further afield than the nearby city park, and why we never took regular family vacations. I found this letter with the papers Mom gave me a few months before she died. In my cursive handwriting, the salutation reads: "Dear Santa Claus (Mom and Dad)." I then proceed to request a joint gift for Barry and me—an electric train set. The letter, signed "Larry & Barry," also notes in a postscript that my brother and I had enclosed six dollars for an extra bridge and additional tracks. No doubt we had perused the home copy of a Sears, Roebuck or Montgomery Ward catalog to determine the cost of these add-ons and came up with the funds by combining savings from our allowances with whatever we'd earned by doing odd jobs for neighbors.

Mom saved that letter in a scrapbook, along with my report cards and reading club awards. She probably thought of it as a sign of my intellectual maturity that I could be so practical in my approach to Christmas presents and the myth of Santa Claus, which I'd never believed in to begin with. I have no idea what Dad thought about the letter. But I wonder if our way of trying to help him play Santa reminded him of all he couldn't provide. Dad seemed content with his job at the post office. Having worked briefly as a janitor in a factory and then at a commercial bakery upon arriving in St. Louis, he must have come to grips with his limited employment opportunities as he entered his mid-fifties. Barry and I learned early on not to expect much, financially, from our parents.

I was too young to recognize those peaceful times Barry and I spent fishing with Dad as gifts of his presence. It made me miserable to see him work so hard at physically demanding jobs, despite his failing health and signs of arthritis. He wore a back brace to work every day and was constantly in search of high-top shoes and arch supports that would allow him to stand on his feet for eight hours sorting mail. After surgery to remove kidney stones in 1951, his physicians had ordered him to lose weight through dieting to help control his blood pressure. As the years passed, I grew despondent about my father's fate as he faced the ongoing challenges of parenting what was left of his ten children, and I projected this dejection onto him.

SUDDENLY IN TUNE with Dad's limited mobility, I abandoned my idea of a walking tour of Harvard Yard that a student working for the Admissions Office might have provided. I decided to enter the Yard at the large gate across from the newsstand at the Harvard Square subway station. I pointed right down the path toward Widener Library where the chairs were being set up for the morning graduation exercises. I moved with Mom and Dad a short distance down the path to gain a more panoramic view and to avoid the crowd entering and exiting the Yard. I stood in front of Matthews Hall, the freshman dormitory where I'd lived, and described the configuration of buildings within the iron-fenced area that made this the Harvard Yard. Freshman dormitories lined three sides of the perimeter fence. The fourth side contained the president's house and some academic buildings. Memorial Church, opposite Widener, dominated the interior space that also contained several academic buildings and one freshman dorm along its crisscrossing paths. In addition to having slowed my gait, my slower speech pattern created space for my parents' questions and comments.

Dad seemed amused by the idea that freshmen lived near the president, who could walk across the Yard to his office in the eighteenth-century Massachusetts Hall adjacent to Matthews Hall. We ambled down the path to admire both buildings. Dad's gaze moved across the grass and paths to the bronze statue of John Harvard in front of University Hall, Harvard College's administration building. Mom wanted to know something about John Harvard's life. Modesty and humility visited me from some distant consciousness, and I replied with the three words a soon-to-be proud Harvard graduate found difficult to say: "I don't know."

Dad, on the other hand, remained intrigued by the architecture of University Hall. His eyes slid up and down and diagonally across the lightly colored granite and he asked, "Do you know when that building was built?"

Something I know a little about, I thought to myself, but nonetheless showed restraint in my answer. "Not exactly, but it was designed by the famous Boston architect, Charles Bulfinch, so probably in the early 1800s."

Mom's ears perked up. She looked skeptically at me and asked: "How do you know who designed that building?"

"I took a course in city planning this past fall when I was thinking of becoming a city planner. With so much urban renewal going on and the controversy over destroying older neighborhoods and buildings, my professor talked about the planning of various buildings at Harvard. He told us how the buildings reflect different periods of architectural history." I paused to make sure Mom didn't have her mouth open before continuing to expound. "You see that tall white building diagonally and outside the Yard's fence? That's William James Hall, designed in 1963 by Yamasaki, the same architect who designed the new airport in St. Louis." Before ending, I added, "By the way, my city planning professor convinced me I should go to law school rather than planning school if I was really interested in getting into city politics."

Mom looked dumbfounded. Dad beamed.

I looked at my watch. I realized they would need some lunch and Dad would need a place to rest before the Radcliffe Class Day exercises. My original plan to hop on the subway and go back to my Central Square apartment for lunch was unrealistic. My mind started to swirl. If I lived on campus in Lowell House in one of the "better" suites that seniors could choose from, I'd take them there. Before I could fall into the abyss of self-castigation for my "mistake" in moving off campus, I had an epiphany.

The furniture store where I worked was just a block away and had several couches on display at all times. My full-time coworkers and the owner had expressed a desire to meet my parents. I announced our destination with a smile, imagining Mom and Dad would be surprised to find a Radcliffe graduate, Tish, running a furniture store with her Russian-born husband, Oleg. My co-worker Michael (another Harvard graduate, about eight years older than I was) had taught me how to use boiled linseed oil to finish the walnut, teak, and rosewood Scandinavian-style furniture the store featured. I envisioned all of us sitting around one of the tables eating sandwiches from a nearby restaurant as I'd often done during the three years I worked there.

After introductions, Michael regaled my parents with stories about how much they were going to miss me, not just at the store, but also the times he and I had spent at his country place in New Hampshire planting winter wheat. Ginny, another co-worker who had attended the University of Wisconsin, added that I'd spent last Thanksgiving Day with her, her husband, and their two small children at their farm in another part of New Hampshire. Mom was aghast when Ginny described how we waited hours for the turkey to cook because she'd tried to use a wood-burning stove in their nineteenth-century farmhouse. Ginny, Michael, and Oleg told stories about how well I related to their various children who ranged in age from toddlers to pre-teenagers. Tish accidentally slipped into Russian when addressing a comment to Oleg, but quickly apologized to my parents. She laughed and noted that I'd become accustomed to hearing Russian spoken not only to her husband but to her two boys who sometimes dropped by the store after school. My inner countenance went from a smile to a frown as I realized how much I'd miss my friends at the store, my Cambridge home.

After an extended lunch and visit at the furniture store, we strolled the two blocks up Brattle Street to the Radcliffe Yard for John Hope Franklin's Radcliffe Class Day address. Harvard and Radcliffe had separate Class Day events and traditions. Radcliffe's Class Day speaker was always someone "related" to one of the graduates; students were allowed to suggest a speaker, which Marian had done. Thus, the president of Radcliffe introduced Franklin as Marian's godfather. After his talk, we took a taxi to the Radcliffe Quad for the dinner in honor of John Hope (as Marian always called him). Since Marian had suggested the speaker, she was given the opportunity to host a dinner in her dorm for the speaker, her graduating dormmates, and their guests.

John Hope delivered a provocative Class Day address that situated the rise of the Black Power movement after the passage of the Civil Rights Bill of 1964 in the historical context of previous Black Nationalist movements. Peering through his brown-rimmed glasses, Professor Franklin was in seminar mode during dinner as the white girls and their parents peppered him with questions. He seemed interested in capturing and elaborating on the nuances behind their questions, perhaps already in his mind revising his talk for publication. He tried to deflect some of the spotlight onto his long-time friend, Marian's father: "Howard," dropping a bit of his oratorical voice with a friendly smile, "tell them about the time we worked as Pullman porters that summer to pay our college expenses."

Howard began in his booming lawyer's voice to address the mostly white people the way he might present a closing argument to a jury in Minneapolis, but cut short his summation by inviting Mom and Dad to confirm his tales of segregated railway travel. As Dad told his story of traveling from Little Rock to Chicago, one could hear a pin drop. Marian's classmates seemed dumbfounded to be in the presence of four college-educated Negroes, ranging from Dad in his late sixties to Howard and John Hope in their early fifties, who had lived through segregated life in the South.

Someone changed the subject by asking about summer plans. Before Marian had a chance to chime in, her father left the gathering, claiming the richness of the food may have upset his stomach after his long flight from Southeast Asia. Mom and Dad used his exit to suggest they were exhausted. I called a cab for them as other parents and guests also began to leave. After Mom and Dad left, John Hope asked Marian and me to follow him outside into the warm summer night to hear more details about our postgraduation plans. I was inclined to listen to John Hope's unsolicited advice.

I'D ALREADY HEEDED advice, albeit accidentally, from another famous professor about where I should attend law school. After I didn't win a Rhodes Scholarship, I applied and was admitted to Harvard, Yale, and Columbia law schools by early March. Over the course of the next few months, I visited Yale and Columbia and sat in on one or two first year classes at Harvard Law. I wasn't impressed with the classes I visited at Harvard, though my opinion was probably biased by something I'd overheard at the beginning of my senior year, when I happened to be in the office of Professor Louis Jaffe with another furniture store employee to deliver and assemble a walnut desk the professor had ordered.

As we entered Jaffe's spacious office in the Law School's Langdell Hall, carrying the heavy desktop between us, I introduced myself as the delivery person, and looked around the office lined with dark mahogany bookcases to determine where the six-foot long desk and two sets of pedestal drawers would fit.

Jaffe, who had scheduled an appointment for the same time, was seated on a burgundy leather sofa with an undergraduate, giving him advice about how to choose a law school.

Professor Jaffe's old desk had been removed, but a burgundy leather desk chair, a matching side chair where a student might sit, and a floor lamp marked the empty footprint for the new desk. My assistant, another Harvard undergraduate, dressed, like me, in coveralls, helped me set the desk top down on the floor. I told Professor Jaffe we needed to go back to our van to get the two pedestals and attach them to the desk. When we reentered the office, carrying the pedestals and our tools, Professor Jaffe was still talking with the student. They barely paid any attention to us as we aligned the pedestals on the unfinished side of the desktop. I used the electric drill to put small holes in the underside of the desk where the brackets would attach the pedestals to the top, and then went to work with my ratchet screwdriver.

My ears pricked up as Professor Jaffe commented, "The advantages of Yale Law School over Harvard are that Yale has much smaller classes and interdisciplinary approaches to the study of law. My son, George, who graduated from Harvard is there and loves it!" I turned the screwdriver more slowly to hear as much of the rest of the conversation as I could. "If you are interested in smaller, more interdisciplinary approaches there is also the University of Chicago," Jaffe continued. "Don't get me wrong, Harvard is a great law school, but there are many other fine law schools to consider. Penn or the University of Michigan, for instance."

From these remarks, I gathered the student must have asked Professor Jaffe which law schools he should consider if he didn't get into Harvard. Jaffe was trying (very gently) to widen the student's perspective beyond the universe of Harvard Square. As the student stood up to leave, he was given one last bit of parting advice: "If you had to choose between Harvard and Yale, I'll tell you what my son told me. Both law schools have about the same number of faculty members (around sixty), but the entering class at Harvard has around five hundred and fifty students, whereas Yale has about one hundred and sixty."

AND SO MY well-honed childhood eavesdropping skills helped me obtain an objective analysis of various law schools from the distinguished Professor Jaffe. Not only did his words dispel the notion that Harvard Law School was The Law School, he also introduced the notion of law school as a form of education of the mind rather than simply professional training.

I sped up my screw-driving, and within a few minutes the pedestals were secure and the desk stood assembled. My assistant and I flipped the desk over for Professor Jaffe's approval, and he handed me a check for the remainder of the bill. As we exited Langdell, I laughed with my fellow worker at how it had never occurred to Professor Jaffe that we might be Harvard undergraduates ourselves. Those coveralls. The same ones we wore in the workshop to protect our school clothes as we oiled unfinished pieces of walnut and completed other messy tasks, had literally been our cover for obtaining advice about law school prospects from one of the leading figures in administrative law at the time. Our working-class appearance apparently allowed Jaffe to speak openly and kindly to an unknown surrogate, the other Harvard undergraduate on the couch, on the assumption that nothing the delivery boys overheard could possibly mean anything to them. How could this professor have known—how could I have known, for that matter—that he was the model of what I would become: a law professor.

I had very high expectations when I visited Yale after my visit to Columbia, where my hosts, all Harvard graduates, had raved about the virtues of being in New York City and Columbia's connection to Wall Street law firms. My Yale visit, also hosted by Harvard graduates, featured a special twist: Haywood Burns, a third-year Negro student who had also lived in Lowell House and who had won a fellowship from Harvard to study at Cambridge University after graduation, was my primary escort. I'd never met him before, but he seemed to know a great deal about me, including my athletic career at Harvard and my finalist status in the Rhodes competition. Haywood had written *The Voices of Negro Protest in America*, based on his research on Black Muslims acquired during his Cambridge fellowship. Having read his book, I expected he'd take me to a class on civil rights law.

Instead, he told me he wanted to take me to his advanced tax class, rather than a first-year class. *Has he sold out to the Man so quickly? I'm not interested in what people who wear green visors to keep the glare off their adding machines learn!*

But I said nothing to Haywood about his choice, recalling Professor Jaffe's characterization of Yale as "interdisciplinary." As Jaffe had predicted, the class was small—fewer than thirty students. The first-year classes I visited at Harvard had over one hundred and fifty students. But the first question Professor John Simon asked made an even bigger impression on me. It had nothing to do with figures or calculations—what I thought tax was about. Rather, he framed a question about the public policy implications of some corporate tax provisions that were, apparently, the subject matter of that day's assignment.

The way the students seized Simon's question and ran away with it in all directions sold me on Yale. With little help from Simon, they carried on their own debate with frequent references to the language in the cases they'd been asked to study. Simon acted mostly as a referee, restating a student's position clearly if a fellow student had mischaracterized it in his zealous advocacy for his own position. My mind spinning, I tried to follow the various lines of simultaneous arguments going on among the students, the excitement in the room palpable. When the professor called for attention to give assignments for the next class, it seemed the fifty minutes had flown by in five.

A few students lingered and talked among themselves, still intent on clarifying points of agreement or disagreement they felt they hadn't had time for during class. Haywood paused to add a short comment to the group still debating as we exited the classroom. I felt as if I were back at Exeter. In the hallway, Haywood smiled at me and said, "That, my new friend, is what Yale Law School is like." He introduced me to several other students, including a few more Harvard graduates: two Negro students I'd met at Harvard and George Jaffe, Professor Jaffe's son. Everyone I met seemed to love Yale Law. At the end of my day, the admissions director told me to take my time deciding, but added that he thought I'd really enjoy my education at Yale. I focused in on "education" on the train back to Boston. Despite my enthusiasm, I also had to think about the practicalities of how I would finance my legal training.

I would continue to be a scholarship boy, but the law schools offered three significantly different financial aid packages. In a nutshell, Yale offered me the least; I would have to borrow some money, at least for my first year, with the hope I might win a fellowship from a foundation that supported graduate study for minority students for my second and third years. Columbia offered me more outright grant money than Yale. Finally, Harvard, through a combination of devices, offered me what today might be called a free ride.

It was so complicated that the dean of admissions at Harvard Law School called me into his office to explain their financial aid package. First, as a Harvard National Scholar I would receive funding to cover all of my tuition. In addition, the Master of Lowell House would offer me a position as a graduate resident tutor that would provide me with room and board in exchange for interacting with the undergraduates at meals and being available for some House functions. The third part of my aid package came from the athletic department: an opportunity in the spring semester to earn some money as a part-time coach with the lacrosse program. Basically, under the Harvard aid package, I would only need to earn enough money in the summer to cover my books and spending money for the fall. As the dean explained, Harvard—the law school, the college, and the athletic department—was doing everything to keep me for another three years.

It surprises me now, given how upset I'd been at the beginning of my sophomore year when Mom told me I was economically on my own because of Dad's disability retirement, that I didn't give the Harvard offer more serious consideration, or, at the very least, discuss my three options for law school with someone who knew me well. My college advisor and thesis supervisor, George Goethals, who had earned his bachelors, masters, and doctorate at Harvard, had assumed I would accept Yale's offer after he witnessed my excitement following my visit there. But we had talked before I realized how much less financial aid Yale would provide. I now realize I'd never shared any of my worries about money with him when we first met during the fall of my sophomore year.

The Ivy League, technically a sports league (though many people think of it as an academic club), had an agreement not to compete for undergraduate student-athletes with different scholarship offers and allowed all eight colleges to see the financial aid offers of any "overlap" students—those admitted to more than one of the Ivy League colleges. This transparency of financial aid offers and the need-based system of all financial aid awards allowed any college to match the financial aid package of another school who admitted the same student. The articulated rationale for this system allowed students without the family resources to pay for an Ivy League education to choose the college that appeared best for him. (Cornell was the only fully coeducational university at the undergraduate level in the Ivy League at that time.) It also allowed the Ivy League to assert it offered no athletic scholarships. But I didn't know this agreement only applied to undergraduate school admissions and that competition for graduate students by offering different financial aid packages was perfectly acceptable.

I didn't trust anyone in my family to help me think through why I was so willing to leave Harvard, a place where I'd flourished. I didn't want any embarrassing questions or comments from my parents or siblings as I tried to weigh the personal, professional, and financial risks and benefits of my decision. Perhaps my economic independence obscured my ability to recognize my need for emotional connection with my family.

I also had to figure out how Marian fit into my decision-making. We'd been in an exclusive relationship since fall semester senior year, and we had several conversations about the future of our relationship after my visit to Yale—without ever explicitly discussing marriage (living together unmarried never occurred to either of us). She hadn't applied to the same law schools as I had, but she was inclined to remain in the northeast. At one point, I offered to attend Harvard if she wanted to attend Boston University Law School. Alternatively, I could accept Columbia's offer if she wanted to attend New York University, which I believed was her preference. She, however, dismissed any path forward that would allow us to live in the same city as law school students. She argued she didn't want me to forego the opportunity to attend Yale, insisting my eyes were ablaze with excitement after my visit. But this left the question of what she would do if I went to Yale up in the air.

Once I had committed to Yale, I decided mid-May to resume my discussions with Marian about our relationship and to talk explicitly about marriage. I did not propose a long-term engagement: waiting until we were both through law school and settled into our first jobs before getting married. However logical, this seemed to me like an unsatisfying continuation of our nine-month dating exclusivity. If Marian pursued her own law degree at NYU we would only be seventy miles apart; if she went to Boston University, one hundred and fifty miles would separate us. I don't know if I mistrusted myself in a long-distance relationship or had fears about Marian finding a more eligible match without me around on a daily basis. None of my older siblings, except for Harold, had opted for long formal engagements. Marriage seemed the most dependable one-way ticket away from Maple Avenue.

In our last conversation prior to agreeing to become man and wife, I remember posing questions to Marian about regret, much in the same vein as when she'd asked me if I would regret turning down Yale. Would she suffer any remorse if she didn't attend law school in the fall, but joined me in New Haven as the latest, most suave, Mrs. Palmer? Marian's musical twenty-two-year-old voice echoed in my head for years afterwards. "Larry, when I'm forty and I look back on my life, I want to have been married to you for decades and to have had our children!"

We made plans to marry in a simple ceremony at the end of the summer in the chapel of Memorial Church in Harvard Yard. I would take a summer job in New Haven at the Yale Summer High School, a national Upward Bound program for underachieving high school sophomores and juniors, and Marian would find a summer job in either Boston or Cambridge so she could plan our wedding and look for a job in New Haven for the fall. We told our friends about our plans—before our parents had even arrived for graduation.

But our plans changed when John Hope took us outside after the Radcliffe Class Day dinner and informed us that it was not an upset stomach that led Marian's father, Howard, to leave the dinner early, but hurt at being excluded from the wedding planning. We quickly acceded to Howard's vision of his only daughter's wedding: a large Washington, DC, wedding with a guest list that included Vice President Humphrey, Howard's political ally since the late 1940s when then Mayor Humphrey of Minneapolis appointed Howard the first Negro judge in Minnesota. After our graduations, Mom and Dad went back to St. Louis, and I went to New Haven for my summer job. Marian accompanied her delighted father to Washington in order to find a job and help execute the new wedding plan.

AFTER MY SUMMER PROGRAM ended, my prenuptial role was to retrieve our possessions from Cambridge and move them into our New Haven apartment. Tish, the owner of the furniture store, had told me I could borrow the store's delivery truck to move our stuff. A week before the wedding, I flew to St. Louis to retrieve my best man, Barry. He would help with the move to New Haven, and we would fly together to DC. More important perhaps than asking family for help with the move or the wedding, a trip to St. Louis gave me an opportunity to see Dad.

During my short visit, neither Mom nor Barry said much of anything or displayed their feelings about my impending marriage. Dad, on the other hand, was always teary-eyed—a combination of sadness and pure delight—whenever we were in the same room together. But I don't remember anything he said. My previous images of him started to collide with my feelings about him since my Harvard graduation. Perhaps I'd learned over my years at school to ignore him, to hold fixed in my mind only the pre-Exeter Dad, the one whose heart was obsessed with how he would provide for all of us. I wanted to talk to him alone, but relatives were always around us, peppering me with questions about my plans post-law school, who was going to be in the wedding, and why I wasn't staying at Harvard for law school. I said goodbye to Mom in the kitchen with a light kiss and told her I would see her at the rehearsal dinner.

ABOVE:
Larry's father, Arglister, 1966

LEFT:
Arglister, around 1963/64

Suitcase in hand, I walked slowly with Dad out the front door to say goodbye, our last chance to be alone, however brief. After the trip for my Harvard graduation, his doctors had advised him not to attempt another trip to the east coast, especially in the August heat. We stood there together on the porch I'd fallen from when I was about four years old, a spill that led to a coma of twenty hours. I put my suitcase down. Dad draped his cane over his right arm, gave me a bear hug, and planted a wet kiss on my left cheek. I picked up my suitcase and walked down the stairs toward Barry waiting in the cab for our trip to the airport. At the bottom of the stoop, I stopped and looked back at Dad. He stood there, his cane supporting him on his right side, dressed in a short-sleeved light blue shirt, a belt holding up his baggy pants. The image reminded me of another Dad, the one I saw when I awoke from that coma in the hospital nearly two decades earlier. Was I now seeing his eyes shimmering like peaceful stars from the porch? Or was I reliving my first memory of him at my hospital crib?

CHAPTER EIGHTEEN

The Widow's Escort

WHEN MY PHONE RANG the Saturday before Labor Day, 1967, I recognized Lela's calmest nurse-voice as she began, "Larry, I've got bad news." Lela explained that Dad, who, with Mom, was visiting her in Los Angeles, had eaten breakfast and suddenly collapsed. She tried giving him CPR and had called an ambulance. "But . . . Dad passed away this morning." As her voice started to crack, I imagined my sister frantically trying to breathe life into our father's ashen face. She cleared her throat, resetting her composure. "They think it was a heart attack, but the coroner won't release the body for burial until there's an autopsy. The funeral will be in St. Louis. I'll call you later with details." I briefed Marian on the call, hugged her, and then slipped into silence.

I don't remember receiving a second call from Lela, but I'll never forget how Urshel drunkenly disrupted her attempt to tell the story of Dad's dying to our assembled family. When I returned to the house after helping Willie escort Urshel out, I searched for Barry. I caught a glimpse of my mother at the center of her own small swarm of relatives and friends who seemed to be giving her farewell hugs and kisses in the middle of the living room. I took a tentative step through the doorway to get a view of the left side of the room and the large window onto the street. My internal radar pinged a warning that Barry was near.

I found him lodged in a corner of the living room near the

hallway. His eyes locked into mine as if he'd been waiting for me to find him, so I moved toward him. Mom, standing with her back to both of us, must have had her own antennae tracking our whereabouts, or she'd picked up on my probing eyes as I entered the room. Before I could say hi to Barry, she untangled herself from a relative's embrace and accosted Barry and me with a command. "I want the two of you to come with me to the funeral home." Before either of us could ask, "When?" she pronounced, "Now!"

Barry drove the three of us to the funeral home, fifteen minutes from the house; we rode in silence. I didn't ask Mom why she was taking only Barry and me, because I already knew the answer. We were babies—twins in fact, in her mind, despite the sixteen months' difference in our ages. She wanted to make sure we experienced Dad's death together, and under her supervision. I was afraid to point out that Barry and I hadn't shared the same life experiences for over a decade. There was something mysterious about the silence that hung in the air. And in the way Mom appeared so calm and determined, not at all my image of a grieving widow overwhelmed by her husband's death. I knew Dad's body was at the funeral home, but couldn't envision why the three of us might need our own private viewing.

It was the middle of the afternoon when we entered the dimly lit room where Dad's body lay in an open casket. Mom grasped our hands—my right and Barry's left—as if we were little boys, and led us across the room. The casket, lined with white satin, was positioned below a multicolored stained glass window that filtered the sunlight. Barry and I stood beside the casket, our hands enclosed for a few moments in Mom's, until she released them to place her right hand on Dad's left cheek. Her forearm partially obscured my view of Dad's frozen lips. I stared at the rest of his face. His skin was darker, yet smoother, than I remembered. With his eyes sealed shut by the embalmer's craft, I had trouble recapturing the tearful twinkle in his eyes I'd been holding onto since I last saw him the year before, when I left to marry Marian.

Mom's quiet weeping shocked me. I'd never seen her cry. This shook me from my reverie and I refocused on her hand, still motionless, on Dad's cheek. She rested it there without stroking or patting his face. I lost sight of Barry right beside us; his presence in the room erased in my mind's eye by the shape of my mother's hand as it sat on my father's cheek. I was desperate for some sign of what I should do. Not a word had been spoken among us since Mom had ordered Barry and me to come with her to this place. Eventually, an inkling arose within me. An intuition of what I, as the older of her two youngest sons, was supposed to do. "It's time to go back home," I whispered, trying to match my voice to the solemnity of the dimly lit room. I reached over and touched Dad's cold brow, dislodging Mom's warm hand. She gave my hand a brief squeeze, quickly letting it go as soon as she turned to leave.

Barry parked the car in front of the house. The swarm of grieving Palmers and sundry relatives and friends had spilled out onto the front porch, buzzing quietly in subdued conversation. Cousin Harvey was puffing on a cigar, talking to a small group perched on the porch rail, their backsides to the street. Cousin Katherine called out, "There's Mattie B!" (a name Arkansas relatives called Mom) as we emerged from the car, and Mom made her way slowly, but with determination, up the concrete steps. Barry gazed up at the group on the porch, and then at me, and sighed, "Let's take a walk."

We started down Maple as we'd done so many times when we both went to Washington Elementary. We walked wordlessly past the other three turn-of-the-century houses on our short block, then on past the corner grocery. Rather than cross Aubert Avenue as we would have done on our way to school, we rounded the corner and walked along the long double block of houses, duplexes, and apartments on Aubert leading to Fountain Park. The same route I'd taken in my unnoticed attempt to run away from home when I was about nine or ten years old.

At Fountain Avenue, I paused to stare at the church where Dad's funeral service would take place the next day. The church overlooked the small green space of Fountain Park. As I admired the church's gray limestone, I thought about the trip we'd just made to see my father's body and the urge I'd felt to remove Mom's lingering hand from his cheek. I remember thinking: forty-three years of love. But I'd also felt something akin to shame for being there, as if intruding on a moment of intimacy in which I deserved no part. Since their arguments over my leaving for Exeter, I'd felt like a child caught in the middle of their battles for emotional control, over each other and me. Once Mom won the Exeter battle, she also took control of the remainder of my adolescence—leaving Dad nearly invisible.

Mom had seemed surprised by her own tears. After I lifted her hand from Dad's cheek, she appeared bent and discomfited, in stark contrast to the upright posture and the calm determination with which she'd summoned Barry and me to go with her to the funeral home. She had looked then as if she were fulfilling some final parental duty. Was this some type of ritual for young children who'd lost a parent that Mom learned as part of her Southern upbringing? I knew our surreal visit to the funeral home was part of some deliberate plan. What other rituals, passed down by Mom and Dad and grounded in our family's very particular emotional dynamics, had I missed out on when I so eagerly departed St. Louis at age fourteen? Would there be other rituals at the funeral the next day that I simply wouldn't understand? Other roles I wouldn't be prepared to play?

I didn't share these thoughts with Barry the way I might have when I was ten. He began to talk, then ramble, and finally to cry as we strolled through the familiar urban landscape of our childhood. His emotionality wakened me from my intellectual musings about my role in our family and forced me to confront the naked fact that we were about to bury our father. Barry began telling me, through his tears, the lesson he'd drawn from the funeral home visit. He wanted to get married, to have a son, and to name him after Daddy. "My Daddy," he'd said, in Southern parlance. I never said "Daddy," preferring the more mature-sounding "Dad." I put my arm around Barry and squeezed his shoulder, half-amused. Our brother Al is already named after Dad, and his son also bears Dad's name: Arglister L. Palmer, III. Suddenly I realized I wasn't even sure if Barry had a steady girlfriend who might someday become his wife. But I kept my silence as we walked along, astounded by the modesty of my little brother's grief-inspired wish.

We meandered the neighborhood on our way back home. As soon as we entered the house, I abandoned Barry and made my way through the crowd to my preferred perch in the kitchen window well as Lela explained to the muted assemblage in the kitchen the logistics of getting our father's casket on the plane. At one point her eyes welled with tears as she described dealing with the Los Angeles Coroner's officials, who had insulted her by asking questions (that she believed were racially tainted) about the possibility of foul play as a cause of our father's death. She had, after all, just seen our father die despite her efforts to revive him. She continued with her story after wiping away some of her tears.

I wanted to talk privately to Lela, suddenly curious about how she had convinced Mom to get on an airplane to fly back to St. Louis with Dad's body. I hadn't been able to convince my parents to avoid the long train ride and fly when they had traveled east for my Exeter and Harvard graduations. Mom had also refused to take a plane when she attended my wedding the year before. But any chance for such small talk with Lela would have to wait until after the funeral.

The next day, Mom made a surprising announcement as we waited for the arrival of the limos that would carry us to the church and burial. She insisted, in front of all my siblings, that I be her sole companion in the head limousine leading the procession. She declared that I needed to be at her side at the church and the burial since the constraints of our law-school budget hadn't allowed Marian, my wife-of-one-year, to make the trip.

THE ONE TIME I didn't disappoint my mother, my oldest sister, Lena, did. Her public breakdown at our father's funeral certainly made me more than a little uncomfortable. I remember hearing, over my left shoulder, a sudden gasping intake of breath as I turned around to glimpse one of the ushers standing in the center aisle, rigid as a signpost in her white, nurse-like uniform, clutching Lena's left arm. I surmised that this woman, who'd been escorting my sister down the aisle to her seat, must have felt Lena's knees buckle as she was about to sit down. Now she scanned the room frantically for someone to assist her as my sister's head flopped backward, then forward, easing Lena down into the pew just as another usher arrived with a cardboard fan to cool Lena, even though the church didn't feel particularly warm that morning. A third usher arrived with a glass of water. It was a production.

After sipping some water, Lena revived and motioned with her hand that her momentary dizziness had passed. She didn't look at me. As the ushers returned to their original duties, my sister sat with her eyes on our father's open casket, which stood below the lectern just a few feet away. I turned my own attention back to our mother, who hadn't shifted her black-veiled gaze from the front of the church to see what was happening in the pew right behind us.

It's impossible for me to say if my mother was embarrassed or simply disappointed that Lena had been so overcome at the sight of our father's body in its open casket. But I was certain that the crowd of several hundred looming at our backs rendered Lena's visible emotionality somehow improper in my mother's mind. I thought of Mom's many admonitions to me as a child, when my older siblings' teasing would reduce me to fits of tears. Had Mom allowed Lela and Harold to tease me and call me snaggletooth because she thought I needed to toughen up to endure the verbal assaults she anticipated the world would throw at me? Perhaps Mom, who had lost her own father when she was only twelve years old and then been sent away from her siblings to live with paternal aunts, had the right to be impatient about Lena's near collapse. Mom's refusal to even look at Lena, to offer my sister a soft pat on her hand, which grasped the back of our pew in her moment of pain and vulnerability, had the finality of a silent order: Act dignified in front of all these people!

I turned my eyes toward the front of the church, fixing on the stained-glass window above the choir loft to distract myself from the scene closer at hand, slowly beginning to understand why my mother had chosen me to sit in the front pew with her. She must have presumed I'd be able to follow the example of her own imposing stoicism during the funeral service. Mom's reaction to Lena's distress communicated her expectations of how I, in my role as the widow's escort, should behave. Or not behave.

Not like Lena now. Not like Barry yesterday after the funeral home visit. My mother didn't want to see any tears or incoherent grief, so I ignored my own embryonic sadness regarding Lena's near collapse and what had occasioned it. There was no place for tenderness in that drafty pew.

CHAPTER NINETEEN

The Family Picture

Mom's black-cotton-gloved hand rested calmly on my right forearm, our arms interlaced, as I stood between her and Al at Dad's gravesite ceremony. As I had at the church earlier that day, I concentrated on mimicking Mom's posture of dignified grief, her tearless eyes focused downward. As Dad's casket wobbled into motion and began to sink on its mechanical scaffolding into the ground, Mom squeezed my arm as she leaned into my shoulder and whispered, just loud enough for me to hear above the complaining cranks and pulls, "Is there only one grave?"

I leaned toward Al, who handled the St. Louis portion of the funeral arrangements, and repeated Mom's hushed question. I straightened my body before leaning back toward Mom to convey Al's response, pretending I was simply offering words of comfort to the grieving widow as I quietly informed her, "One."

The casket came to rest inside its rectangle of shadow and, for several seconds the only sound I could hear was my mother's quiet breathing through her black mourning veil. Until she hissed, "Fix it!"

After hugs, kisses, and tears, the crowd dispersed into their various cars, and Mom silently entered her limo, leaving me behind with Al. He eyed me, shrugged his shoulders, and laughed, "I didn't think I was supposed to buy a grave for someone who was still alive." He'd surmised, without my saying a word, that Mom wanted a double grave, although she hadn't shared that important detail with him at any point during the confusion of getting Dad's body released from the Los Angeles County Coroner's Office and flown back to St. Louis. Al didn't seem bothered by the fact that Mom and Dad hadn't already made their burial arrangements, or at least let him or Lena know their wishes. The matter of fact manner with which he accepted his unspoken assignment to help me "fix" the one-grave problem demonstrated yet again how our Palmer DNA communicated the most complex desires and expectations of our parents and our brothers and sisters.

We stepped into Al's car and drove along a gravel road to the cemetery office. Although Mom had given me the order, I knew she meant for Al and me to figure out together how to acquire a new gravesite for Dad and for her. I also knew to defer to Al as the oldest son. He explained the circumstances of his purchase of a single gravesite to the person in the office and shared Mom's belated declaration that she wished to be buried alongside our father after her death. The cemetery representative acted as if a change of burial plans at the last moment was at least not uncommon. She informed us that Dad's body would have to be moved to a double gravesite nearer to the office, pointing out the window to the very spot as she explained the additional charges for a double headstone, the new site, and the relocation of Dad's body. Al didn't have his checkbook with him, but I had mine, so I wrote out the check, knowing Al would see to it that I was immediately reimbursed as soon as we got back home to Maple Avenue.

We didn't wait around to watch the cemetery workers remove our father's casket from the ground and, without any ceremony, rebury it. Without discussion, we both sensed that Mom would have no peace of mind as she presided over the brood back at the house, preparing for the post funeral meal for family and friends, until she heard from us that the only man she would be sleeping next to, even after her own death, was our father. Whatever fights and arguments I may have witnessed or imagined they'd had over money, my education, or the assorted futures of my siblings, I finally had an inkling of what her quiet tears and the way her fingers lingered against Dad's death-cold face at the funeral home the day before might have meant. Maybe something as simple as that last caress allowed her to escape the prison of her own strong mind and feel herself inside her own grief, a woman—bereaved but fully human.

When we got home, Al stopped just inside the front screen door and communicated to Mom in the same discreet, hushed manner that we'd employed during the interment that we had solved her one-grave problem. Before rejoining the crowd gathered for the repast she had so meticulously organized, she went upstairs to write me a check, already preparing for another departure later that evening: mine.

I made my usual beeline for the kitchen, figuring I could lose myself in the crowd of friends and family gathered there—though such gatherings were becoming increasingly lonely events for me. As I walked through the kitchen, Lela stepped right in front of me, blocking my path to wherever I thought I was going, and said, "Larry, you haven't shed a single tear. You've got to get your grief out." Without knowing if what I said was true, I mumbled something about how I didn't grieve by crying. But it was true that I'd already moved on, intellectually, planning my journey back to New Haven and worrying about the law school classes I'd missed, just as the semester started. But, out of respect for my sister, I stood there. Shedding not a tear. Saying not a word.

I broke my silence by moving toward the hallway. No longer in her funeral attire, Mom reappeared. Before she joined a slice of the celebratory gathering of my sisters, brothers, nieces, nephews, cousins, aunts, uncles, and in-laws squeezed in among the neighbors and members of my parents' church reminiscing about Dad in the living room, I met her at the foot of the stairway. She grabbed my hand and squeezed it as an inconspicuous means of handing me a folded check.

Someone shouted out, "We need a family picture!" The murmurs of approval reverberated through the living room, dining room, kitchen, front porch, and backyard. Standing somewhat apart from the crowd in the hall foyer, I wondered how the "family" would be defined. I thought no amateur camera could capture the crowd of possibly fifty or more people if everyone related by either blood or marriage constituted the Palmer Family. Even though I was a gangly second year law student at Yale, I listened, as I'd done as a small child, to hear how the adults would resolve who besides me, Mom, and my nine sisters and brothers would take part in this family picture.

I couldn't tell who mediated the competing conversations, but a consensus emerged that only people who had at some time lived at Maple Avenue while Dad was alive should join the Palmer siblings in the picture. I suspected Al helped engineer this consensus. I heard him summon several of my younger nieces and nephews, whom he called gophers, to find all my siblings who might be anywhere on the premises and tell them to come to the living room for the family picture. Cousin Archie, from Mom's side of the family, shouted above the hum of conversation to Mom, whom he called Mattie B, that he had a camera to capture this historic moment of all ten of her living children actually congregating in one place.

Willie took charge of deciding who stood or sat where for our amateur photographer, Cousin Archie. Willie may have taught in the public schools, but his passion was photography. He directed us to assemble in the living room in front of the large window that looked out on the street. I picture him now drawing back the tan curtains and closing the blinds above the peach couch.

As "the next to the baby" (a phrase often used to refer to me at large family gatherings), I knew my thoughts about how we should be positioned for the family picture wouldn't be welcomed. The muted hum of relatives, church members, and neighbors became an oddly comforting background noise as we all waited, inside our individual silences, for Willie's orders. I hung back in the front hallway as Mom and my siblings congregated in the living room, watching as Willie, without any debate, assumed the mantle of photographic director.

Willie approached Mom's mother, Grandma Lela, almost hidden in a corner of the living room in her black long-sleeved funeral dress, and escorted her to the couch in front of the living room window. I'd almost forgotten she had lived with us at Maple Avenue off and on during the previous two decades. Growing up in that house, space was always a contested matter: who sat where at large family dinners, where one slept, and with whom you shared a room. As Willie motioned to Grandma Lela to sit on the couch to the far left and approached Mom, I thought that the spatial layout for the photograph would reflect, to some extent, the rules for space distribution at home, with oldest to youngest as the organizing principle. After he seated the women on the couch in age descending order—Grandma Lela, Mom, Lena, Lela, and Louise—Willie walked over to my brothers standing in the living room and touched Mac's shoulder.

Willie ushered Mac to a spot behind the couch, directly behind Lena. Willie asked Al to stand on Mac's right and Barry, the youngest son, on Mac's left. So, age would not be the organizing principle for our placement in the frame. After Al and Barry took their spots, Willie stood Harold (the fifth oldest son) next to Al, and Urshel (the third oldest son) next to Barry. Willie's aesthetic pattern became clear to me before he turned to tell me where I should stand. My brothers, attired in their black funeral suits, white shirts, and tastefully dark-colored or gray ties, appeared progressively taller as my eyes moved from Mac's left and then to his right. I knew I was taller than both Urshel and Willie, which meant Willie and I would need to fill out his tableau by taking our own places on Mac's far left and right.

I caught Willie's eyes resting on me. Without a word from him, I walked into the living room and went to stand next to Urshel and behind Louise. Willie took his place next to Harold at the other end of the row of Palmer sons, just behind Grandma Lela. Cousin Archie, who'd requested the photograph in the first place, had disappeared, perhaps drifting into a conversation in the kitchen, bored with standing there in the center of the living room during Willie's slow process of arranging all of us. Suddenly Cousin Katherine, Archie's wife, standing in the opening between the living room and dining room, shouted, "Archie, get your behind in here and take this picture before everybody scatters again!" Cousin Archie, who stood several inches shorter than his wife, scampered out of the kitchen like a dog answering a whistle, his camera in hand.

The family picture Willie composed for Cousin Archie's masterpiece consisted of Mom, her ten children (ranging in age from

Palmer family photo taken after Larry's father's funeral, 1967

their twenties to their forties), and her mother, Grandma Lela. Although I cherish this color photo as an irreplaceable family artifact, it is, at an objective level, an aesthetic disaster. Though Willie shut the blinds behind the couch to block out the bright sun of that September afternoon, the glare still casts shadows upon the brown faces of some of the Palmer sons. Those not in shadows—Willie, Harold, and Al—recede into the curtains of similar hue to their tan complexions that framed the large window behind the couch. Willie's arrangement of our white shirts, growing progressively taller on either side of Mac and shining out as they do from under our black suits, emphasizes him as the center of attention among the sons. And yet, it's hard to make out Mac's actual facial expression in the picture.

Among the women perched on the couch, Grandma Lela and Lena are the only ones still in their funeral dresses. Mom, in her sleeveless dress, is prepared for the warm, although not humid, September day in St. Louis. Lela, on the other side of Lena, is wearing a bluish short-sleeved dress she might have last worn to a sophisticated summer party in Los Angeles. Louise, in a light silver three-quarter-sleeved dress looks like she might be ready to go to a well air-conditioned church. In this lineup, Lena, seated in front of Mac, occupies the center of the picture among the women, a space that should have belonged to the matriarch and widow.

I often wonder what, if anything, our mother thought about how Willie placed Lena at the visual center of Cousin Archie's family photograph. I suspect if Mom had any complaint at all about that day it would have been that Lena had fainted at the funeral. If Willie's arrangement had perturbed Mom, she showed no sign. Mom considered too many of the people at Dad's repast "company" for her to complain out loud about anything.

Despite the fact that Willie's arrangement perhaps altered the message the picture should have conveyed, those black suits, the way they sweep the viewer's eyes into the center of the frame toward Lena sitting in her black dress on the center of the couch, is the only good thing I see in this family treasure. Cousin Archie failed to notice the backlighting problem caused by the window blinds. All that sunlight, filtering out of the northwest, down across St. Louis's rooftops, through the dusty slats of the blinds and into this scene of our shared grief, creates slanted, distorting silhouettes around Mac, Barry, Urshel, and me. Mac, Urshel, and I are nearly invisible in the photo's blur.

To add insult to injury, whatever Cousin Archie (or Willie?) said to get us all to look at the camera didn't work. Grandma Lela, Lena, and Lela are looking at something to their right. Mom, looking directly through her light blue pear-shaped glasses at the camera, appears to know she's posing for a photograph of an important occasion. Harold, like the conscientious son he was, is focused on Cousin Archie. Willie, too, is standing at a slight angle and looking directly into the camera, which I attribute to his photographic experience. I imagine there was a momentary somber silence before Cousin Archie snapped the picture, but Urshel's under-his-breath joke, "I usually get paid to have my picture taken," definitely broke it, causing both Louise and me to giggle and turn away from the camera toward him. My face is invisible, my profile casting a silhouette on the blinds behind me. We understood Urshel's joke as an allusion to the way he'd earned his living as an extra in Hollywood movies since running away in 1948. I wondered: Did he get paid to be in those porn shots I'd found in his room before he ran away? Because of Urshel's humorous disruption, only the side of Louise's jaw and some of her beautiful teeth are visible as she looks up at our strikingly handsome brother. His eyes closed, Urshel is standing with his back to the window, not at a slant like the rest of the Palmer brothers. The photo does not do him justice.

Looking at all ten of us Palmer children gathered together as adults has led me to reflect on the psychic price I paid when I left my siblings in order to spend my adolescence in a mostly white world. It would be many years before I could understand that when I left home the fears of my father and siblings were planted deep in my soul—along with my mother's ambition. Even today, despite its photographic defects, Cousin Archie's attempt to capture this historic moment in my family's life has a formidable impact on me. Every time I look at the photo I say to myself: There they all are, the people I thought I'd left behind to become a scholarship boy.

ONCE AGAIN APART from my family, floating 30,000 feet above the earth in a plane headed east, I realized I didn't know for sure where Dad's casket would be, or where the decaying and transforming mass of his DNA would come to rest. My siblings, other than Al, thought they knew the spot, since we'd witnessed his casket being lowered jerkily into the ground. I wondered if Dad's body had been moved yet or if the burial workers might put off the task for another day. I pushed back the instinct to call Al as soon as I got back to New Haven and tell him to check and make sure Dad's body had been moved. My gut panic was probably just a budding lawyer's instinct to make sure he had all the facts straight. I chuckled to myself, and relaxed, and the churning in my insides about Dad's death subsided. It seemed that years of geographical distance, combined with my intellectual ability to deflect difficult emotional situations, had created in me a wholly analytical disposition.

The double helix of our Palmer DNA would eventually clarify who knew, who thought they knew, or who simply took it on faith that they knew how to find their way back to where what was left of our father connected us all to the earth. My own little cloud of complex proteins and genes, mutations and metabolic processes, took it on faith, because my shared experiences with Al had made me believe that he, at least, would do the right thing when it came to our family.

THREE WEEKS AFTER Dad's funeral I awoke in the middle of the night, in tears, with one thought: I missed my Dad. I should have followed Lela's lead through my blues as I had all those years before, learning to slow dance with her.

As I lay there restlessly trying to get back to sleep, I thought about how I'd never again see Dad laugh so hard he'd cry. Never see the teary twinkle in his eye, like the one he sported the day of my Harvard graduation, overjoyed and proud as he was to see me. The last thing I remember thinking about before falling back to sleep was the sloppy kiss he gave me, little more than a year earlier, a few months after I graduated from Harvard, as we said goodbye. How he'd stood there on the porch, leaning harder on his cane than I may have realized. It grieved me even then to see him so frail, but it took a long time for me to shed any tears.

It dawns on me now. I was grieving the many opportunities I'd missed to simply see Dad for who he was. My father, who loved me.

Acknowledgments

This book has had a long maturation period, starting over thirty-five years ago, when I had a long conversation with two friends I had known since my freshman year in college about memories of people and events I thought I had forgotten. Although I was intrigued with my friends' suggestion that there might be a book inside of me, the project never became my main priority until I retired in 2011.

I pay tribute by name to only a few of the many individuals and institutions who helped me translate my long-held thoughts and feelings into a book. I am grateful to my fellow participants in the 2013 Kenyon Review Writers Workshop in Nonfiction. These writers and instructors exposed me to many ways of discovering not only the transformative events of my life, but also the reasons why I wanted to write about it. I left Kenyon with a draft of what would later become "The Haircut," published in *New England Review*. James "Randy" Marshall, whom I met after Kenyon, deserves special recognition because he not only read numerous drafts, but also helped me to develop the book's structure. I returned to Kenyon again in 2014 and received valuable critiques on my writing from another set of generous colleagues, leading to "Urshel: The Beautiful Black Sheep," published in *Blackbird: An online journal of literature and the arts*. After more than five years of writing and rewriting, I thought the manuscript was ready to send to a publisher. Irene Hoge Smith and John Irving read and commented on the final draft before I sent the manuscript into the world. Heartfelt thanks to Irene and John for their generosity. My wife, Suzy, has listened with her ears and heart to my retelling of my stories over the past 25 years. In addition, she has offered me the benefit of her keen editorial eye in reading and discussing numerous drafts of the manuscript.

I express my gratitude to Paul Dry, along with his colleagues Julia Sippel and Mara Brandsdorfer of Paul Dry Books, Inc., for their careful editing and design. I also thank *New England Review* and *Blackbird*, the publishers of previous versions of two chapters noted above.

The writing of this book was propelled by my desire to understand how my relationships with my nine sisters and brothers shaped who I am. My journey of discovery throughout the writing process was at times painful but ultimately beautiful. Once I embraced how differently I related to each of them growing up, I was able to celebrate the richness and depths of the bonds within our family.